MAGICAL MAGYARS

MAGICAL MAGYARS

THE RISE AND FALL OF THE
WORLD'S ONCE GREATEST FOOTBALL TEAM

DAVID BAILEY

First published by Pitch Publishing, 2019

Pitch Publishing
A2 Yeoman Gate
Yeoman Way
Worthing
Sussex
BN13 3QZ
www.pitchpublishing.co.uk
info@pitchpublishing.co.uk

A CIP catalogue record is available for this book
from the British Library.

ISBN 978 1 78531 544 2

Typesetting and origination by Pitch Publishing

Printed and bound in India by Replika Press Pvt. Ltd.

Contents

Introduction 9

'When Hungary's football history is told, Jimmy Hogan's name should be written in gold' 13

'The game boils down to the 'three B's'. Brains, Ball control and Balance' 23

'Sebes was a real narrow-minded, iron-fisted communist' 33

'Little money, little football. Big money, big football' 43

'The time of sport being funded by patrons is over' 51

'They both wanted things their own way – they were huge rivals' 63

'Football should be played foremostly with the brain' 75

'I felt like I was in a madhouse and that nothing and nobody made any sense' 86

'The play of the others would range between brilliant and mediocre' 99

'When we arrived in England in 1953, we were welcomed with a friendliness that touched us deeply' 115

'Best team I ever played against? Hungary in 1953' 127

'105,000 people watching the match at Wembley' 140

'The Battle of Berne' 151

'It is not possible to stop the Hungarian attack but theirs is a defence that lets in goals' 161

'Traitors!' 170

'After the Wolves v Honvéd match we held a post-match dinner 180

'Two friends are sitting in a bar' 189

'Had Hungary won the 1954 World Cup there wouldn't have been a revolution' 200

'I didn't leave Hungary, I just didn't come back' 214

'Who is this FIFA to tell me what to do in my own country?' 227

'You must shoot immediately shoot, shoot and shoot again!' 240

'I was where I had to be. I did what I had to do' 249

Appendix 1: Unbeaten 256

Appendix 2: Epilogue 261

Endnotes 278

Bibliography 286

Acknowledgements 295

Index 296

In memory of
Alan and Jenny Bailey

Introduction

The match of the century

FROM the moment they stepped out on to the pitch, it was evident that they were something very different. They were lithe, confident, daring to juggle the match ball – quite unlike the other foreign teams, who were always clearly intimidated by the sheer size and passion of the home crowd. The kit the visitors wore was sleek: their cherry-red shirts V-necked and tight-fitting, their shorts cut above the thigh and boots cut below the ankle. In comparison, the England team looked suddenly old-fashioned in bulky, collared shirts, knee-length shorts and cumbersome boots, like workhorses trudging next to thoroughbreds. London's Empire Stadium was cold, wet and packed solid. 'Wembley' being full was nothing unusual in those days before football matches were televised live, but what was remarkable was the speed at which tickets had sold out: weeks beforehand and in a matter of hours; even more so considering the match was held on a workday afternoon, meaning the majority of the punters had had to forsake a day's pay to be there.

Why the massive interest? Well, Hungary were the first nation from behind the Iron Curtain to visit England, and were an enemy of sorts, having sided against Britain in both world wars, and circa 1953 the Cold War was getting colder. There was intrigue: Hungary were a team made up of soldiers, policemen; one, Major Bozsik, was even a member of parliament. There was interest in Major Puskás, one of the world's greatest players. And there was the no small matter of Hungary being the current Olympic champions and maintaining a three-year, 24-match undefeated run.

But none of this overly concerned the English. The Hungarians may have had Puskás, but he wasn't a patch on the world's best player,

Stanley Matthews. Hungary's Olympic gold? An amateur tournament, easy to win when you fielded a team of professional 'shamateurs' as had the Hungarians. And Hungary's unbeaten run? Admittedly impressive, but what was it to England remaining unbeaten at home to non-British opponents? Within 45 seconds, Hungary took the lead, and what followed was a lesson from the pupils that the masters never forgot. The 6–3 scoreline was one that didn't do the Hungarians justice. They were unlucky not to score ten. The English lucky to snatch three. The Wembley crowd were stunned, not knowing whether to cry or applaud. Their England, the sport's very inventors, had been demolished, humiliated even, on their own hallowed turf, their cherished unbeaten record rudely smashed. But at the same time those present had witnessed the future of football. The Hungarians had brought with them a style of play never seen before in Britain. Short passing, long passing, movement, interchanging, control, backwards, forwards, sideways.

The embarrassed masters, claiming an off-day, demanded the pupils give them a rematch, which the Hungarians duly did five months later in Budapest. This time, in front of their own, they were even more impressive, beating England 7–1: a defeat that remains England's heaviest ever. The Hungarians dubbed their boys the 'Golden Team' – the English press, waxing a little more lyrical, the 'Magical Magyars'.

Over 50 years later, and this Englishman was living in Budapest. Never one to miss a natter about football, the conversation often turned to Hungary's historic victories over England. Now, while I knew of both defeats, it was not something that English football history books tended to dwell upon. I knew enough of the England team (Alf Ramsey, Billy Wright and Matthews), but of the Hungarians, except for Puskás, I knew almost nothing other than that they were an exceptional team that had taught England a lesson. I can recall one Hungarian friend genuinely disbelieving that I, as a football obsessive, knew nothing of Sebes, Hidegkuti, Lóránt, Bozsik, Czibor, Kocsis, Kubala, Béla Guttmann ... well, I'd heard of Guttmann, but that was because of his success in coaching Benfica – I didn't realise he was Hungarian. And the rest I knew of – vaguely – were they any good? I thought Hungary were a one-man team led by a Galloping Major?

Apparently not. Apparently (and my friend was neither the first nor last Magyar to tell me this) the Puskás-captained Hungarian team of the 1950s were, in their time, the greatest football side in the world bar none. And not just great, but revolutionary with it, changing the very way the sport was played. The only reason why they didn't prove that they were the best team in the world was that dark forces didn't want a communist nation winning the World Cup – they were robbed of it in the last minute of the 1954 final against West Germany by a corrupted referee, an Englishman no less!

My interest piqued, I began searching for a definitive book that explained to me not just what the team achieved but *how*? How on earth had this tiny and at times troubled nation (at 74th in FIFA's world rankings at the time of my search[1]) ever managed to produce a team that had revolutionised football? But no such book in the English language existed, so I sought one in Hungarian, with a mind to translating the version which told the story in full. But here was the stumbling block: while there are books aplenty in the Hungarian language on the team's achievements and exploits, the books' authors take it for granted that their readers know the participants, background and history. I didn't. And as I read, questions led to more questions, and what emerged was a gripping tale of friendship, betrayal, greed, death and ultimately revolution, set against and aided by the most brutal Stalinist regime in the entire Soviet bloc. A regime that imprisoned and murdered more of its own people than any other Soviet satellite, and that is saying something. This was no ordinary football team riding their luck with good players and timing; this was the culmination of decades of investment and preparation. It just so happened that it all came to fruition during Hungary's darkest days, as did the team's abrupt, chaotic and angry end.

And while my friend was wrong about the World Cup Final referee being corrupt, he was correct that Puskás was the Maradona, Messi or Ronaldo of his day, and for a brief period in the 1950s the Magical Magyars were the greatest football team in the world; and, more than this, they really did revolutionise the game. I found their story fascinating. I hope you do too.

Note: Where a quotation has been translated from Hungarian, this is indicated by '†' in the endnote.

CHAPTER 1

When Hungary's football history is told, Jimmy Hogan's name should be written in gold.

Gusztáv Sebes

THE origins of the ancient Hungarians are much debated, but the accepted theory is that they stemmed 6,000 years ago from tribes who lived in Russia's Ural Mountains on Europe's border with Asia.

By AD 463, these proto-Hungarians had migrated south-west into the lands of the Turkic Empire (modern-day Ukraine), and, by interbreeding with Turks and the Mongol followers of Attila the Hun, burgeoned from a simple nomadic farming people into a 400,000-strong tribe. They were a formidable fighting force, renowned for their horsemanship and the accuracy of their arrows, and thus called the 'Onogurs': in ancient Turkish, 'on' meaning 'ten' and 'ogur' meaning 'arrow'.

In the ninth century, one of the Onogurs' largest sub-tribes, the Megyers, migrated further westwards, settling upon a fertile terrain they named 'Magyarország' – 'Magyarland'. The term 'Hungary' is derived from 'Hungaras', the Latin spelling of 'Onogurs'.

After five centuries of relative peace under the rule of a succession of Magyar kings, in the mid-16th century vast swathes of Hungary was conquered by Turkey, to become the western outpost of the Ottoman Empire. The Turks remained for almost 150 years until they were driven out by the armies of the Austrian-dominated Habsburg Monarchy. The Habsburgs had their own agenda for Hungary, and made the country one of their empire's principalities under direct rule from Vienna. In 1848, the Hungarians revolted: a bid for independence that was ruthlessly quashed by the Habsburgs begging the military assistance of Russia. However, for the Hungarians, the defeat was not in vain. The revolution unsettled the Habsburgs, and – fearful that the Hungarians would rise again – they reached upon a compromise in which the Austrian Empire and the Kingdom of Hungary combined as one to form the Austro-Hungarian Empire.

The dual monarchy was one in that the Hungarians may have felt themselves to be the poor relation, but it was undeniable that the investment by the powerhouse that was the House of Habsburg was responsible for evolving Hungary from a rural backwater into one of the most powerful countries in Europe. And in 1873 a capital city befitting of Hungary's new status was established, made by the joining of two towns that stood on opposite sides of the River Danube: Buda to the west and Pest to the east. Budapest.

The sport of football was first brought to Hungary in the late 1870s by students returning from studying in Britain. But their lack of knowledge and regard for the rules meant their games of 'kick-ball' were bloody, chaotic and short-lived. Such mayhem was all rather distasteful for the gentlemen's athletic and gymnastic clubs that had sprung up across Hungary, catering for the country's new middle classes, and it wouldn't be until a decade later that they took the game up with any seriousness. The first official football match in Hungary took place in October of 1897 when the Budapest Torna Club (BTC), Hungary's most prestigious gymnastics club, faced the Vienna Cricket and Football Club in Budapest. 'The Cricketers' arrived with a team including seven Britons, two of whom were the sons of the match's referee. A well-heeled crowd of 2,000 dressed in their finest crammed Pest's Millennial Racetrack to watch the match professing much amusement at the referee's whistle-blowing antics. The 'Austrian' veterans (their team had been formed two years earlier) won 2–0, their goals met with warm applause from both the Hungarian spectators and players.

By the turn of the century, a further 17 clubs had followed BTC's suit and set up football teams, for not to have done so would have meant abstaining from what had fast become the nation's most popular sport. For the gentlemen participants clad in flannel shirts, knickerbockers and ankle-high boots, the emphasis was purely on attack and glory.

For the spectators, suppressed in their daily lives by the constraints of society, the joy was in being able to yell, swear and cheer at will. Football had come to Hungary, and the Hungarians loved it.

In 1901, a football association[2] and a Budapest league were established and the same year an English professional club[3] visited Budapest for the first time – Southampton FC, soundly thrashing BTC 8–0 and the *next day* a select Hungarian team 13–0. Hereafter, British clubs began to make Budapest a regular pre-season destination, assured of a warm welcome and bolstered by the assurance that they wouldn't be beaten. For this reason, in 1908, the English national team chose Hungary (and Austria) for their first international matches outside of the British Isles.

So one-sided was the match that the Hungarians, in losing 0–7, never left their own half for the entirety of the 90 minutes. 'I cannot possibly comment on something I have not witnessed in action,'[4] was the reply of England captain Vivian Woodward when he was asked afterwards what he thought of Hungary's attack. Though, perhaps feeling he'd been a tad harsh towards his hosts, Woodward, a stickler for fair play and manners, did single out one Hungarian player for praise: Imre Schlosser, a 16-year-old debutant who Woodward, correctly, predicted would become 'Hungary's best player for the next decade'.[5]

The emergence of Schlosser as Hungary's star player was reflective of the direction that football in the country had taken. As the sport became the favourite spectator pastime of the masses, rowdier working-class crowds replaced the well-heeled ones that had treated matches as social events. Schlosser was a hero of the former and appalled the latter, though in fairness his habit of spitting into the opposition's goal after scoring was never going to endear him to the gentry.

Schlosser was everything that Hungarian athletes had hitherto not been. A street urchin with legs so bandy, due to childhood malnutrition, that they were a decisive advantage to 'Slozi' on the football field, as he hopped and lopped, leaving opponents unable to anticipate his next move. In addition, Schlosser wasn't even what the gentry considered a pure Hungarian; he was a Swab, a German-speaking Hungarian, at a time when Hungary was straining to retain its own identity in the shadow of the all-controlling Austria.

Swabs made up almost a quarter of Budapest's population. Their heartland was the Pest district of Ferencváros, and the local football club, Ferencvárosi Torna Club,[6] provided them with an outlet through which they could voice pride in their ethnicity.

The only other club who could remotely match Ferencváros's support and finances was MTK,[7] the club of Budapest's Jews, who likewise numbered roughly a quarter of the capital's population. The club was formed in 1888, by Jews but not solely for Jews. MTK's football team was formed over a decade later and was a success from the very start, winning the league title in only their second season.

Over the next 24 years, such was the domination of the two clubs that no other clubs would win the league title: MTK winning 13 titles to Ferencváros's 11. In 1911, Ferencváros constructed a brand new stadium boasting a grandstand and a clubhouse complete with restaurant. It was considered the finest stadium in Europe – at least until a year later, when, one kilometre up the road, MTK built an equally grand home stadium.[8]

The drive behind MTK was the club's colourful chairman, Alfréd Brüll. A former champion wrestler, Brüll had the ambition of making MTK the biggest and best football club in Europe by utilising the full support of Hungary's Jews, one of the largest populations of Jews in Europe. He was always on the lookout for ways to progress *his* club, regardless of feathers ruffled. Brüll decided that MTK's pristine new stadium was deserving of a star player, and thus seized upon an argument over money between Imre Schlosser and Ferencváros and brought Slozi to MTK, supposedly luring the player via his socially ambitious wife with kitchen furniture and a grand piano. Ferencváros were furious that their rivals had stolen their best player, a player so revered that the local council were in the process of naming a street after him. Ferencváros complained to the FA, who, never having faced such a predicament, dithered, then banned Schlosser for six months, hoping this would be long enough for him to 'change his mind'. He didn't.

Brüll then proceeded to disregard Hungarian football's amateur ethic by employing the services of a *professional* coach, and a foreigner to boot: Jacky Robertson, a former Scotland international. Brüll had purposely sought a Scotsman, and only a Scotsman, based on Scottish footballers' new-found reputation as the best in Europe. Scots had won this accolade after their nation's footballers had invented 'passing', an acknowledgement that rolling the ball to a team-mate was not an act of cowardice. Scotland's footballers further recognised that once a player released the ball, it was productive for him to quickly move to an unmarked position to make himself available for a return pass. In hiring Robertson, MTK obtained one of the more credible, canny retired Scottish footballers venturing into Europe. The 34-year-old was a man of firsts: Chelsea's first signing, scorer of their first-ever league goal and the London club's first-ever manager. The 'Scottish Passing' that Robertson[9] introduced would become MTK's signature over the next decade and beyond when they dominated Hungarian football. In all Robertson spent just over one season at MTK before returning home to Britain.

Robertson's departure was timely for just a year later Europe was enveloped in war, with Britain and Hungary on opposing sides. Events had been sparked by the assassination in July 1914 of Archduke Franz Ferdinand (next in line to the Habsburg throne) and his wife while on a visit to the Bosnian capital, Sarajevo. The assassin was a Serbian separatist, and, in retaliation, Austria–Hungary declared war on Serbia. To Serbia's aid came Russia, which declared war on Austria–Hungary. Germany allied with Austria–Hungary and declared war on Russia, and two days later France. Britain allied with France and declared war on Germany.

Without further ado, Hungary's mostly conscript armies were despatched to the Eastern Front to fight against the might of the Russian army, where, ill-supplied, outmanned and outgunned, they suffered one heavy defeat after another.

In 1916, the elderly Emperor Franz Joseph died, and the Habsburg throne was passed down to his nephew Karl. The new Emperor was a leader more aware of the Hungarians' grievances, and as public dissatisfaction over the war mounted, he surrendered his powers as King of Hungary to one of the Habsburgs' most vocal opponents – a radical nobleman called Count Mihály Károlyi, nicknamed the 'Red Count'. Károlyi's party had won the public's favour through an anti-Habsburg and, more importantly, an anti-war stance. And as thousands of Hungarians took to Budapest's streets to cheer the new government, the irony wasn't lost on Hungary's now precarious aristocracy that one of their own had ended 350 years of Habsburg rule in Hungary.

For the first two years of the war, football in Hungary was suspended; but such was the public demand for the sport that the first division was resumed, albeit with fewer clubs and under the name 'War League'. It was a league dominated by MTK, again due to the chutzpah of their chairman, Alfréd Brüll. Throughout the league's suspension, Brüll had continually searched for a replacement for Jacky Robertson. Alas, Scottish football coaches in wartime Hungary were thin on the ground, so Brüll settled for second best and an English one.

Jimmy Hogan was well known in English football as a master of ball control, but whether he was well liked was a different matter. He was odd. A non-swearing fitness fanatic, he was sarcastically nicknamed 'The Parson' by his team-mates for his preference for attending church over joining them at the pub. Coaches distrusted him; he was pushy, meddlesome and annoyingly inquisitive – offering unsolicited advice, questioning instructions and (perhaps most annoyingly of all) scrutinising contracts. He'd arrive for training sessions first, leave last, and in between constantly harangue for practice with a ball instead of just being satisfied, like everyone else was, with the traditional training of laps, sprints and star jumps. It was a reputation for meddling that meant that he spent the bulk of his playing days a level beneath his abilities[10] in the English lower divisions, and when he retired (with a knee injury aged 30) put club chairmen off from taking a chance on him.

However, not *everyone* in English football was dismissive of 'The Parson'. James Howcroft was England's leading referee, and after officiating a 1912 match in which Austria drew at home to Hungary, was approached by Hugo Meisl, the young and ambitious president of the Austrian FA. Meisl[11] asked Howcroft's opinion as to how the Austrian team could improve, to which Howcroft recommended that Meisl employ an assistant from outside Austro-Hungarian football, one who could offer a new way of thinking, and it so happened he knew just the man …

Hogan recalled that moving to Vienna was 'like stepping into paradise'.[12] His wife, their children and he lived in a luxury apartment, and his evenings were spent being feted in Vienna's sporting coffee houses, where football was famously discussed and dissected with a high-brow intellectualism. Work too was a labour of love. The Catholic Hogan, son of a Lancashire mill worker, and the Jewish Meisl, son of a rich banker, clicked from the start, finding common ground in a shared obsession with a belief that intelligence in football would always triumph over stealth.

But, for Hogan, the good times in Vienna did not last. On the outbreak of the First World War, he was interned in a camp for foreign aliens, while his pregnant wife and two children were left to fend for themselves, only managing to flee Austria with the help of the neutral American counsel. Meisl was powerless to help, and Hogan never really forgave him: 'Thrown into prison with thieves and murderers, the Austrian FA broke my contract and left us to starve.'[13] Although in his own way Meisl did help, by letting it be known that Hogan was in internment. The news reached the ears of Alfréd Brüll, who in turn had Baron Distay, the Cambridge-educated vice-president of MTK, use his contacts with the Red Cross to have Hogan released and brought to Hungary. Hogan, not wanting to look a gift horse in the mouth, immediately accepted the Baron's offer, and a week later arrived in Budapest to be greeted warmly by a large delegation and introduced to all as a Scotsman.

If Hogan had liked Vienna, then he was positively enraptured by Budapest – 'Europe's most beautiful city'[14] – and the Hungarians: 'I can never forget their kindness or their hatred of the Austrians and Germans.'[15] And it was no wonder. The new office and the facilities that awaited Hogan at the MTK stadium were superior to anything else in Europe, and the only restriction placed upon him as an enemy alien was to promise not to speak about the war. MTK also supplied him with an interpreter, a recently retired team captain called Dori Kürschner. The two quickly became firm friends – similar minds, fascinated with the tactics of football – and Kürschner's interpreter role soon merged into that of an invaluable coaching assistant.

Away from his family and with time on his hands, Hogan dived into his new job, a blank canvas at his disposal upon which to place his long-thought ideas. He'd long calculated that in an average game a player is, at best, in contact with the ball for just two minutes. Therefore the standard Hungarian training of two practice matches a week meant that the players were in contact with the ball for only four minutes a week. For Hogan this was utterly insufficient, though better than in England, where ruled the belief that players in training should be starved of the ball so that come matchday they would be 'ball hungry'. Hogan was glad he'd left such nonsense behind, and in doubling MTK's weekly training sessions, he had his new charges repetitively working with a ball and nothing but a ball. With self-demonstration, Hogan drilled the players in his 11, self-taught, ways of trapping the ball. He had them learn tricks and feints, and sharpened their dribbling by having them run around sticks at full speed with the ball at their feet, first controlling it with the outside of the foot, then afterwards with only the inside. He further handed the players a long list of stretching exercises designed to keep them supple, exercises that he expected them to do in their own time outside of training – just as he had done as a player.

The team's elder players, led by Imre Schlosser, were taken aback by the intensity of their new coach, especially when Hogan ran his critical eye over their lifestyles, and then, much to their astonishment, ordered them to cut down on cigarettes, beer and goulash, and replace them with early nights, water and steamed vegetables. How was a man supposed to compete on cabbage? Mr Robertson had never been this pernickety.

The young players, however, were far more responsive – showing an eagerness to learn that was one of the main reasons why Hogan warmed so much to Hungary. With most of the adult first team conscripted into the army, Hogan had to assemble a team made up of schoolboys, veterans and players on war leave. The pick of the bunch was a 16-year-old by the name of György Orth, who Hogan had spotted playing for the Budapest club Vasas, urging Brüll to do whatever it took to get the lanky full-back to MTK: 'A player like this only comes about every hundred years.' Hogan placed Orth in the centre-half position to act as a 'playmaker' pulling strings in a team that used skill and guile, rather than brute force, to break down defences. Hogan's players, drilled in the art of ball control, were instructed to attack as one tight-knit unit with Orth as the pivot, keeping the ball on the ground, working up the field with short, incisive passes, retaining possession, remaining onside and pushing back the opposition defence. 'Scottish passing' evolved into 'Danubian passing'.

In November 1918, the Austro-Hungarian armies surrendered. Alfréd Brüll begged Hogan to stay, to bring his wife and children over to live in Budapest. But Hogan couldn't – he hadn't seen his family or country for four long years, and furthermore he was convinced that his time in Hungary would land him a job at an English club. It was Hogan's dream to become a success in English football, to silence the sniggers that dogged his name. If he had been able to win the league (twice) in a country with an impregnable language and with a rag-tag team of veterans and schoolboys, what heights could he achieve in English football with full-time professional footballers?

For Hungary, the Great War was nothing but an unmitigated disaster. An estimated one million of their troops were killed, and an almost equal number were injured or captured.

At home, people's blaming the aristocracy for leading them to slaughter led to a host of protests and crippling strikes. The foremost agitators were the Hungarian communists, their numbers considerably boosted by the return of thousands of prisoners of war, who, while in the captivity of the Russians, had been converted to Bolsheviks. The beleaguered government of Count Mihály Károlyi was impotent to prevent the chaos enveloping Hungary, and eventually the 'Red Count', now seemingly not red enough, relented and conceded power to the communists' leader, Béla Kun – 'The Hungarian Lenin'.

The *idea* of communism had initially greatly appealed to Hungary's downtrodden masses, but the reality of the Hungarian Soviet Republic was wholly different. The workers and peasants quickly saw that they would be even worse off under the communists' radical reforms, which were intended to place all industry and land under government ownership. Their dim view was darkened further by the communists' wont to despatch thugs to quell and arrest dissenters.

Hungary's communist government was no more popular with other European governments, including that of France. The French, wary of the threat that Bolshevism posed in their own country, backed the Romanians in invading Hungary, forcing Béla Kun and his government to flee after just 133 days in power. But while Kun may have fled (to Russia), the Romanian army remained, plundering and laying claim to Hungarian territories which they believed were rightfully Romanian. It was only when a group of military-backed nationalists filled the power vacuum left by Kun that Romania withdrew its troops. The leader of the nationalists was the highest-ranked military man among them: Admiral Miklós Horthy, a former commander-in-chief of the Austrian-Hungarian navy; and his being of minor nobility allowed Hungary's parliament to elect him as regent.[16]

Horthy was a dignified and sober man, until confronted with a Bolshevik – then he would turn a shade of murderous. Indeed, his first move in government was to begin reprisals against those involved or associated in any small way with the communists. In terms of people murdered, imprisoned and exiled, the 'White Terror' far outdid the 'Red Terror'. It was an ominous beginning to what was to be more than two decades of Horthy rule.

CHAPTER 2

The game boils down to the 'three B's'. Brains, Ball control and Balance.

Jimmy Hogan[17]

MTK continued their domination of Hungarian football throughout the 1920s, winning nine league titles in a row, with football that adhered to the Jimmy Hogan-taught crisp, accurate passing and intelligent player movement. Bolstered by their domestic success, the 'Golden Team'[18] began thinking big, really big. Tours of Europe and America were planned; were going to show the world how to play football …

And then in 1925, everything changed with the introduction of a new offside rule, the one in existence today. The 'new' rule replaced the previous rule that had meant a player was offside unless at least three opponents were between him and the goal. Now, only two were needed. The 'old' rule had certainly fulfilled its design in preventing goal-hanging, but, at the same time, it had made for dull, low-scoring matches. The 'new' rule handed the advantage back to the attackers, and as such attacking became easier: teams no longer had to build up play with thought when a ball launched towards the opposition goal was just as effective. MTK's moving up, down and across the pitch in one tight unit, with probing passing, became ineffective, outdated overnight. Play became regimented, as teams took to holding to formation lest they get caught out of position.

The drop in quality led to an inevitable decline in crowd levels, also compounded by an exodus of Hungarian footballers to Italian football. The first ones[19] had gone in 1920, when Italian clubs were 'amateur' in name only, openly paying wages. By 1923 the trickle had turned into a torrent, as at least five teams' worth of *Ungheresi* (Hungarian fotballers) flooded the Italian leagues. Ultimately the problem of Italy having its own talent frozen out and Hungary being stripped of its best players was solved in 1926, when the two FAs simultaneously adopted professionalism. The Italian FA went one further and implemented a rule stating that its clubs could not employ more than two foreigners; one year later this was made one foreigner, and a year after that none. As the surplus Hungarian footballers returned home, so began a scramble for limited professional contracts, which were heavily in the clubs' favour.

Into this tide of pessimism returned Jimmy Hogan, lured back into Hungary by MTK, who were convinced that he was the one man who could reverse their change in fortunes. In the seven years since Hogan had left Hungary, he'd been asked more than once by Alfréd Brüll to return to the club, which Hogan had persistently refused to do, or rather his wife had.

Mrs Hogan's reasoning for not going anywhere near Hungary was based on the condemnation that her husband had faced in England for his coaching in Hungary during the war. Hogan had hoped that his experience at MTK would land him a plum coaching job in English football, but instead he was labelled a traitor for helping the enemy. The first sign that all was not well had been when Hogan had gone cap-in-hand to the English FA only to have a pair of socks flung disdainfully at him by the FA chairman: 'The boys on the front were glad of those.'[20]

The furious Hogan had little choice but to work outside of football, taking a job in a Liverpool tobacco factory, labouring unhappily until one day, a year later, he was contacted by Teddy Duckworth, the English coach of the Swiss national team. Duckworth, a former Blackpool player, knew Hogan well. 'Was "The Parson" interested in coaching the Berne club Young Boys?' Of course Hogan was: he would have walked to Switzerland for the job in bare feet once he'd learned that also coaching in Swiss football was his friend and former MTK assistant Dori Kürschner.

Kürschner had replaced Hogan as MTK coach in 1918 but only remained for one season. Kürschner was a Jew and, like tens of thousands of other Hungarian Jews, chose to emigrate rather than tolerate the anti-Semitism of the Horthy regime any longer. Until the end of the Great War, Jews had lived reasonably peacefully for centuries alongside Magyars, and they only became a target for hate with the onset of Horthy's 'White Terror'. The communist leader, Béla Kun, was a Jew, as were many of his ministers. Horthy wanted Bolshevism in Hungary exterminated, and Jews in his eyes were Bolsheviks in the making.

Kürschner's leaving was Hungary's loss. After a successful spell coaching in German football, he moved to Switzerland, where he would make his name as a coach. Indeed as a coach Kürschner would go on to supersede Hogan as a pioneer, first laying the foundations in Swiss football for their famous 'Swiss Bolt' sweeper system, and more notably later in Brazil, where he is revered as the importer of modern tactical football.

Duckworth recruited Kürschner and Hogan to assist in coaching the Swiss team at the 1924 Olympics, winning silver, still the greatest success in the history of Swiss football. And yet while Hogan and his family were happy in Switzerland, and he was eternally grateful to Duckworth and Kürschner, his considerable ego couldn't bear being third best. Hogan was a man used to being either ignored or adored. He hankered after Budapest, where he had been the latter. When, sure enough, Alfréd Brüll was back in contact with talk of money and MTK ruling Europe with Hogan at the helm, Hogan let himself be convinced – against the advice of both his wife and, more notably, Dori Kürschner.

It was advice that Hogan would rue not heeding. He was quick to find that the Hungary he'd been so nostalgic for no longer existed. In his absence, the civil wars – the Red and White Terrors – had scarred the nation. In Hogan's eyes, she was a harder, more sceptical place, openly mistrustful of foreigners and none more so than towards a man whose nation had played a pivotal role in the greatest humiliation in Hungary's 1,000-year history: the Trianon Treaty.

In June 1920, delegates from the Great War's victors – Britain, France and Russia – had met at the Palace of Versailles in France to sign a treaty designed to punish Hungary for its role in the war. When the first member of the Hungarian delegation read it, he fainted. The Trianon Treaty[21] stripped Hungary of almost two-thirds of its lands, handing disputed border territories to its neighbours Austria, Czechoslovakia, Poland, Italy, Ukraine, Romania and the Kingdom of Serbs, Croats and Slovenes. Three and a half million Hungarians were condemned to new lives as minorities subjugated to hostile foreign governments. Hungarians greeted the ratifying of the treaty as a day of national mourning. Shops and businesses closed, the national flag flew at half-mast, and thousands protested on the streets. Even today when the subject of 'Trianon' is broached, many Hungarians voice a bitter sense of injustice and a longing for the return of the mighty pre-Trianon Hungary.

In what remained of the now landlocked and wounded Hungary, anti-foreign sentiment rose to the fore. The government introduced an aggressive policy of Magyarisation, the intention being to turn Hungary from a nation where the peoples spoke and practised a myriad of different languages and religions into a nation that was distinctly Magyar. The possession of a foreign surname was deemed unpatriotic. Thus hundreds of thousands of people changed their (Jewish, Slav, Swab or Slovak) surnames to something more suitably Magyar.[22]

To add to Hogan's sense of isolation, soon after his arrival his MTK captain, György Orth, suffered a broken leg (nobbled according to the Hungarian reports) in a friendly match in Vienna. Hogan burst into tears on being told: his protégé had been by far Hungary's best player for almost a decade, the lynchpin of both MTK and the national team – 'The most versatile, greatest and most intelligent player I have ever seen.'[23]

Without Orth in his team, missing the friendship of Kürschner, and no doubt conscious of Mrs Hogan impatiently awaiting his return, Hogan accepted an offer from the central German FA to work as an adviser. His departure from Hungary went mostly unnoticed, and his legacy would not bear fruit for another two decades.

However, many a Jewish Hungarian footballer was not so ready to turn their back on the style that had given them a great sense of pride. A Jewish Hungarian was now expected to play a certain way, with skill. A small number of them upped and moved to Vienna, specifically to play for Hakoah Vienna, a club who wore the Star of David and for whom only Jews could play. Hakoah (the name meaning 'strength' in Hebrew) was a sanctuary for Jewish footballers from right across Europe and thus able to recruit from a plentiful and willing pool. Its spine, though, was Hungarian; its stars József Eisenhoffer[24] and Béla Guttmann, adherents to Danubian football, and men who would both go on to become world-renowned coaches. In only their fifth season Hakoah won the Austrian league title, a national success that encouraged them to become the first-ever club to undertake a world tour[25].

The success of the tour was watched with avid interest in Vienna by Hugo Meisl, coach of the Austrian national team. Meisl was never a footballer himself – he was a banker by trade who'd joined the Austrian FA voluntarily, and by his early thirties had manoeuvred his way up to the association presidency, a position from which he was then able to appoint himself national team coach. With no hindrance from a meddlesome selection board, Meisl had time to experiment with tactics, formations and line-ups. Meisl hated the strength-over-intelligence route that football had reverted towards, and witnessing through Hakoah that Danubian football was not obsolete gave him food for thought. What he saw was that whereas the new offside rule had forced teams to maintain their formation when defending, it wasn't necessary when attacking. Meisl, therefore, had his five-man forward line interchange at will, pushing up, dropping back, swapping wings – the 'Danubian Whirl' and the 'Vienna Waltz'.

The 'Wunderteam' were football's first great international side. In a 27-match period between May 1931 and May 1934 they lost only twice, their peak being in 1932, when they thrashed Hungary 8–2 in Vienna – a loss that was Hungary's heaviest to date.

The humiliation of losing so heavily to Austria was for Hungarian football a wake-up call that change was necessary, and the Hungarian FA even went so far as to permit the re-forming of a coaches' union, which five years earlier they had prevented coaches from joining.

The 'Trainers' Society', *Edző Testület*, was designed to raise coaching standards as well as look after the welfare of coaches in the new world of professionalism, but to the authorities, it had reeked of a trade union. The second time around, and with active encouragement to do so, Hungary's coaches flocked to join. Theirs was a sense of patriotic pride in the desire to uphold the reputation of Hungarian coaches as being among the finest, if not *the* finest, in Europe. Hungarian coaches had spread far and wide across the continent: besides Dori Kürschner in Switzerland, the Swedish national team was coached by former MTK defender József Nagy, French champions Olympique Marseilles by József Eisenhoffer, and in Italy, at one point during the 1930s, there were 31 Hungarians coaching in all three professional divisions.

In the Trainers' Society's monthly meetings, members were encouraged to discuss and divulge new ideas and training methods, and from this developed a consensus as to *how* Hungary should play: a combination of the Hungarian desire to attack, the Austrian Wunderteam's finesse, English physicality and the tactical discipline of the up-and-coming Italians.

The 1934 World Cup, Hungary's first tournament, gave Hungarian football the opportunity to measure its progress. However, in the quarter-final they ran up against the Austrian 'Wunderteam', and what should have been an eye-pleasing 'Dual of the Danubians' on the world stage, instead degenerated into an ugly, spiteful affair. It was won 2–1 by the ageing Wunderteam, who themselves would go on to be beaten in the semi-final by the host nation and eventual winners, Italy.

Hungary's having to lower themselves to devious ways and the Wunderteam's failure not just to win but to make an impression at the tournament marked the beginning of the end of the golden age of Danubian football, and a sea change in how the game was played. The triumphant Italians brought new ways: cynicism over flamboyance, hard tactics over luck and defence over attack. Their first and foremost measure was to contain the opposition by any fair or foul means, with danger men and playmakers smothered by man-marking or bruised into submission. It wasn't attractive football by any means, but was, as Italy's domination of the 1930s would testify, very effective.

Four years later, Hungary would have their chance to measure the progress of their football against the Italians, when the two faced each other in the final of the 1938 World Cup. The tournament, held in France, wasn't one of history's strongest. Argentina and Uruguay abstained in protest at the tournament being held in Europe (for a second time); England and Scotland refused to enter; Spain, engulfed in civil war, were denied entry; and Austria couldn't enter, their country no longer existing, having been incorporated months earlier into the German Reich.

The weak field gave Hungary cause for optimism, but they raced to the final even more easily than they could have hoped for, with a goal ratio of 13 to one – defeating Dutch East Indies[26] 6–0, Switzerland 2–0 and, in the semi-final, Sweden 5–1. And, on the eve of the final, they fell apart.

Before the tournament the Hungarian FA had, finally, relinquished team selection to the new team coach – though it was Dr Károly Dietz, the former head of the selection board. It was a move in the right direction, but with the wrong person. Dietz, a former chief of the Budapest police, was an unbending man with little regard for fancy football and even less for players' opinions. On naming his team for the final Dietz inexplicably, and without explanation, omitted three of Hungary's very best players, Géza Toldi, Lajos Korányi and Vilmos Kohut. The left-winger Kohut was in particular considered an asset to the team. He played in France for József Eisenhoffer's Olympique Marseilles, and Dietz, in selecting him for the World Cup squad, had gone against the FA's policy of only selecting players who played in Hungary, with the aim of winning the support of the French public, who'd long taken to the fast and powerful 'le canon Hongrois'.

A rumour spread among the squad that Mussolini had asked Regent Horthy to allow Italy to win the World Cup for the good of fascism and therefore Dietz was under orders to deliberately lose. It was a rumour that was taken seriously by a good number of the Hungarian team. Fascism was on the rise across Europe, and nowhere more so than in Hungary, and those players who had been affected by its consequences had no desire to aid its growth further. One key player, József Turay, even went so far as to refuse to play in what had been dubbed the 'Final of the Fascists'.

Such discord was no preparation for a World Cup final against the reigning champions, whom Hungary hadn't beaten in 13 years. The Italian coach, Vittorio Pozzo, *technico* for 19 years, remembered his team of '38 as his strongest. The Azzurri, backed by the Mussolini fascist government's almost unlimited funding, had prepared for the tournament for a month, the Hungarians for a week on a shoestring. The Azzurri were fit, experienced, organised – in short, world champions. They were also very cunning: shirt-pulling, blocking, tripping, toe-treading and questioning the referee. To the Hungarians, this was all new, but they'd too learn in time. The Italians invited the Hungarians to attack, and once they'd spread themselves too thinly, hit them on the counter-attack. Hungary scored twice, the Italians four times, a scoreline that didn't do the reigning world champions justice.

While the Italian team returned to Rome to be feted as heroes and granted a personal reception with Benito Mussolini, clad for the occasion in his famous white suit, the returning Hungarians returned to a somewhat darker homecoming. A police escort and an enormous brooding crowd awaited them at Budapest's Keleti railway station with Dietz being the main focus of their ire. Obviously not a man to take a hint, it would be weeks before Dietz resigned and then only after placards labelling him a traitor were plastered all over Budapest. In his resignation letter, Dietz stated that no outside forces had influenced his World Cup Final selection. Few believed him.

In April 1941, Hungary entered the Second World War on the side of Nazi Germany. Hitler had cultivated its support with trade deals and by forcing Czechoslovakia to return to it territory lost in the Trianon Treaty. In return, when the time came for Hitler to launch Operation Barbarossa, the German Reich's invasion of Russia, he demanded Hungary's military assistance.

But, as Hungary's losses on the Eastern Front mounted, Hitler's popularity nosedived as Hungarians came to realise that this war was but a repeat of the First World War, with Hungary as a sacrificial lamb for another nation's battle.

Regent Horthy too saw the war as futile, and he was grieving for a son, István, killed on the Eastern Front. Horthy rued allowing his government to become indebted to Hitler, whom he loathed: a common infantryman and Austrian to boot. Horthy entered secret talks with the Western Allies mooting the idea of Hungary surrendering, talks that were so secret that Hitler knew of them before they took place. For Horthy's betrayal, Hitler had German troops, albeit bloodlessly, invade Hungary.

Hungary remaining Germany's ally was of huge importance to Hitler, so Horthy was permitted to remain as its leader, though all further policies were decided in Berlin. The most significant was the deportation of Hungary's Jews, who, due to their government's allying with Nazi Germany, had hitherto been spared transportation to concentration camps, although they had had to live under harsh anti-Jewish laws which had forbidden them from employment and owning businesses.

During a period of 55 days during the summer of 1944, half a million of Hungary's 760,000 Jewish population was transported to Auschwitz. This, however, did not sit well with Horthy. While no lover of the Jews, Horthy was fearful of later repercussions from the Allies for both himself and Hungary, especially with the Soviet army nearing ever closer to Hungary's borders.

Hitler perceived Horthy's abrupt ceasing of the deportations as 'weakness'. And, his patience at an end, Hitler had Horthy's remaining son kidnapped from the family's palatial home and placed in a concentration camp, his 'well being' depending on his father's compliance in handing over power to Ferenc Szálasi, leader of the Hungarian Nazis.

At any other time, Szálasi would have been a hard man to take seriously. His speeches were rambling and incoherent, and he believed Jesus to have been a Magyar and the Bible to have been written in a Magyar-like language. Even Hitler was suspicious of Szálasi's uber-patriotism, but reasoned (as much as Hitler could reason) that a Szálasi government would rid Hungary of Jews, political opponents and anyone else they deemed undesirable, before the Soviet army reached Budapest.

Szálasi and his henchmen didn't rid Hungary of all of the above, but in the three months that they were in power they did try, and with a bloodlust that shocked even the Nazi Germans. The Arrow Cross were only tempered by the Red Army surrounding Budapest in the winter of 1944–45, setting the stage for one of the most critical battles of the war: the 'Siege of Budapest', a hundred days of bitter house-to-house fighting between the Soviet and German armies, with pockets of Hungarians fighting on both sides. By the time the isolated German command surrendered in February 1945, the death toll of civilians was 25,000, many from starvation and cold. A quarter of the city's buildings were destroyed, not a bridge remained over the Danube, and every animal in the city zoo had been consumed.

It was a sorry end to a sorry war, and as the smoke cleared and the bedraggled citizens of Budapest climbed out of their basements, some hoped that the Russians would be better than the Germans; others hoped that they wouldn't stay for long. Others weren't so sure …

CHAPTER 3

Sebes was a real narrow-minded, iron-fisted communist.

He did not believe in God, or man. He believed in communism.

Gyula Grosics

AS a reward for victory, the Soviet army command awarded their troops three days to 'enjoy the spoils of war', triggering a revenge-fuelled orgy of raping, robbing and looting upon the beleaguered Hungarian populace that lasted weeks.

The barbarism was advocated by Moscow, who felt Hungarians to be deserving of their mistreatment – after all, theirs was an enemy nation whose armies had themselves committed atrocities in Russia and upon being invaded had refused to surrender or turn against their German occupiers. For the 80,000 Soviet lives lost in the 'liberation' of Hungary, a price had to be paid.

Hungary's womenfolk fared the worst. It is estimated that 200,000 Hungarian females were victims of rape at the hands of marauding Soviet troops, starved of home leave and possessing the belief that the enemy's womenfolk were fiar game. In Budapest alone, 10 per cent of the entire female population were raped. The vast majority of victims were infected with sexual diseases, a matter made worse by the chronic shortage of medicines. Abortion was made legal and free to cope with the levels of unwanted pregnancies.

Hungarian males too had good reason to avoid any dealings with the Soviet patrols. During the battle for Budapest, the Soviet command, in their reports to Moscow, had hugely exaggerated the number of Hungarian troops defending the city so as to appease Stalin's annoyance at the battle taking so long. Thus in the battle's aftermath the Soviet command, to fulfil their lie that they had captured 110,000 Hungarian POWs, simply rounded up 50,000 civilians to make up the shortfall. This number was then substantially added to by the post-war Soviet Union's need for slave labour on which its economy had come to rely, resulting in around 200,000 Hungarian civilian males being deported to Siberian Gulags, and of whom only a third returned, many years later. German-speaking Swabs were supposed to be specifically targeted for deportation, but the Soviets were indiscriminate in their selection. Males who appeared to be fit for labour were rounded up by trigger-happy Soviet patrols barking 'malenkaya robot!' – the Russian for 'a little work'. Many even went so far as to join the Communist Party in the hope that a card-carrying membership would be enough to prevent them being carted off – alas, it was not. Communists, Jews and Roma found themselves in equally dire circumstances as they had been at the hands of the Nazis.

But when it came to looting, the Soviet troops truly surpassed themselves. A Soviet soldier raised in the stark poverty of communist Russia, on reaching Budapest, was confronted for the first time in his life with a Western metropolis. No matter how nonsensical the item or whether they knew its use, if the Soviet troops thought it was worth *anything*, they took it. Stories remain in Hungarian folklore of the Russians drinking out of toilets in the belief that they were for that very purpose and, once their thirst was quenched, taking away the toilet. Entire apartment blocks were stripped of furniture and fittings, farms of livestock; churches and cemeteries were ransacked and banks emptied. Civilians were robbed of clothes and valuables, wristwatches being a particular target. Even Moscow was in on the plunder, despatching to Budapest art and history experts to relieve the city's museums of their most valuable items.

The Soviet Union's ultimate plan was to make Hungary a satellite state whose sole reason for existence would be to serve the motherland. Stalin had insisted that wherever in Europe the Red Army reached, the Soviet Union would have 100 per cent control. As it was, the Soviets had long made preparations to seize political control in Hungary, readying for the task some thousand Hungarian communists who, during the Horthy regime, had fled Hungary and found refuge in the Soviet Union. Known in Hungary as 'Muscovites', these men and a small number of women had spent their time in Moscow being trained in espionage and educated in the running of specific governmental departments, their fate depending on the paranoid whims of Stalin, and with every right to be nervous. Even Béla Kun, founder of Hungary's Communist Party, was a victim of Stalin's purges. Arrested on spying charges in 1939, Kun was transported to a Siberian Gulag, where he died soon after.

By 1945 the most senior Muscovite was 46-year-old Mátyás Rákosi, notorious in Hungary for his active and bloody role in the 'Red Terror'. Rákosi was a complex man: witty, charming, clean-living, faithful to his Mongol wife, and a murdering psychopath. He was a Jew, born Mátyás Rosenfeld, the tenth child of a provincial greengrocer. A photographic memory enabled him to earn a scholarship to a prestigious Budapest university (as well as learn ten languages and never forget a slight), after which he entered a career in banking, working in both Berlin and London.

He returned to Hungary to join the army on the outbreak of the First World War, fought on the Eastern Front, was captured by the Russians, and at the war's end was one of many thousands of POWs who returned home as converts to Bolshevism. Few, though, were more violently committed than Rákosi, for which Béla Kun rewarded him with a ministerial role once the communists took power. However, Rákosi's time in parliament, as Hungary's youngest ever minister, was as brief as the 133-day communist government.

He fled Hungary, then returned incognito, and was recognised, arrested and sentenced to 15 years' imprisonment (three of which he served in solitary confinement). On his release Rákosi headed to Moscow, to be paraded as a hero, and even given the honour of standing next to Stalin for the 1940 anniversary celebration of the Russian Revolution held in Red Square. And yet despite the show of comradeship, the anti-Semite Stalin loathed Rákosi, never failing to make derogatory remarks about his humped back and bald dome or accuse him of being a British spy. But Rákosi survived because he had his uses: the foremost of which was that he slavishly followed edicts to the letter, without question and delay.

In February 1945, the self-styled 'Stalin's best pupil' (Hungarians preferred 'arsehead') was despatched back to Hungary to take immediate control of the Hungarian Communist Party.

If you were today to ask a Hungarian of their opinion of the Soviet Union's regime in Hungary, after a snort of derision you would probably receive an answer mentioning rape, corruption, oppression, concrete housing blocks, empty shops, alcoholism, suicides, prison camps and secret police. Pushed to find any positives, most will admit that crime was almost non-existent, jobs were secure for life, streets were kept free of litter, the later regime of the 1970s and 80s was nowhere near as harsh as that of the earlier Stalinist regimes, sport facilities were excellent and plentiful, and Hungarian athletes were among the very best in the world.

From the start, the Soviets ensured that sport was under their control. Besides the entertainment for the masses that sport provided, a nation of fit and occupied young persons was less likely to turn its energies and attentions to the goings-on of the government.

The Soviets, on overseeing the forming of a provisional government made up of leaders from Hungary's left-wing parties, placed sport under the governance of the Education Ministry, which in turn oversaw the re-forming of the Hungarian FA and the appointment of one Tibor Gallowich as Hungary's new national team coach.

The 45-year-old Gallowich was a former goalkeeper but had become better known as a sports journalist, and after that as coach of the Budapest club Vasas. Founded in 1900 by the Metalworkers' Union (Vasas being the shortened term for *Vás és Fémmunkasók Sport Klub* – 'Iron and Metalworkers' Sports Club'), the club was quick to gather a loyal following of socialists and trade unionists.

In 1941 Gallowich, who via his sports columns never made any secret of his political leaning, was appointed the club's coach, but he lasted only two years before being targeted for arrest by the Nazis, as they stepped up the persecution of left-wing opponents. He quit Vasas and went into hiding, but one day, having gone out in search of food, was run over by a tram. Rather than be hospitalised, which meant running the risk of capture, Gallowich insisted on being taken to the home and care of his elderly father. The Gestapo learned of this and sent an arresting party. Gallowich clambered down a lift shaft, slipped and plummeted to the ground, knocking himself unconscious, breaking even more bones but escaping arrest – and to learn that being hunted by the Gestapo placed a man in good stead in the new socialist Hungary.

Yet come his appointment as national team coach, Gallowich still had not fully recovered from his injuries, so the Hungarian FA found for him an assistant, a former MTK player by the name of Gusztáv Sebes.

The 40-year-old Sebes was a dour, humourless man whose playing and coaching career had produced little of note – thus his appointment to one of the most prestigious coaching roles in European football came as a great surprise to many until it was pointed out that Sebes was a genuine communist, and not one of the many thousands of 'chancers' who'd joined the party in the wake of the Soviet liberation, raising the Communist Party membership from 2,000 to 500,000 within six months. Even during the Stalinist regime's darkest days, when it was obvious that things had gone seriously awry, Sebes's belief in communism never wavered, yet this is no great wonder, considering how well communism served him, that a man as loyal and honourable as Gusztáv Sebes would only choose to serve it back in return.

Football history often describes Sebes as the 'mastermind' behind the Magical Magyars – an all-seeing, all-controlling coaching genius, the source of all innovative ideas and tactics. This is as over-simplistic as it is over-generous – Sebes was no genius. He was, though, a competent coach who *possibly* would have been successful in his own right. Unarguably his great fortune was his being a communist at the 'right time'. This is not to do Sebes an injustice – a lesser man would have failed to seize the opportunity that was handed to him, and Sebes did so with such ambition, dedication and determination that it would have to be eventually prised from his grasp.

Football and communism were the two constant threads throughout Sebes's life. He was a Swab, born in Ferencváros, a stone's throw from the Ferencváros stadium. His cobbler father was a communist, another POW convert of the Russians during the First World War. Such beliefs, though, in Horthy's Hungary led to blacklistings, and, ever unable to find permanent work, the family suffered. Sebes was consequently forced to leave school early, but, tarred with the same brush as his father, he too failed to hold down a permanent job; and he too became involved with the communists, who would send agitators to recruit men and women from labour exchanges – though Sebes's breaking into the Vasas youth team at the same time kept him occupied and away from becoming too immersed.

Aged 18, Sebes joined his brother Ferenc (also a communist) working in a factory in France. In Paris, Sebes began playing for a team of Hungarian émigrés who played to a reasonable standard in the French Workers League, and in 1926 was selected to play for the French Workers XI against a team of visiting Russians. His performance in the match drew the attention of the coach of Olympique de Billancourt, the team of the Renault factory, who duly lured Sebes with an offer of better-paid employment as a fitter. But concern for his elderly parents and a desire to make a success of himself in Hungarian football had Sebes returning home after little more than a year.

Back in Budapest, he began playing and working for MOM, a sprawling glass factory in Buda, whose works football team played in the lower divisions. Sebes though was of a standard way above this level and was soon signed up by the mighty MTK, or 'Hungária' as the club had become known having turned professional a year earlier in 1926.

While Sebes professed to abhor professionalism in sport, believing that financial reward as an incentive corrupted sport's very ethic, he also had to admit that being paid to play football was better than working elsewhere. So perhaps to hide his embarrassment, on joining Hungária Sebes changed his surname from the Swabian 'Scharenpeck' to the Hungarian 'Sebes', a word that translates to 'swift' and was a tongue-in-cheek recommendation by Hungária coach Ágoston Weisz in joking reference to Sebes's notorious lack of speed. Marking out a forte as a utility player, willing to carry out instructions to the letter, Sebes remained at Hungária for the next 13 seasons, playing some 200 times for the club and much to his eternal pride once for the Hungarian national team.

Sebes was 34 years old when he left Hungária, after anti-Jewish laws that forbade Jews from owning a football club and even indeed earning money from the sport in any capacity, forced the disbandment of Hungária. Sebes took a job as a repairman with the Budapest Electricity Board, and was soon coaching their football team –

Elektromos – in the nation's reduced 'War League'. Success there led to two equally successful coaching spells at first division clubs, Szentlőrinci AC and Csepel SC respectively.

Sebes spent the war years quietly coaching Elektromos in the reduced war league, went back to school to finish the exams denied to him as a child, and kept his opinions very much to himself. But as the Nazis began to take more control in Hungary, Sebes began to worry more: he'd never made a secret of his being a communist, but, as a man of few words, he'd never bragged nor politicised it either. But now, with the Arrow Cross executing any perceived enemy on sight, Sebes had to walk a tightrope between avoiding all contact with known Nazis and at the same time, as part of his job, assisting them in disconnecting the electricity of apartments in Budapest's Jewish ghettos. Yet nothing cemented Sebes's hatred of the Nazis more than their shooting dead his brother Ferenc in the early days of Budapest's siege. Ferenc Scharenpeck had been Sebes's best friend, and his death affected Sebes for a lifetime, especially the memory of having to inform his elderly parents of the tragic news.

But then came a reverse in fortunes. As the Siege of Budapest came to an end, Sebes was sought out by an old acquaintance he knew as János Csermanek. The two knew each other from playing together as youths at Vasas, formed a friendship of sorts based largely on their both being communists, and then went their separate ways. By 1942 Csermanek was the leader of the clandestine Communist Party, and was using the pseudonym János Kádár (meaning 'cooper'), a name that he thereafter kept for life.

But post-war, because Kádár was a 'Hungarian communist' (i.e. one not trained in Moscow), the Soviets did not trust him to lead the party, and so replaced him with the Muscovite Mátyás Rákosi.

Nonetheless, Kádár remained of use. He was popular with Hungary's home-grown communists, and his domestic knowledge was used by the Soviets to appoint secretaries for the newly formed district Communist Parties springing up across the country. Kádár was careful to bestow the appointments upon persons he personally knew to be unequivocal communists.

At the same time, the Hungarian FA was in the process of searching for an assistant for Tibor Gallowich, and what coach had better credentials than Comrade Sebes – party secretary for the Buda district of Budafok?

Hungary's domestic football resumed in May 1945 with an 11-week 'Summer League'. The Hungarian national team resumed in the August, playing two matches in successive days against Austria in Budapest.

The new dawn of socialist football broke on a sweltering summer's afternoon at a sold-out Ferencváros stadium. Hungary won by a comfortable 2–0 against an Austrian team playing their first match since their country had been released from annexation by Germany.

For the next day's match, Tibor Gallowich, bolstered by Austria's under-par performance, decided to select four debutants, one of whom was a cocksure inside-left by the name of Ferenc Puskás.

In selecting the 17-year-old, Gallowich made Puskás (pronounced *Push-kash*) Hungary's youngest ever debutant. It was an international debut much awaited by the Hungarian public, but against hardened internationals Puskás failed to shine as he did at league level, and, despite Hungary winning 5–2, provided no real glimpse as to his talents. But he did provide an insight as to what team-mates could expect …

In the game's 12th minute, Hungary captain Gyula Zsengellér found himself with only the Austrian goalkeeper to beat, but rather than shoot he instead passed to the unmarked Puskás, who had called politely for the ball by shouting 'Uncle Gyula!' On collecting the squared pass, Puskás calmly rolled the ball into the empty net for Hungary's first goal.

Minutes later, Zsengellér again rounded his marker, and as he bore down on the Austrian goal, Puskás again called for the ball – but Zsengellér, instead of passing, chose to shoot, a shot that sailed wide. The teenage debutant turned to Hungary's 1938 World Cup star: 'Fucking hell, Zsengellér! Couldn't you see I was unmarked?'

In November 1945, the Soviets oversaw the very first democratic elections in Hungary's history, and the first in which the vote was extended to women and the peasantry. But 'democratic' was a loose term. Right-wing parties could not enter because they were forbidden to exist, and before giving permission for the election to go ahead, Moscow insisted that, whatever the result, the government was to be a coalition, ensuring the communists a seat in parliament.

Come election day, the Smallholders' Party, a centre-left party formed by farmers and small businessmen and led by a Calvinist minister, Zoltán Tildy, won the majority of the vote: 57 per cent to the communists' 17 per cent. But in reality Tildy was only ever to be a figurehead president. The real and absolute power lay with the Soviets. And it was only when Tildy came to designate government departments that the reason for the Soviets' uncompromising stance on a coalition government became apparent: Moscow wanted control of the Interior Ministry, the department responsible for the nation's policing and inland security.

The man appointed Minister of the Interior was a hard-line home-grown Hungarian communist by the name of László Rajk (pronounced 'Rike'), under whose jurisdiction the Soviets placed the Department of National Security – Államvédelmi Osztály (ÁVO).

The ÁVO stemmed from the Department of Political Security – Politikai Rendészeti Osztály (PRO) – an organisation set up by the Allies to capture and prosecute Nazis. Quite without irony, and perhaps to save on transporting evidence, the PRO had made their headquarters in the very same Pest building that had been the headquarters of the Hungarian Nazi Party, a building abandoned with subterranean cells and torture apparatus still intact.[27] By implementing hastily passed laws allowing them to intern people indefinitely on suspicion of having associated with the Nazis, the PRO ensured the arrest and execution of hundreds of 'war criminals', including Ferenc Szálasi and four of the Horthy regime's former prime ministers.

Once the PRO had served its purpose, the Soviets, not wanting such a ready-made 'secret police' to go to waste, changed the name to 'ÁVO', kept the staff and headquarters and ordered a new target for arrest: opponents of the communists.

Rákosi, with a secret police at his disposal, was able to begin what he would notoriously boast to be his 'salami tactics', slicing away opponents one at a time. Rákosi's first prominent target was a particularly outspoken critic of his: Béla Kovács, a popular Smallholders politician who (naively) believed that his parliamentary status gave him immunity from political arrest. In the winter of 1946–47, Kovács was arrested and taken to the ÁVO headquarters, where, under torture, he confessed to treason, for which he was transported to the Soviet

Union for punishment. Béla Kovács would not return to Hungary for nine years, during which time his family did not know whether he was dead or alive.

Rákosi's next target was the prime minister, Ferenc Nagy. In the coalition government, the majority Smallholders leader, Zoltán Tildy, was president; Nagy, as leader of the second-largest majority party, the Social Democrats, was prime minister; and Rákosi deputy prime minister. President Tildy was of too high a profile internationally for Rákosi's 'slicer', but Nagy was an obstacle that Moscow no longer chose to tolerate. In May 1947, Nagy went on a trip to Switzerland and in his absence, Rákosi, as deputy prime minister, called a cabinet meeting at which he produced a signed confession by Béla Kovács from his captivity in Siberia incriminating Nagy in a conspiracy to overthrow the government. On learning of the charges brought against him, Nagy simply refused to return to Hungary, instead announcing his resignation as prime minister – although only once his five-year-old son had been delivered to him safely at the Swiss border. Ferenc Nagy never returned to Hungary.

The purgings of Kovács and Nagy were met with disapproval in Western diplomatic circles; but, other than some cross words, none of the victorious Allied governments were willing to risk a backlash from their own war-weary people by picking a new war with Soviet Russia – especially over Hungary, a nation that had so readily sided with Nazi Germany.

Hungary was on its own.

CHAPTER 4

Little money, little football.
Big money, big football.

Ferenc Puskás

FERENC Puskás was loud-mouthed, boastful, loyal, funny, generous and a football genius who became by far and away Hungary's greatest ever footballer. He was the original 'number ten' playmaker – the predecessor to Eusébio, Pelé, Cruyff, Maradona, Zidane and Messi. His funeral in 2006 was a day of national mourning, and his grave lies in the crypt of Budapest's Saint Stephen's Basilica, an honour bestowed upon only the most revered of Hungary's national heroes.

His father was Ferenc Purczeld, a professional footballer who at the time of his only son's birth played for Vasas, moving out to the outskirts of Budapest to join Kispesti AC when Puskás was a year old. It was once in Kispest that he Hungarianised the family name from Purczeld to Puskás, meaning 'gunner'.

Kispest (meaning Little-Pest) is today a suburb of Pest, but in 1928 it was a town in its own right, the sixth largest in the country. The club provided Purczeld with a part-time job in a local slaughterhouse and subsidised housing in a tenement block.[28] The apartment was cramped and with no running water but, for the boy Puskás at least, had the bonus of overlooking the Kispest pitch. His first memory was hearing the roar of the Kispest crowd from his kitchen window. By the time he could toddle, Puskás was out on the local grounds, amusing and amazing the older kids with his juggling, dribbling and vocabulary of colourful curses. He was affectionately nicknamed 'Öcsi' ('Oochy'), meaning 'little brother', a nickname by which Puskás would be known in Hungary (by those that liked him) for life.

By the age of ten, Puskás was playing for Kispest youth team, albeit under another player's name to get around the fact that he was underage. The identity of the wonder kid was an open secret, and it wasn't as if he was a shrinking violet who needed protecting. Although the other boys all towered over him, Puskás was the best player by far, but his habit of bossing *everyone* was too much for the team coach, Nándor Szűcs. A local greengrocer who ran the team voluntarily, Szűcs objected to being told what to do by a child, and handed the club an ultimatum: either the boy goes or he does. Kispest replaced him with Puskás's father.

In his later years, Puskás would credit his father as the most significant influence upon the way he played football, thanking him for 'all the things he didn't teach me'. Puskás senior was no overbearing parent, pushing his offspring to excel at all costs. So overjoyed was he that his son shared his passion for football that he encouraged and indulged the boy all he could, letting him run training sessions and turning a deaf ear to his running mouth.

Puskás's traits of ball-hogging and over-reliance on his left foot stemmed from his being left to his own devices. It also allowed him to develop his own style of play, which as he matured made him almost impossible to dispossess with the ball at his feet, as testified by the highly respected Scottish international Tommy Docherty (later to become manager of Manchester United) when given the role of man-marking Puskás during a Scotland–Hungary match in 1954:

> He was a master at screening the ball, and even though he looked a little portly even then, he used every part of his body to full effect. When he received the ball, he would turn his back to me. When I came around to his side he would then twist and turn, an arm would come out to fend me off. If not an arm then he would use a shoulder or his backside. All I could do was constantly reposition myself, harass and hustle the man until he inadvertently offered me a glimpse of the ball, whereupon I'd attempt to get a toe on it and hopefully knock it away. One thing I noticed about Puskás was how he always held his head high when the ball was at his

> feet. Not once did I see him look down to see where the ball was, which enabled him to assess the movements of his team-mates and opponents alike. He was more than just a stylish creator; I found him quite aggressive.[29]

But it was a father's overindulgence that was also to Puskás's detriment. The boy Öcsi became the man, and the adult Puskás was equally crude, dismissive of authority and unwilling to accept even the most well-intentioned of advice. It was a side to his character that some found amusing, perhaps because they themselves lacked the courage to backchat and insult, but many others were less than impressed.

There was one person, however, to whom Puskás did defer: his best friend and next-door neighbour, a quietly spoken boy with piercing blue eyes called József Bozsik. The same József Bozsik who would go on to become the first player to represent the Hungarian national team 100 times.

In football history, world-class footballers coming from the same district is unusual, but two coming from the very same tenement block at the same time is unprecedented, though not a coincidence. The town of Kispest produced a disproportionate number of professional footballers. The standard of play on the local grounds was famously high. A professional contract at a club was one viable escape, if not from the town, then from the drudgery of working in a local factory. All five of the Bozsik brothers would go on to play football at a league level, and even by Kispest standards their upbringing was poor. The family father, a factory labourer, suffered from tuberculosis, a disease that not only rendered him unemployable for long periods but would kill him while his sons were still boys.

The Puskás family were positively wealthy by comparison, security which allowed their only son to adopt a gregarious and reckless attitude. Bozsik, knowing the facts of life, was the complete opposite. The older by 18 months, he provided for Puskás the role of a surrogate elder brother – a bond that would, though, prove especially beneficial for Puskás as his fame and ego grew. Surrounded by sycophants, Puskás had to continually act up to being the 'Puskás' people expected. But in Bozsik he had someone he didn't feel pressure to make laugh or impress. They remained close friends for a lifetime.

The right-half Bozsik made his Kispest league debut two years *before* Puskás, and his international debut two years *after*; against Bulgaria in 1947. Puskás was absent; Hungary won 9–0. When Puskás returned for Hungary's next game against Austria in September 1947, he and Bozsik lined up for the first time together. Hungary lost 4–3.

Quickly, though, Puskás became a target for Italian clubs. After Hungary played in Italy in 1947 (and lost 3–2), Puskás was approached by representatives from Juventus, offering him a large sum of cash, a brand new car, an apartment and a role for his father on the club's coaching staff. In dubious disbelief, Puskás asked for time to consider the offer before quickly conferring with his team-mates, who confirmed that the Fiat-backed club could indeed easily afford to fulfil such generous terms.

But, as sorely tempted as Puskás was, he was to accept he was in no position to make the move. The welfare of his paternal family, German-speaking Swabs, very much depended on Puskás's loyalty to the new socialist Hungary. Because of Hungary's Swabian population's links with Germany it was they who were explicitly targeted for deportation by the Soviets. In January 1945, some 35,000 of them were rounded up and deported to the Soviet Union. And within a year, double that number had been sent 'back' to Germany, where a differing future awaited depending on which zone of Germany they were deported to, West or East. Puskás's aunt (his father's sister) and her family would have been among them had her famous nephew not intervened.

Another reason for Puskás remaining was that money-wise, at least compared with the average Hungarian, he wasn't doing too badly. Kispest, to entice him and Bozsik to stay, supplied the pair with a shop selling kitchen utensils, although what they knew about pots and pans was anyone's guess. He also went on tour with Ferencváros to Central America in the summer of 1947; during the negotiations for this tour, he is supposed to have said, 'Little money, little football. Big money, big football.' It is a comment for which Puskás is notorious in Hungary, often reeled out to portray him as the (grand) father of money-greedy footballers. And although he always denied saying it, Puskás did do very well out of the tour – the $1,500 he earned was enough to buy a house in Kispest[30] and still have some money left over.

Lesser-known footballers had less reason to stay. The financial incentive of playing in Italy outweighed any reason to remain in Hungary, where a succession of poor harvests and the nation's crippling obligation to supply the Soviet Union with produce and war repatriation payments had spiralled the currency into the most extreme bout of hyperinflation anywhere, at any time in history.[31] Matters were stabilised somewhat with the introduction of a new currency, the forint (still in use today), but it did not replace people's savings or pensions, or alleviate the queues in shops for the increasingly expensive, but increasingly meagre, goods on offer. Circa 1947, no laws existed in Hungary that prevented citizens from freely leaving the country (this would soon change). And as Hungary's footballers began to head to Italy in large numbers, FA president István Ries, fearing a repeat of the exodus to Italy of a generation of Hungary's footballers in the 1920s, resorted straight to pleading:

> We ask you to come home. We await with love everybody who wants to take part in the rebuilding of Hungarian sport. There will be no repercussions if within a month you return. Come back! Hungary calls you! We need you! Whoever can manfully and respectfully see that they made a mistake, we will respect you even more. Come home! Do not carry the unforgivable sin of going into exile from your homeland![32]

When pleading failed to stem the flow, the amnesty was extended for another month, and then again a month after. And still players kept disappearing, and none returning. At the end of the second amnesty, the government came to the end of their tether. There would be no more amnesties and no more tolerance towards athletes leaving Hungary. They had been warned.

In the summer of 1948, Hungary's two leading political parties, the Communist Party and the Social Democrats, merged to form the Hungarian Socialist Workers' Party. The Social Democrats had had no say in the matter, and nor was their leader, the president, Zoltán Tildy, given a role in the new party – in fact quite the opposite.

Tildy, a deeply religious, honourable man, had long been a nuisance to Moscow, refusing to do as they bid. The Soviets wanted rid of him, but as president he was too internationally visible to be arrested on trumped-up charges – so instead his family was targeted. Tildy's diplomat son-in-law was arrested and charged with 'illegal activities' (corruption and adultery), sentenced to death and hanged. The terrified Tildy resigned, and he and his wife were placed under house arrest, where they would remain for nine years.

Tildy was replaced by Árpád Szakasits, a leading Social Democrat, a communist stooge and a man prepared to do as ordered. Szakasits would remain in the figurehead role for a year, until he served his purpose of demonstrating democracy, and moved aside to allow Rákosi to become president.

One of the last ceremonies Zoltán Tildy performed as president was to cut the ribbon on a proposed 80,000-capacity national stadium. Ideas for a national stadium had been mooted for decades, but due to wars, costs and political squabbles, none ever developed any further than the drawing board. The communists, however, were determined to construct a stadium that was on a par with, or indeed better than, any in the world, no matter what the cost. Future visitors to sports events in communist Hungary may have to go through endless hoops to be able to attend, but once there, they could not fail to be impressed, overawed even, with what the Rákosi regime had achieved. Well, that was the plan anyway.

A further plan for the stadium was for it also to be the home of the first-division club Vasas. The club of the Metalworkers' Union was considered the 'club of the workers', and when the communists came to recognise the propaganda value of football, Vasas was deemed the perfect club to be associated with. In the communists' taking over of the club, János Kádár, the Communist Party wartime leader, was appointed its president, with Mátyás Rákosi as honorary president. But, in truth, neither Kádár nor Rákosi held any more than a passing interest in football. Kádár much preferred chess, although as a schoolboy he had played for Vasas's youth team, and as an adult he had occasionally turned out for the Communist Party team alongside Sebes and Tibor Gallowich. Rákosi didn't mind the spectacle of the sport, but the unpredictability of large crowds made him uneasy.

Therefore Vasas was run by the club's former president, Gyula Hegyi, who had been allowed to remain as managing director. A veteran communist, Hegyi was also appointed minister of a newly formed Sports Ministry, established to control the running of sport in Hungary. But, like all who were in positions of political influence in Stalinist Hungary, the former lathe operator Hegyi was not his own man. Ordered by his communist bosses to form a committee to prepare Hungarian athletics for the summer's London Olympics, Hegyi was further instructed to appoint as his president an old adversary: Gusztáv Sebes.

The two hated each other dating back to the 1920s, when Sebes played for Vasas's youth team and Hegyi was a club administrator. Their paths crossed again a few years later in France when they both worked in the Renault factory in Billancourt. Hegyi, as the Hungarian workers' trade union representative at the factory, was jealous that the newcomer Sebes, as the star of the factory football team, held more sway with the factory management. Sebes was no less enamoured with Hegyi: 'I only ever saw him trouble himself with beer, wine and palinká. Not once did I see him dealing with the union's workers.' Twenty-five years later, the relationship remained thus.

Sebes, while proud at being chosen, was as loath to serve under Hegyi as he was to vacate, even temporarily, his role with the national football team. It was evident that Tibor Gallowich could not remain head coach for very much longer. The injuries he'd suffered during the war had begun to take their toll on him as he aged, and to cope he turned to drink. A half-pissed Gallowich became a figure of quiet exasperation, changing line-ups without a word of explanation and giving rambling, incomprehensible team talks in which he would quote philosophical works to his bemused charges. He left the task of training the team to his overbearing but trustworthy assistant. In fact, Sebes did everything except select the team.

Having made himself indispensable, Sebes was reluctant to release his grasp, even going so far as to approach one of the most fearsome men in the country, the Muscovite Minister for Transport, Ernő Gerő. Sebes told Gerő that he felt he did not know enough about athletics to accept the Olympic Committee's presidency. It was an excuse Gerő brushed aside, replying, 'It is an assignment, and treat it as such. What do you think I knew about transport before I became transport minister? I simply bought a ticket and boarded the train. Surround yourself with people who know what they are doing, and you will be fine.'[33]

The sinister Gerő was not a man easily refused, and besides it was good advice that Sebes would use from there on. And, as it was, once in London he began to enjoy himself. The Olympics opened up a new world for Sebes. The meter reader was listened to, respected. He had come a long way. But, as ever, there was a cloud: while in London, Sebes learned that Tibor Gallowich had recruited two temporary assistants. The first was Gábor Kléber, a journalist for *Népsport* ('Peoples' Sport'), a popular sports daily formerly called *Nemzeti Sport* ('National Sport') until it was taken over in 1945 by the Communist Party's propaganda ministry. Kléber's arrival did not overly concern Sebes – the two were friends, having played together for MTK during the 1920s; and in 1946 Kléber had written an article in *Népsport* in which he lavishly praised Sebes as the future of Hungarian football.

The second coach, however, was a name that was enough to give Sebes sleepless nights – coach of the league champions, Újpest: Béla Guttmann.

CHAPTER 5

The time of sport being funded by patrons is over. The Communist Party are now the funders of sport. We want to grow a nation of fit and strong workers! We want sport to be in schools, factories and offices. We want the people to be fit mentally and physically so that we can build the country. This is why we are supporting sport. And us communists, when we make a promise, we keep it!

Zoltán Vas, Mayor of Budapest

THE two greatest Hungarian coaches, Gusztáv Sebes and Béla Guttmann, were of the same generation, were both Danubian-taught in the same mould, were born of the same city, played for the same club – and were complete opposites.

The Swab Sebes was thrifty, saving for his pension from the day he left school; the Jew Guttmann was a big spender, a gambler who'd die penniless. Sebes was prepared to kowtow, Guttmann was intolerant of interference and loathed all forms of totalitarianism. Sebes was loyal, Guttmann was always angling to hawk himself to the highest bidder. Sebes thought in the long term, Guttmann's theory was that players respond better to a new coach and that spending any more than two seasons at one club for a coach was fatal. Sebes was the son of a cobbler, Guttmann was from a middle-class family. Sebes was a home bird, Guttmann a perennial wanderer.

Sebes was a patriot, Guttmann held little affection for his land of birth.

Béla Guttmann was born in 1899 in Budapest, the son of dance school teachers. Indeed he himself, when work in football was slack, would teach dance. The poise and balance Guttmann learned from dancing helped him greatly as a footballer, but the gracefulness he possessed was overshadowed by his intolerance of being told what to do. And he had a temper. His time at his first club, MTK, came to an abrupt end when he fell out with manager Herbert Burgess[34] after the Englishman dared to drop him. Guttmann replied as he always would once his ego was piqued: disregardful of the consequences, he quit. He headed to Vienna to join Hakoah Vienna, the 'Unbeatable Jews'. When Hakoah toured the east coast of the United States in 1926, Guttmann decided to remain in New York, where in between discovering the Manhattan high life he found time to play for a series of clubs. Then, in 1932, the Great Depression struck, the US league collapsed, and a bankrupt Guttmann returned to Europe; he spent three years coaching in Austria and Holland before heading back to America.

In obtaining a visa for the United States, Guttmann was extremely fortunate. The Americans could afford to be choosy, inundated as they were by hundreds of thousands of European Jews looking for a safe haven far from Europe. Yet while Guttmann liked America – a Jew with chutzpah could make it there – there was one major problem: there was no football. Therefore, on learning that the coach of Újpest, a friend and fellow Jew by the name of László Sternberg, was on his way to America to escape growing anti-Semitism in Hungary, Guttmann threw caution to the wind, contacted Újpest and headed back to Budapest.

It was 16 years since Guttmann had last been in Hungary, and for a brief while he was glad to be home. At Újpest he won the league in his first season, but by the following season anti-Jewish laws forced him to quit, and he was conscripted into an unarmed Jewish labour battalion.

Labouring alongside Guttmann was a fellow football coach by the name of Ernő Erbstein. The two knew each other from their days playing in the United States. Like Guttmann, the Wall Street crash had had the Transylvanian Erbstein heading back to Europe. In Italy, he became 'Ernesto Erbstein' and coach of Serie A Torino, lasting but a season before Italy's anti-Jewish laws forced him and his family (despite their converting from Judaism to Catholicism) to make a reluctant return to Hungary.

Who knows what emotions Guttmann and Erbstein felt once they'd recognised each other – shock, relief, maybe even shame? The last time they'd met had been as two affluent young men in Manhattan. Now here they were back in Hungary, half-starved, in slave labour. One evening, while sleeping in a railway siding, Guttmann and Erbstein (and three others) took their chances and escaped.

Guttmann raced to Újpest to hide out the rest of war hidden by his Catholic fiancée's family, while Erbstein went to an address in Pest that openly offered shelter to Jews, in an apartment under the fragile protection of Swedish Red Cross workers and diplomats.

The moment the German army surrendered, Erbstein wasted no time in collecting his wife and daughters (they had been hidden by a priest) and returned immediately to Italy and Torino, where his former job was waiting for him. Guttmann too would most probably have left just as sharply had it not been for his fiancée, soon to be wife, who wanted to remain in Hungary. He found work as coach of Vasas as the replacement for the new national team coach, Tibor Gallowich. Yet Guttmann and Vasas chairman Gyula Hegyi were always going to be at odds with one another. Guttmann's demanding his wages in food and clothes, rather than Hungary's hyperinflationary currency, instantly peeved Hegyi. Guttmann only lasted a year before accepting a better offer from the Romanian club Chinezul Timisoara, but this again only lasted a season before a director's questioning of his team selection had Guttmann packing his bags and returning to Budapest and Újpest, where again he led the club to the league title.

It was a triumph that earned Guttmann an invite from Gallowich to assist in Hungary's game against Italy in June 1947. The word from Italy was that Italian national team coach Vittorio Pozzo was intending to field for the match ten outfield players from the Serie A champions – Ernő Erbstein's Torino. The information gave Gallowich the notion of following suit and selecting a Hungarian XI made up of nine players from Újpest (Puskás and Ferencváros's Ferenc Rudas were the exceptions). Guttmann's invitation into the fold had Sebes simmering with jealousy; however, come the day of the Hungarian squad's departure, (much to Sebes's relief) the only aeroplane available to fly the entire team to Italy did not have space for Guttmann. Hungary lost 3–2.

A year later, and with Sebes away in London for the Olympics, Gallowich again invited Guttmann into the fold, and duly Hungary won four of their five matches on a summer tour of the Balkans. Towards the end of the tour, Gallowich fell ill and quit, jumping before he was pushed. Guttmann fancied himself as his replacement – why wouldn't he? Well, one reason: the sports minister, Gyula Hegyi.

Hegyi was the man responsible for appointing the replacement new coach, and would be the one having to face the consequences for any error in judgement. As brilliant a coach as Guttmann was, Hegyi wasn't going to risk his own career by choosing him. The only other apparent candidates to hand were Gábor Kléber and Sebes. But Hegyi thought Kléber too inexperienced and hated Sebes, although he had to admit that the meter reader could be trusted to be unswerving in his duty. Hegyi, therefore, hit upon a compromise of Kléber and Sebes taking charge.

Guttmann shrugged his shoulders – he'd survived worse. This, after all, was a man whose father and sister had been murdered in Auschwitz. Undoubtedly, had he been offered the position, he would have accepted: how long he would have lasted is another matter. But it does beg the question: what greater heights could the Magical Magyars have achieved had Guttmann, or, for that matter, Ernő Erbstein, been at their helm?

Days after his omission from the national team, Guttmann joined Kispest, after quitting Újpest following a training ground bust-up with the club's president. Kispest, on learning that Guttmann was going free, had immediately sacked Ferenc Puskás senior – a decision that the Kispest directors had not taken lightly, knowing that Puskás junior would not take the news well. But it was a change that the club felt necessary in recognising that they possessed a team of players capable of winning league titles and beyond … but not all the time Puskás's father was in charge. Ferenc Puskás senior was not a bad coach per se, but his allowing his son to do as he pleased *was* bad coaching. Kispest's directors had feared that unless the Puskás clique was curbed, more and more of the club's players would follow the example of fringe international József Mészáros, who had quit Kispest for Ferencváros.

As expected, Puskás cursed, sulked and threatened at his father's sacking. Yet in the short term, there was little he could do, bar refusing to play, which would have only earned himself a ban. Even leaving Kispest was no easy matter: transfers in which the selling club was a reluctant participant could end up taking many months, and besides, Puskás did not want to leave Kispest – he *was* Kispest! If anyone would be going, it would be Guttmann.

So began a battle of wills. While Puskás did everything he could to unsettle his new boss, Guttmann set to ridding the club of the lax regime of Puskás's father. Guttmann, a man after Jimmy Hogan's own heart, was notorious for training his players to exhaustion. He doubled the Kispest training sessions, put an end to lunchtime drinking sessions (he even sent a hungover Bozsik home) and began jettisoning fringe players whose gripes at not playing were, Guttmann believed, the source of most unrest.

Matters finally came to a head when Kispest played away to Győr, a town in western Hungary. Late in the second half, Puskás, who had been in a belligerent mood all game, hurt himself fouling a Győr player. Bearing in mind that the following week Kispest were to play stiffer opposition in Ferencváros, Guttmann berated Puskás for his recklessness and told his players: no more fouling. However, centre-half Mihály Patyi ignored the order and carried on as before, to which a furious Guttmann yelled from the touchline for Patyi to come off, preferring to play the final minutes with ten men (no substitutes were allowed). But as Patyi made to leave, he was thwarted by Puskás telling him to stay. Patyi looked hesitatingly between Guttmann and Puskás, finally deciding to obey his captain rather than his coach. Guttmann, unable to disguise his disgust, resigned there and then. He spent the rest of the game in the stands reading a newspaper, and on the train back to Budapest sat in a separate carriage to the team, refusing to speak to anyone.

Not everyone at Kispest was happy to see Guttmann go: many had respected him and thought Puskás's behaviour disgraceful. Puskás, for his part, was initially unconcerned that he had overstepped the mark – he was just happy that his father was to be reinstated as coach. But it was a smugness that soon dissipated when he was hauled before an FA disciplinary board for an earlier misdemeanour in a match against Bulgaria in Sofia.

Throughout the match, the Bulgarians had systematically punched and kicked Puskás whenever the referee's attention was elsewhere. Late in the second half, Puskás finally snapped, raking his studs with full force down the thigh of one of his tormentors, Trinkov. While the prone Bulgarian was carried off, Puskás was sent off – but, boiling at the injustice, had to be forcibly removed from the pitch. In the dressing room, he was no calmer. When a team official criticised his behaviour, Puskás retorted by threatening to never play for Hungary again, saying he would be better off accepting one of the many offers from foreign clubs keen to sign him, for there at least fucking idiot club officials would speak to him with respect!

In front of the disciplinary board, Puskás, his head bowed like a scolded child, wasn't so colourful or forthright in his choice of words. In truth, to the board, Puskás's violence in Sofia was inconsequential, but what they couldn't leave unpunished was his threat to leave Hungary. He burst into tears on being told of his one-year ban from international football.

> Trinkov angered me so much that I could not control myself. I was irritable straight after the match and I was still irritable in Győr when I had a difference of opinion with my coach [Guttmann]. Why? Maybe until then everybody had simply let me do whatever I wanted. I believed I could get away with a lot more than a lesser player could. In Győr, I made a mistake. The sentence made me realise this. If I had been sentenced a week earlier then the incident in Győr would never have happened. I also read the criticisms about me in *Népsport*. I must say they pointed out a lot of things to me that up until then had not even crossed my mind. I also want to point out that I never wanted to or want to play abroad. It is true that I have been invited more than once, but there is nothing with which they could tempt me to leave here …'[35]

For his troubles, Guttmann too was banned: for one month for walking out on Kispest. But Guttmann didn't care. He had no intention of ever again working in Hungarian football, despite numerous offers. He applied to leave Hungary and, much to his surprise, permission for him and his wife was granted. Guttmann was one of the thousands who flooded the passport office in the aftermath of the communists' removal of Zoltán Tildy, realising that it would be their last opportunity to leave the country legally. It was a rush that the Soviets tolerated to a point, taking the pragmatic view that it was better to have future annoyances leave now rather than having to deal with them later. But by the winter of 1948–49 the Soviets tolerated no more, and Hungary's borders were closed. Anyone caught attempting to leave without permission would be committing the crime of treason, and just so footballers understood the seriousness of the situation, the FA president István Ries spelt it out for them …

> Firstly the FA will never grant the player permission to play abroad. Secondly, five years in prison awaits anyone who leaves the country without a passport, and those that assist them can also expect five years. Thirdly, if anyone does make it abroad they will instantly lose their citizenship, and therefore can never return home. There have been numerous examples of players who have foolishly gone abroad and, now there, find themselves in dire straits having been cruelly discarded by the very people who tempted them to go. This is why every Hungarian footballer should trust in us; we care more about the players' futures than they do![36]

The sealing of Hungary's borders was a turning point in Mátyás Rákosi's behaviour towards the Hungarian people. Hitherto he had at least made an effort to create the illusion that he intended to build a democracy, but with the borders closed there was no need to continue the charade. 1948 was what he later described as the 'Year of the Takeover', and the year culminated in Rákosi eliminating the last and most potent opposition to communism in Hungary.

Cardinal József Mindszenty was not the most powerful man in Hungary, but, with two-thirds of the population being of the Catholic faith, he was undoubtedly the most influential, and he despised the communists. On Boxing Day 1948, Mindszenty was arrested and taken to the ÁVO headquarters, where he was subjected to 29 days of interrogations, finally confessing to the most ludicrous of crimes including plotting to steal Hungary's crown jewels. In January 1949, a haunted-looking Mindszenty stood trial, admitting all the charges against him, for which he was sentenced to life imprisonment. With the cardinal breaking rocks, Rákosi added insult to the Church by demolishing the magnificent Regnum Marianum, one of Hungary's most beautiful churches, which was situated in Pest's City Park. Two years later, and a stone's throw from the site, a four-metre-high statue of Stalin was erected – lest Hungarians forget that in a Stalinist regime there could only ever be one God.

Hungarians met the imprisonment of Mindszenty with silence. People were petrified – even the Nazis had left the church alone. It was just as Stalin wanted. The Soviets knew that peoples across the Eastern bloc would never take to communism willingly: they had to be terrorised into compliance, and to this end KGB-style secret police forces were used.

The Hungarian secret police, the ÁVO, was the biggest of all government departments, staffed by some 48,000 personnel – keeping files on one million people, over 10 per cent of the population. It was an organisation fed by informers who, on the whole, were ordinary people thrust into an impossible situation where refusal to cooperate was not an option. However, not all informed to save their own or loved ones' skin: many people soon found that feeding information to the ÁVO, be it true or false, was a solution to settling a grudge or dispensing of a love rival.

Once in the ÁVO's clutches, arrestees were at the mercy of guards, recruited from the criminal classes and under orders to be brutal in their treatment of their charges. Special humiliations awaited those who had been of a higher rank or had proved to be a particular nuisance. They were taken to the ÁVO headquarters on Pest's Andrássy Boulevard, where, in the basement cells, they were readied for their interrogation with sleep deprivation and beatings. Interrogations lasted as long as it took for the ÁVO to extract a signed confession (drafted by an ÁVO officer) admitting guilt and incriminating others (a genuine signature was required).

Those that survived the gallows were sent to one of four specially built Soviet-style labour camps that had been constructed deep in the countryside. Prisoners were totally and utterly isolated from the outside world, receiving neither visits nor letters, and worked from dawn until dusk on rations so meagre that they barely staved off starvation.

It is calculated that between 1948 and 1953 some 1.3 million Hungarians were brought before the courts, of whom 695,623 were given life sentences. A further 2,350 were sentenced to death and executed. Double this number are thought to have died in ÁVO custody before reaching trial.

The joke became: 'There are three types of classes in Rákosi's Hungary: those that have been in prison, those that are and those that will be.' Only it was no laughing matter: the fear and terror the ÁVO spread was insidious. Friends and neighbours avoided each other lest one be an informer; suicides became rife and alcoholism soared. Within three years of its being established, the ÁVO turned Hungarians from a warm, gregarious and generous people into a paranoid nation full of mistrust, suspicion and resentment. It was perhaps the ÁVO's worst crime of all.

The national team coaching partnership of Sebes and Gábor Kléber never clicked, and after only a few games together in charge, the two men's friendship cooled to a rivalry. Sebes was the chief instigator. Being in partnership forced him to contain his natural authoritarian personality, in the fear that if he were too strict with the players, they would voice a preference for the more congenial Kléber.

Eventually, matters came to a head when it was learned that Kléber had been encouraging the players to attend church, a heinous crime which made it impossible for him to continue in his national team role. For good measure, his now former friend Sebes put the knife in:

> The squad has an outstanding selection of players, but Kléber could not mould them into a team. Kléber cannot teach, and since he is incapable of teaching it is not suitable that in today's society he should occupy such a role. Across all sport, we need to produce strong and brave people, the type who are always ready to defend their work and socialist home. We want to produce the type of athletes who recognise our classless society and can fit into the thoughts and minds of the nine million Hungarians and eight

> hundred million populace of the peace camp [Soviet bloc] in their fight for peace. But how would Kléber be capable of producing such sportsmen if he is not respectful of those minds whose endeavour it is to show us the road to peace?[37]

Sebes was appointed Hungary's coach on 22 January 1949 – his 43rd birthday. He didn't have to take stock of his situation to know what an enviable position he was in as coach of a national football team. At his disposal was a golden generation – none of whom could leave the country of their own free will. Furthermore, Sebes was to be funded financially like no other Hungarian coach before or since. Hungary's finishing third at the London Olympics had prompted the Rákosi regime to invest in sport.

He was also fortunate to be the first 'footballer' to be appointed Hungary's national team coach: all previous head coaches had been primarily administrators. Sebes was a combination of both, and this is where his strength lay. As a player, he had been versatile – he understood football and footballers, but he was no master tactician or man motivator. He was, however, a solid and excellent organiser, one wholly dedicated to his task, unselfish in his wanting Hungarian football to be the best. He had a dedication that a 'better coach' would have been unlikely to match. His first move as coach was to form a six-man coaching committee, composed of various league club coaches whose combined role was to keep him informed, at fortnightly meetings, of the goings-on in the leagues regarding injuries, tactics and players worthy of possible national team selection. Of the six, Sebes entrusted his friend and former MTK team-mate Jenő Kalmár as his assistant.

The 41-year-old Kalmár, as a former Hungarian international, had the full respect of the players and would prove the perfect foil to the disciplinarian Sebes:

> Kalmár – Okay lads, training starts tomorrow at 9am.
>
> Puskás – Why so early? Why not make it later?
>
> Kalmár – I am in charge here and what I say goes! Training tomorrow starts at 11am.

One of Sebes's first priorities was to have Puskás's ban cut short. Hungary needed their best player, and in Sebes's opinion, five months of his year-long ban was time enough for the boy to have learned his lesson. Five months, incidentally, in which Hungary had played not one international game.

The early return of Puskás from his ban was mud in the eye of many who had hoped he would get his comeuppance under Sebes. And yet quite the reverse happened. Sebes placed a protective, even indulgent, arm around Puskás, so much so that it was obvious that Puskás was his favourite. Whether Sebes privately approved of Puskás's behaviour is doubtful, but he knew that Puskás was going to be, with or without him, the lynchpin of the Hungarian national team for the next decade and beyond. If Sebes was going to be successful, he needed Puskás, and if that meant tolerating the boy's backchat then so be it. This leniency, however, was reserved for Puskás only.

Another priority for Sebes was to instil some hardiness into his pampered charges. A fortnight before his first match in charge (against Czechoslovakia in Prague), he gathered the A, B and C teams for a ten-day training session at the Hungarian athletics training camp on the outskirts of the small town of Tata, 60 miles west of Budapest. The camp was purposely isolated and spartan to prevent the athletes from being distracted by frivolous entertainments. Alcohol was banned, and the athletes slept in dormitories, washed in communal showers and ate in a communal dining room. Sebes loved the place, believing that its hardships made his pampered charges hardy. The footballers hated it. Most had grown up in poverty and had no desire to enjoy its discomforts again. By the time the team arrived in Prague, they were exhausted, and they lost 5–2.

Sebes acknowledged that he was to blame for the defeat, claiming that he'd made the mistake of listening to others, and selected the best players but not the best *team*. Half-heartedly, he even offered to resign, but FA president István Ries refused to accept the offer, as Sebes probably knew he would. Ries was a socialist, Sebes a communist; if there was any sacking to be done, it would be the other way around.

Népsport also backed Sebes. The communists' mouthpiece refused to criticise the new manager, noting that on the train journey to and from Prague, the mood had been full of good cheer and song.

Days later, Sebes received a letter from a member of the public offering the advice: 'Sebes! You fucking halfwit! You should teach the fuckers to play football, not sing!'

CHAPTER 6

They both wanted things their own way – they were huge rivals. They were both so hungry for the ball that they were crazy. Sometimes I'd make it to the byline and look up and I'd see Puskás pointing to his left foot and Kocsis pointing to his head. I'd say to them, 'You two need a ball each.'

László Budai[38]

THE first act of defiance towards Soviet rule in the Eastern bloc came not from the oppressed masses but from the communist dictator of Yugoslavia, Josip Broz Tito. In 1948, Tito declared that he would rule *his* country with a 'nationalistic' form of communism, independent from the Soviet Union.

Stalin was furious, but bar going to war with Yugoslavia there was very little he could do in retaliation. There was no Soviet military based in Yugoslavia, and Tito had firm control of the country's secret police. Stalin therefore took steps to prevent any similar future acts of defiance, by purging from other satellite states communists who were thought capable of 'Titoism'. Comrades perceived as being more patriotic towards their own nations than they were towards the Soviet Union were the primary targets.

In Hungary, this meant the 'Hungarian' communists, i.e. those not trained in Moscow. The first and most significant Hungarian comrade to be arrested was the foreign minister, László Rajk – an arrest met with incomprehension right across the Hungarian-speaking world. Rajk was the establisher of the ÁVO and had been the leader of the underground Communist Party for a period during the Second World War, for which he'd been arrested and placed in a concentration camp. And now the Hungarian public was informed that all along Rajk had been, in fact, a fascist spy!

At his trial, Rajk, reading from a script, admitted to all the charges set against him and was sentenced to death, a verdict that the audience met with collective clapping. His wife, Julia, received six years' imprisonment, and their baby son, László junior, was placed in a state orphanage under a different name. Rajk was executed at Budapest's Fő Street prison on a gallows specially constructed under the window of his wife's cell.

Rajk was but days in his unmarked grave before Mátyás Rákosi's portrait began appearing everywhere in government buildings, shops, factories and offices. Not a public speech was given in which the bald and paunchy psychopathic former bank clerk wasn't praised, thanked or credited with saving Hungary from ruin. In 1949, at the School Sports World Cup, the sports minister, Gyula Hegyi – rather than praise the athletes – thanked Rákosi for his vigilance:

> … in recognising the danger that those Western imperialist dogs the Titos and Rajks wanted to heap upon us. Today we have come to celebrate, but again we should remember that the crushing of these traitors is the reason we can celebrate our victory in sport![39]

And *Népsport* 'quoted' Vasas goalkeeper István Turai as saying:

> It was appalling us having to listen to that stubborn and emotionless villain Rajk. I extend my eternal gratitude and praise to our party and nation's leader, Mátyás Rákosi. Only with similar devotion, sacrifice and vigilance can we continue freely living, working and playing sport.[40]

Unlike Hegyi, who publicly praised Rákosi, it is doubtful that Turai actually said what he was quoted as saying, but who was he going to complain to?

It would become a regular occurrence with Hungary's star footballers that they would read of themselves lavishing praise on the merits of the Rákosi regime having uttered no such thing. None of them were ever comfortable with the quotes being made up in their name, being only too aware of the possible future repercussions of their being documented as supporters of the regime. The dilemma for many a footballer was: stay in Hungary, stomach the regime, and run the risk of being labelled a communist lackey; or give up football.

There was one other option, however, but it meant running the risk of arrest or worse: Italy. The Hungarian authorities kept under wraps the success of Hungarian footballers there, but among Hungarian footballers it was no secret at all. Two footballers in particular had done very well for themselves. The foremost was a former Újpest forward, István Nyers, who'd left Hungary in 1946 as a 22-year-old and within two years was playing at Inter Milan as Stefano Nyers; in his first season there, he was the leading scorer in Serie A. Nyers had been one of Hungary's bright young prospects, and his loss was felt keenly by Hungarian football. In a combination of revenge and warning to others, Újpest attempted to blemish Nyers's name by reporting that the reason for his swift departure was his being caught red-handed stealing from a dressing room, a 'crime' for which Újpest banned him for life.

The second was Gyula Schubert, or 'Julius Schubert' as he was known in Italy, a former player for Ganz, the team of a sprawling Pest metalworks. Via Czechoslovakian football, Schubert made his way to Italy to star for the Serie A champions, Torino. It was a club coached by Ernő Erbstein, who (as you may remember from Chapter 5) escaped alongside Béla Guttmann from a Jewish labour battalion during the war. Erbstein returned to his former post at Torino, and repaid the club's loyalty by leading them to four successive Serie A titles. And while Erbstein may have made a vow never to return to Hungary, he still made a concerted effort to keep up to date with Hungarian football, which was how he came to learn about Schubert.

Erbstein encouraged Schubert to keep up correspondence with players back in Hungary who he thought would fit into the playing style of the Torino team, and, as it turned out, Schubert knew just the player: a young Vasas forward by the name of László Kubala.

Kubala and Schubert were childhood friends, both born to Slovak immigrant parents in the Pest district of Rákoshegy, and together progressed from the local grounds to begin their careers together at

Ganz. Schubert was good, but Kubala was better. Brash and bustling, with a mop of blond, curly hair, Kubala was a distinctive presence on and off the pitch, and rated by many as Ferenc Puskás's equal.[41] He also shared other traits with Puskás, such as a distaste for taking orders, hence in 1947, rather than endure national service, Kubala left Hungary on a false passport to join his friend Schubert at the Czechoslovak club ŠK Bratislava. In Czechoslovakia, the Slovak-speaking Kubala took citizenship and was immediately selected for the national team, for whom he would play six times. He also married the sister of the ŠK Bratislava coach, but, a Budapest boy at heart, Kubala never felt quite at home in provincial Bratislava – even less so when he received his call-up papers for the Czechoslovak army. In October 1948, he decided to return to Budapest and sign for Vasas.

> I know they are angry with me in Budapest, and I also know that I have a lot of enemies. My best friends in Kálvaria Square are also angry with me. They say I cheated everybody. I know that I am a wrongdoer, but I have suffered for my wrongdoings and now that I am home I hope to be forgiven. When I was playing for the Czechoslovakian national team, I was always wondering, 'Am I good enough to play for Hungary?'[42]

Kubala was indeed good enough, and within a week of his return, Tibor Gallowich gave him his debut for the Hungarian national team. But Kubala's determination to remain in Hungary did not last, as demonstrated by his aversion to soldiering. Kubala was a man unable to tolerate petty rules and regulations, and could not see himself settling in to life in a communist Hungary. And as soon as his old friend Gyula Schubert contacted him with an offer to join him at Torino, Kubala began plans to reach Italy. He found an accomplice in a Vasas team-mate, György Marik, and in January 1949 the pair disguised themselves as soldiers, got into a military truck with Russian registration plates and smuggled themselves into Austria, and after that into the American sector of Vienna, where they paid a smuggler to take them across into Italy to a refugee camp.

Vasas reacted to Kubala's defection by denouncing him as a fraudster for taking the signing-on money for his contract and then fleeing. The

Hungarian FA agreed and began to secure a formal extradition request on account of Kubala's alleged fraud, his fleeing from the country without permission and his failure to do military service. FIFA backed the FA and imposed a one-year ban on Kubala, and also upon Marik for good measure.

The intrepid Marik headed for the newly rich Colombian league, while Kubala remained in Italy after Torino offered to pay his wages on the agreement that he would sign for them once his ban was over. Thus Kubala became a Torino player in all but name, training daily with them and accompanying them to matches. But despite the security offered at Torino, it was, however, still an anxious time for Kubala. He had to wait for his wife and baby son to join him in Italy, and by the time they arrived they were sick with exhaustion, forcing Kubala to take time off to nurse them, meaning he missed travelling with the Torino squad for a match in Lisbon. Two days later, on 4 May 1949, the Italian Airlines flight carrying Torino back from Portugal got lost in fog and crashed into the side of a mountain, killing all on board, including Ernő Erbstein and Gyula Schubert.

Kubala's near escape and the death of his team-mates, but in particular his friend Schubert, left him deeply shocked. But help arrived in the form of his former coach and brother-in-law Ferdinand Daučík, arriving at his sister's request to alleviate her homesickness as well as to be company for the despondent Kubala.

As coach of ŠK Bratislava, Daučík had tracked down Hungarian first-division players of Slovak descent (such as Gyula Schubert and Kubala) and enticed them to the club with the lure of their being able to represent the Czechoslovak national team. In Italy, Daučík was no less resourceful. What Kubala needed was to be playing football, not sitting around moping! Daučík immediately set about forming a team made of dissenters, players like Kubala, who had arrived in Italy from eastern Europe and were banned for their troubles. He appointed himself as the coach, named Kubala as captain and chose the name 'Hungária' because in his opinion a Hungarian football team would attract bigger crowds on the planned tour of Europe.

Spain was the first country Hungária toured, and the last. In all they played six matches, the last of which was in Madrid against a full-strength Spanish national team preparing for a 1950 World Cup qualifier. One can only imagine how impressively Kubala must have played that day, for straight away the watching Real Madrid and Barcelona presidents both raced to obtain his signature.

The match having been played at Real Madrid's stadium meant naturally that the Real president cornered Kubala first to offer him a contract that few, if any, would refuse. Only Kubala did, insisting that he would only sign if Daučík was given a coaching position at the club. In the following days, while Real dithered, unsure whether to give in to what in their eyes was tantamount to blackmail, the Barcelona manager, Pepe Samitier, approached Kubala. 'I want the same as this,' Kubala said, pulling out the contract Real had offered him, 'and my brother-in-law to be appointed coach.'

Samitier agreed in an instant. Barça handed Kubala an enormous signing-on fee of 300,000 pesetas (over £100,000 in 2019 values) and a contract with a weekly wage that was double the amount paid to the club's highest-paid player. Daučík would remain in charge for the four years. Furthermore, Barça paid 12 million pesetas (worth £4.4m in 2019) to the Italian club Pro Patria, for whom Kubala had made a handful of appearances and who held his licence, and a further 300,000 pesetas to Vasas, on the understanding that they would not press the Hungarian FA to extend Kubala's ban once it ended in a few months' time. Vasas, the team of the Communist Party, readily accepted the money.

Hungary's communist press condemned and rubbished Kubala, informing their readers just how miserable, unwanted, homesick and regretful the 'Slovak mercenary' was in his new home. But those that knew the truth of Kubala's success were dumbfounded. Sure Kubala was good, but he wasn't even the best footballer in Hungary!

It was a thought that occurred to, among others, one József Járay, a football-loving opera singer famous in both Hungary and Italy. Járay had contacts with Italian clubs who paid him commission to bring them Hungarians. But it was a sideline that was sidelined by Hungary's closed borders. So instead, Járay looked to copy the success of Ferdinand Daučík's Hungária by planning a similar team formed of Hungarian international footballers, and with the intention of using Italy as a base from which to tour Europe and, if successful, beyond.

Járay contacted the one footballer he knew would be more than interested: Gyula Lóránt, a Vasas defender and fringe international. Lóránt was unusual for a footballer in that he had a university education. It wasn't only this that set Lóránt apart from other footballers: he was an aloof man, with a reputation as a dirty player and being greedy for money. He had no love for the communists and nor they he: the son of a Horthy regime policeman, the well travelled and educated Lóránt (born Gyula Lipovics) was not fooled for a moment by the propaganda dished up by the communists. As a youth during the war, he'd spent time in a refugee camp run by Americans; he'd turned down a chance to be repatriated to the States and had regretted it ever since. As an economics graduate, Lóránt also had business ambitions of his own that he knew were highly unlikely to be fulfilled under a communist government, and neither was he willing to further himself by joining the Communist Party.

Lóránt agreed to Járay's proposal, and, once he had collected enough names to form a squad, arranged a secret meeting at a nondescript pub in the Pest suburb of Csepel to finalise details of exactly how, when and from where players would leave. It was agreed that the group of 14 would split into four smaller groups and meet at different points across Pest, from where each group would be driven to the Yugoslav border, where Járay had a contact who was a border guard.

The would-be dissidents were made well aware of just what the consequences of leaving Hungary illegally would entail. The decision to leave their homeland was one that none took lightly. They may have awaited adventures and riches, but their families left behind could face serious repercussions. Being a relative of a person classed as a dissident would not necessarily mean arrest and imprisonment, but certainly would place a cloud of heavy suspicion over the family name, giving the vindictive authorities reason to make life a misery for them. Siblings could be denied housing, nieces and nephews refused entry to university, fathers and uncles demoted at work, grandparents receive inferior medical care, and so on.

But, 24 hours after the meeting, it was learned that the ÁVO knew of the plot and had been searching the pubs of Csepel the previous evening. The players scrambled to inform each other that the escape was cancelled, rushing to give themselves alibis. However, there remained one player who wasn't notified of the cancellation: Gyula Grosics, a goalkeeper for first-division MATEOSZ. He stood at his designated meeting point, a street corner in downtown Pest, waiting for three of his team-mates, when instead he was confronted by two ÁVO officers.

With his suitcase at his feet and his football boots strung around his neck, Grosics said he was waiting for a lift to go and visit his parents. 'We'll take you,' he was told.

The 22-year-old Grosics was very much in Sebes's plans, which may be why, when he was taken to the ÁVO headquarters, he wasn't beaten. He was, though, slung into a cell, deprived of sleep and questioned for hours. Grosics stuck to his story, even when he was told that in the next room two of his fellow conspirators were spilling the beans. Eventually, Grosics was released, placed under house arrest and told to return in two days, and when he did Sebes was waiting for him …

> Sebes spoke, saying that it would be good if I was to give the whole story. 'Uncle Guszti,' I replied, 'I have already told what happened, that I was going home to visit my parents.' I stuck rigidly to my lie. They, of course, wanted to hear what they already knew, but I was not going to be a willing participant in that.
>
> 'If this is the case, then it is regrettable,' said Sebes, 'because there will be repercussions!' At that moment I thought that the two ÁVO men were going to grab hold of me and take me away. But this didn't happen – instead, Sebes continued. 'Forthwith you are banned from all league football matches for one year, but this ban will be suspended for two years. However, you are banned from representing the international team for one year, and we are taking away your passport.' It was laughable. I didn't have a passport. I didn't mind, though; I felt that I had got off lightly.
>
> The only person I had told of my plans to leave Hungary was my mother, to whom I posted a letter a few days before I was meant to defect. That evening, when I returned to my parents' house and knocked at their door, my mother clung to my neck and sobbed with relief. All I told her was that I had been caught and taken to Andrássy Avenue. My mother had no idea about the place – nor did my father, and he was more informed. The church circles they

> mixed in never spoke of the ÁVO. They didn't perceive that it was possible such a place existed.[43]

Grosics did indeed 'get off lightly', certainly compared with the four players accused of being the plot's ringleaders: Gyula Lóránt, József Mészáros, Béla Egresi and Károly Kéri. In *Lóri*, a biography of Lóránt, his wife, Ibolya, described the moment of her husband's arrest:

> A car pulled up uninvited in front of our house. It almost sunk in the dry sand, and there was a cloud of dust behind it hundreds of metres long. Two policemen and a civilian stepped out of the car, clamped some handcuffs on Gyula and took him away without a word. I sprinted after them, begged them, why and where are they taking him??? They just ignored my questions. That's the way it was in those days.[44]

Lóránt tried to explain that he wanted to leave Hungary due to the stress of his wife's first husband (who had been assumed dead) returning from Soviet captivity and demanding his family back via threats on Lóránt's life. And although this was true, it wasn't the truth the ÁVO wanted. As ringleader, Lóránt was given a harder time than Grosics, and once he duly confessed, he, Mészáros and Egresi (Kéri was released) were taken for indefinite internment at the notorious Kistarca labour camp. They were also banned from football for life.

Nine of the other ten conspirators received bans of between three months and one year; the one exception was the Ferencváros centre-forward Ferenc Deák, who got off scot-free. It was suspected that Deák was the one who informed the authorities of the group's plans, though why he should do this is not explained. Gyula Grosics, for his part, was convinced that the informer was the fiancée of one of the players, not wanting him to leave her.

Lest it be forgotten that among all the arrests, show trials and hangings, Sebes was preparing for his second game in charge. The match was against Austria in Budapest, and one that Sebes daren't lose. Getting thrashed by the Czechoslovaks in his first match had been bad enough, but at least the blow had been softened by Czechoslovakia being a fellow communist state. Austria, however, was not only Hungary's biggest football rival, it was also a capitalist nation.

Against the Czechoslovaks, Sebes had gone against his instinct and erred on the side of caution, and paid the price; against Austria he went the other way and fielded the most attacking first eleven at his disposal. Hungary duly won 6–1, with Puskás scoring a hat-trick, but he wasn't the star of the show – that honour befell a 19-year-old debutant called Sándor Kocsis.

Kocsis, at his club, Ferencváros, had broken all schoolboy goalscoring records, mostly with his head. As an exponent of heading a football, there is probably none better than Kocsis. He was only of average height but had an abnormally long and powerful neck, a high forehead and a lithe upper body coupled with powerful squat legs, enabling him to jump head and shoulders above other players. His emergence into the national team sparked not a little jealousy in Puskás. The first time the two played against each other was in 1947 when Kispest visited Ferencváros, and it was Kocsis and not Puskás who was acknowledged in the next day's press as the game's best player. It was the beginning of a lifelong bitter rivalry between the two – an animosity originating from Puskás, who became envious of not just the accolades Kocsis received for his goalscoring but also the praise he got for the humble manner in which he carried himself. It was a shyness that in time Kocsis would shed, and he would become vocally resentful of all the accolades Puskás received. Yet the two's dislike of each other was in no way damaging to the team; in fact, it was quite the opposite. Such was their determination to usurp each other that any attempt at scoring was snatched in the blink of an eye, but both were also professional enough to pass or lay the ball off if necessary – but only ever as an absolute last resort.

Over the next three games, Sebes tweaked his attack. He played Puskás on the left wing (he sulked) in a 1–1 draw against Italy, dropped him for his sulking for the next game, a 2–2 draw away to Sweden (Sebes relented and brought Puskás on at half-time), and dropped Kocsis in an 8–2 win over Poland in which Puskás and Ferenc Deák scored four goals apiece.

But, as pleasing as the run of four unbeaten matches was, Sebes couldn't help but notice that in each of them Hungary had conceded at least one preventable goal. What he needed was a defender who could rule the defence: someone strong, intimidating, that someone being Gyula Lóránt.

Fortunately for Sebes, his old comrade János Kádár had been recently appointed as interior minister, the man with the power to release people from prison. Kádár was reluctant, but understood the importance of Lóránt to Vasas and the national team, and released Lóránt on the condition that Sebes take full responsibility should he once again attempt to defect.

Lóránt was released (along with Mészáros and Egresi) from Kistarca labour camp after serving three weeks. But he was far from free. Releasees from camps had to sign a paper admitting to being 'an enemy of the State', a tarnish that meant they could be re-arrested at any time for any reason. No signature meant no release. Furthermore, if they spoke of their time in the camps, they would be sent back for any period between six and ten years. Releasees often lived lonely existences, shunned by relations, old friends and neighbours terrified that through association they would attract the attention of the ÁVO. Having survived the brutalities of the camps, many releasees were unable to cope with the silent pressures of life on the outside.

When Lóránt hadn't arrived for training at Vasas for a week or more, Sebes sought him out at his home. He was shocked to see the player in such a dishevelled state. Sympathy was never Sebes's strong point, and he curtly informed Lóránt that he was disappointed by his betrayal and that he had only himself to blame for his current dire situation. Sebes further explained to Lóránt that the reason for his release was his value to the national football team, but if he was of no importance, then what was stopping him from being re-arrested?

It wasn't a threat by Sebes but a fact, and one which Lóránt grasped. From here on in he became a dutiful servant to Sebes, following his instructions to the letter. If an opposition player was known to be easily intimidated or a young bright spark needed to be disciplined, Sebes would assign the task to Lóránt. Lóránt was dubbed the 'Blond Rock' by the press, but the emphasis on his hard-man image disguised just what a good player he was. Technically adroit, he was dominant, decisive, a steady presence in the back line who would instil confidence in his team-mates and fear in opponents.

Indeed Lóránt was everything Sebes believed a proud Swab should be, except, that is, a communist.

Lóránt's return to international football in October 1949 against Austria in Vienna was his first full match: a 4–3 victory, with Deák and Puskás scoring two goals each, sealing Hungary's first win in Vienna in 12 years. A fortnight later, Bulgaria visited Budapest and were dismissed with ease 5–0; three weeks after, Sweden were the visitors, and they too were beaten 5–0, Sándor Kocsis scoring a hat-trick in a match so one-sided that Hungary's inactive goalkeeper, Géza Henni, was substituted because he was cold.

CHAPTER 7

Football should be played foremostly with the brain.

Márton Bukovi

You stupid dick! Can't you see what colours we are wearing?

Ferenc Puskás's standard reaction to any team-mate who misplaced a pass

FOR Hungary's beleaguered citizens, the 1950s began with Mátyás Rákosi pushing through parliament an endless stream of pro-Soviet legislation, the first steps of a 'Five Year Plan': the time frame given to him by Moscow to turn Hungary into a fully fledged Soviet state, i.e. a smaller version of the Soviet Union. Within a matter of months, the framework around which Hungary had existed for centuries was dismantled. Private enterprise, land and property were placed under government ownership. Hungarian traditions and national holidays were disregarded and replaced by those of the Soviet Union. Hungary's armed forces adopted Soviet ranks and uniforms, and the teaching of Russian was made compulsory in schools.[45]

This Sovietisation of Hungary allowed Rákosi to purge the Hungarian parliament, once and for all, of people who were not Communist Party members. The result was the arrest in June 1950 of the country's two leading Social Democrats: the former president Árpád Szakasits, and István Ries, the justice minister and president of the Hungarian FA. Szakasits was sentenced to life imprisonment on charges of spying, while the 65-year-old Ries never made it to his show trial, dying from a heart attack during his interrogation.

Whether Gusztáv Sebes believed for a moment that Ries was a spy, he never said, but Sebes couldn't deny that the death of his (former) boss cleared the path for him to carry through his own plans unhindered. Sebes and Ries's working relationship had begun on good terms, but had deteriorated after Ries refused to pay for Sebes to travel to Vienna to watch the Austrian national team. Ries had felt that Sebes needed taking down a peg, whereas Sebes had seen Ries as a relic from the past, whose sole intention was to block every move towards progress. Of course the national team coach would want to see future opposition play first-hand!

Ries was replaced by the FA's youngest member: Sándor Barcs, a 34-year-old journalist. The appointment of Barcs was his reward for being a judge at the László Rajk trial – not that Barcs was in any way legally qualified. He had been personally 'asked' by the ÁVO chief, Gábor Péter, to sit on a four-man panel and find Rajk guilty. Later in his life, when the emerging truth of the Rajk trial cast a shadow over his good name, Barcs would condemn the trial as 'theatre' and admit to his frustration at knowing of Rajk's innocence but, out of fear for his own family's welfare, choosing to remain silent.

The multi-lingual Barcs would remain president of the Hungarian FA until 1963. But during Sebes's time as coach, Barcs's power as president was nothing more than that of an administrative figurehead, at best as a translator for the squad. His ideas and plans were ignored, and his mail from abroad systematically opened before it reached him. In his dealings with representatives from foreign football nations, Barcs would stand at an embarrassing loss when they asked why their correspondence to him always went unanswered. A Communist Party member but not a communist, Barcs held no sway over Sebes, and that was the way Sebes liked it.

Finally free to select his own assistants, Sebes recruited into the national team fold two friends and former MTK team-mates, Pál Titkos and Gyula Mándi, as FA secretary and first-team coach respectively. Titkos was a member of Hungary's 1938 World Cup Final team, but Sebes preferred to utilise his experience in an administerial role as the FA secretary, an invaluable set of eyes and ears for Sebes at the FA's headquarters. Gyula Mándi, on the other hand, was brought in to train the A team on a full-time basis, replacing the flagging Jenő

Kalmár, who was stretched thinly, juggling the demands of coaching the national team with his other job as coach of first-division club Dorogi FC. As a player Mándi had been an established international and famed as the first 'cultured' defender in Hungarian football, though when Sebes sought him out he was down on his luck. He'd endured the war serving in a Jewish labour battalion, and by 1949 was in poor health, scratching a living as a tailor. Sebes's invitation gave Mándi a new lease of life, for which he repaid his friend with nothing less than unswerving loyalty.

And yet while he was clearly a 'Sebes man', Mándi was also a kindly father figure in whom the players could confide. The players' fear of being belittled or bellowed at did not exist with Mándi: he simply gave them the encouragement to express themselves and play to their strengths. Gyula Grosics notably referred to Sebes by his surname and Mándi by his forename when he explained:

> The two men were total contrasts. It is perhaps an exaggeration, but Sebes was a dictator with the power over life and death. He always kept a distance of three paces. Gyula was quite different. If need be, he was a friend; if need be, he was a trainer. If we needed advice, we always turned to him. He was a fantastic person who really understood football at the top level.[46]

Entrusting Mándi to train the players as he saw fit was one of the wisest decisions of Sebes's time as head coach. Sebes disliked training the players, and it was joked among them that he only ever put on a tracksuit when a photographer was near. Giving Mándi a free hand allowed Sebes to concentrate on delegating and organising, roles in which he excelled, and which were bringing reward.

The six-man coaching committee that Sebes had had the foresight to form on his appointment as head coach was beginning to pay dividends. The information that the committee gathered on Hungary's first- and second-division footballers, such as strengths, weaknesses and personality, helped Sebes choose a pool of 25 players. From this number, he formed 'A', 'B' and 'C' teams. If an A team player was unable to play for any reason, his replacement in the B team would be primed to fill his place, and so forth with the C team, and beyond them to the Budapest, northern Hungary and southern Hungary first elevens. Each team played with the same formation and style, and, if logistically possible, all on the same day.

Sebes had the A, B and C teams train as one at the Hungarian athletics Olympic training camp, on the former monastery site in Tata, which the players hated for its spartan regime. After one complaint too many (led by Puskás), Sebes acknowledged the players' gripes and had them train thereafter in Budapest on the city's Margaret Island, an oasis of calm situated on the Danube between the banks of central Buda and Pest. The island was far more to the players' liking, a place where Budapest's residents go to enjoy greenery and fresh air, and it was here the squad would train in the stadium of the one-time Magyar Athletic Club (MAC).[47]

Alongside Titkos and Mándi, there was also another coach with a strong MTK connection who was invaluable to Sebes, but one that he went to lengths to keep away from any training ground involvement with the team. Márton Bukovi was the highly respected coach of MTK, but neither a former team-mate nor a close friend of Sebes's. It was not personal: Sebes simply felt intimidated by the presence of a man who was considered one of the best coaches, if not the best, in Hungarian football.

A former Ferencváros and Hungarian international centre-back, Bukovi spent the last two years of his playing days in France, from where he moved to Yugoslavia. There, he became coach of Gradanski Zagreb, where he remained for a decade until 1945, when the club merged with three other clubs and became Dinamo Zagreb. Bukovi was chosen as the coach of the new club, and remained at Dinamo for two seasons until MTK lured him back to Budapest in 1947.

When in 1948 Sebes vacated his position as president of the Trainers' Society, Bukovi was the man that his fellow coaches voted in as his replacement, and under his guidance the society flourished.

By the early 1950s, the number of qualified coaches in Hungary stood at an unprecedented 900, responsible for coaching some 100,000 registered footballers. A decade earlier there had been 15,000 players. Bukovi set out some unwritten rules, the first and foremost of which was that training sessions were to last for not more than two hours but not less than 90 minutes, during which time the players were kept continually on the move. The sessions had to be stimulating, and progress made on each occasion, however slight. Equipment was to be laid out in advance, and any player arriving late was forbidden to partake.

When the coach was giving a talk, footballs were withdrawn so the players would concentrate on what was being said. But, for the most part, Bukovi encouraged coaches to be innovative in their own right, instructing them to teach players by any method possible, as long as it produced the desired results. With this in mind, Hungary's coaches set to finding numerous ways to make sessions productive, fun and inventive, with names to match ...

Blind Man's Bluff: A player would put on a blindfold and attempt to hit team-mates calling his name with the ball.

Where Is Red?: A player would stand with his back turned a short distance away from a line of team-mates, one of whom would be wearing a red bib. On a whistle blow, the player would have to turn and, in one movement, aim the ball directly at his bib-wearing team-mate.

The Wall: A wall the height and width of a tall man was constructed, with pieces of brick poking out at differing angles. One player would blast a ball at the wall, while another had to control the unpredictable return.

Hit the Umbrella: An umbrella was hung from the crossbar, and players would line up to hit it with the ball from all areas of the pitch.

Five Touch Goal: Five players would line up in a forward line against a three-man defence and a goalkeeper, and each attacker would only be allowed to touch the ball once, meaning the fifth touch had to be a shot at goal.

Silent Football: Players had to play in complete silence to learn to use their sight to find their team-mates.

Walking Football: A full-size match was played at a leisurely stop-start walking pace, so the coaches could continually stop the game and point out tactical errors and plan moves.

Thus by 1950 Sebes had at his disposal the players, the coaching team and the facilities, but what he did not have, and what he wanted, was a distinct Magyar style of play, one that differentiated Hungary from other football nations. Sebes, Mándi and Titkos sat down and planned. Each had been an MTK player during the club's 1920s heyday, and therefore was indoctrinated in the Jimmy Hogan school of control and movement. And while they wanted to continue this legacy, at the same time Sebes and his assistants also wanted to bring Hungary up to the modern era, and in doing so looked to the Soviet Union.

The Dynamo Moscow team of the early 1940s were the team that the Magical Magyars' whole administrative and coaching structure and playing style would most closely resemble: disciplined, super-fit and controlled by a Stalinist regime. Dynamo was formed in the late 19th century as *Morozovtsi* by two English brothers, Clement and Harry Charnock, owners of a Moscow mill. They formed the club from their mill workers, dressing the team in the blue and white of their home-town club, Blackburn Rovers. In 1923 the club was taken over by the Russian secret police (formed in 1917 after the Russian revolution with the mind to protect the Communist Party's interests and thwart any counter-revolutions, the force would become known by several names over the next 80 years: GPU, NKVD, KGB and so on). When known as the GPU, the organisation formed the Dynamo Sports Society for its personnel. Requiring an established football team in Moscow in which to incorporate, the society chose Morozovtsi, changing the club's name to Dynamo Moscow. By the late 1930s, Dynamo's patron was Lavrenty Beria, head of Stalin's secret police, now called the NKVD. Beria (himself an ex-footballer) recruited the services of Boris Arkadiev, the best young coach in Soviet football.

Beria provided Arkadiev with everything he needed to create a winning team, and in turn, Arkadiev developed a style of play that if viewed from above appeared to be a series of cogs in motion. The Russians called it 'passovotchka'; the Western press 'organised disorder'. Players did not hold one specific position but moved around the pitch according to the flow of the game, taking up position where necessary, interchanging and connecting with short, fast passes. Individualism did not exist, and to emphasise this the players did not wear numbers on their shirts. Dynamo was the perfect communist football team: no individuals, everyone equal and the head of the police taking all the credit. But Arkadiev was no authoritarian who ran his team on fear. He counselled his players' views and treated them to trips to theatres and art galleries, purposely high-brow so as to make them feel, and therefore act, intelligent.

In almost every way, Sebes copied Arkadiev. He had the Hungarian team's kit streamlined and the boots made lighter. He made the players' health, mental and physical, of paramount importance, even going so far as to corner players' wives to remind them not to neglect their husbands' sexual needs. The medical treatment the players received was carried out by the country's very best doctors at a specialist sports hospital in Budapest. Emphasis, though, was placed more on prevention than cure, and through gymnastics, pre-match warm-ups and attention to diet Hungary's footballers would remain remarkably free from the niggling muscle strains that blighted so many other national squads. The players were warned of the dangers of a bad diet, smoking and alcohol (although, among others, Grosics, Bozsik and Czibor all smoked heavily) and provided with foods of quality and quantity that their fellow countrymen could only dream of. And, again like Dynamo, during the mid-winter break Sebes ordered the players to remain in shape by playing indoor sports such as basketball, handball and volleyball. During the summer break, he would arrange, every Wednesday, for the squad to travel to towns in the countryside to play practice matches against local clubs. The friendly games were hugely popular. The arrival of Puskás and co. was a huge event for the town involved. Shops and factories shut early, and the players were often paraded pre-match in the town square. The players themselves also enjoyed the games – the provincial crowds greeted them with warmth and appreciation, not something they always received from the more critical and less easily impressed football followers in Budapest. The term 'friendly match', though, was alien to Sebes: he demanded that, regardless of the quality of the opposition, his players should never give anything other than their all. Hence scores often reached double figures, and rare consolation goals met with huge cheers and ironic congratulations from Puskás: once telling a fortunate goalscorer (a local mayoral candidate), 'You're one lucky bastard – that fluke has just won you the election!'

In 1945, Dynamo got to test themselves against clubs outside of the Soviet Union when they undertook a four-game tour of Great Britain. The best that British football had to offer withered in the face of the Soviets reared on a diet of puritan living and marathon training sessions. Chelsea were held to a 3-3 draw. 'We could hardly keep up with them,' puffed the Chelsea full-back Albert Tennant. Cardiff City were beaten 10–1, Arsenal 4–3 and Rangers battled for a 2-2 draw in front of a 92,000 crowd at Ibrox. Dynamo returned home as heroes. Their historic tour had been followed avidly across Europe, and in Hungary by no one more so than an ambitious young communist by the name of Mihály Farkas. Farkas was a Muscovite, trained in Moscow as a propagandist and sent to Hungary in 1944, where on arrival he changed his name from the Jewish 'Hermann Löwy' to the more distinctly Hungarian 'Mihály Farkas' ('farkas' ominously meaning 'wolf'). In Moscow, Hermann Löwy had been known as a dedicated student, but in Hungary, as Mihály Farkas, he became a crude and boorish bully, ballooning in weight due to the good life he enjoyed as a government minister. When appointed defence minister, he began to dress in a general's uniform, complete with a chest full of medals that no subordinate dare question the authenticity of.

Of all the senior Muscovites, Farkas was the only one who had a genuine interest in football. His impoverished upbringing (he was the result of a brief liaison between a chambermaid and unknown father) gave him an understanding of the sport's popularity, unlike some of his better-educated comrades – self-proclaimed men of the people, who had hated what the people liked.

On a more selfish level, Farkas recognised that his being an integral cog of an internationally successful football team could only bode well in Moscow's watchful eyes. The perfect opportunity to fulfil his designs to become the 'Hungarian Beria' arose when his appointment as defence minister coincided with Hungarian football being brought into line with football in the Soviet Union. Amateurism was re-adopted, substitutions were introduced, and once the 1949/50 season ended, Hungary's football seasons changed so that they ran parallel with football in the Soviet Union.[48] The most significant change, however, was the placing of Hungary's football clubs under the ownership of government departments, industries and trade unions. And Farkas, in his position as defence minister, made sure that the army was to have the first pick of clubs, and asked Gusztáv Sebes to find one suitable.

Sebes was taken aback by Farkas's sudden interest in football, and not a little unsettled. But, in no position to refuse the request, Sebes decided to take the pragmatic view that Farkas's presence could also have its advantages, in that a man as powerful as Farkas could arrange for Hungary's first team to all play at one club. Sebes ran through a list of Budapest-based first-division clubs. Vasas, as the club of the worker, appeared to be the obvious choice, but the communists had had their fingers burned with the club, and wanted nothing more to do with it. Their ambitious plan to make Vasas the biggest club in the land had blundered to a halt. The Communist Party had grandly imagined that their involvement in Vasas would boost match attendances, yet quite the reverse happened. People may have been prepared to lower themselves in joining the party, but very few were going to cheer them. Sebes then considered Ferencváros. *Fradi* remained the biggest and best-supported club in Hungary, but Sebes knew that continually having to quell the club's prominently right-wing support would prove more trouble than it was worth. Újpest too was a club with parochial and partisan support that Sebes didn't trust, and MTK he deemed would be too unpopular among the masses due to the club's reputation as the team of wealthy Jews.

This left Kispest AC, and the more Sebes looked, the more he realised that the club was perfect. The town itself had been incorporated into Budapest only a few months earlier, fulfilling Farkas's criteria that the club be Budapest-based; the club's support was quite substantial and well behaved; and the club was in dire financial straits, desperately looking for new owners. But, best of all, the base of Hungary's first team was already there: Bozsik and Puskás.

In December 1949, at a celebratory dinner marking Kispest Athletic Club's 40th anniversary, it was publicly announced that the club was now that of the Armed Forces Ministry and forthwith was to be called 'Budapesti Honvéd Sport Egyesület' – 'Honvéd' for short: 'hon' meaning 'homeland' and 'véd' 'protect'. The club's entire staff were given military ranks, with the players conscripted as lowly privates and despatched for three months' basic training at a Pest barracks. However, while they coped easily enough with the physical rigours, they resented having to remain confined to barracks for the entire duration. The leading dissenter, Puskás, was mollified somewhat by both he and Bozsik being promoted to the rank of sergeant major. But even this did not quell Puskás's indignation at having to miss his home comforts, so a compromise was reached in which the players spent the mornings doing light military duties and the afternoons playing football, and, unlike the other conscripts, were allowed home of an evening.

The benefits of being 'Honvéd' were immediate. The players were treated to new kit, new boots and refurbished training facilities. But despite this progress, many at the club felt a sense of unease and regret that their once beloved small-town local club had been stripped of its identity, to become the domain of Mihály Farkas.

Indeed, they had reason to be fearful. Farkas wanted Honvéd to be his and his alone, which meant ridding the club of its president, László Sólyom. A former head of the Budapest police force and a communist, Sólyom had a genuine love of football, hence his involvement in Kispest AC. He was on first-name terms with the players and, still being a relatively young man, enjoyed participating in the team's training sessions when he could. Farkas, however, was less endeared with Sólyom's popularity, which he jealously perceived as a threat. Thus, only three months into his presidency, Sólyom was arrested as part of a purge by Rákosi of Hungary's top military (Sólyom having been given the rank of lieutenant general on the club becoming Honvéd). On 20 August 1950, after the now obligatory show trial, Sólyom, along with six other senior military leaders, was sentenced to death and executed. Farkas oversaw Sólyom's replacement at Honvéd by his parliamentary deputy, General Sándor Nógrádi, a man Farkas knew would keep him abreast of all the goings-on at *his* club.

Within months of Kispest becoming Honvéd, every other league club in Hungary likewise came under the control of either the military, the police, trade unions or heavy industry. Budapest's domestic police force took control of Újpest, recruiting the club's players as policemen and changing the club's name to 'Budapest Dózsa'.[49] MTK came under the control of the powerful Textiles Workers' Union and hence became 'Budapest Textiles'. Meanwhile, the Caterers' Union took control of Ferencváros (a particularly strong union in the district known as the 'Stomach of Hungary' for its numerous flour mills), changing the club's name to 'ÉDOSZ', an acronym of 'Élelmezési Dolgozók Szakszervezete'. Only Vasas, already the team of the Metalworkers' Union, remained exempt from new ownership, although the club's name did change to 'Budapest Vasas' as only the Budapest branch of the union remained in control of the club.

Similarly, across Hungary, club names were changed en masse to reflect their new owners. If the local steelworks had control of the club, the new name would consist of the town's name followed by 'Vasas'. If it was the local railways, 'Lokomotív' was used; if the coal mines, 'Bányász'; if the police then 'Dózsa' and if the army had control, 'Honvéd' would be included in the club's name: for example, Debrecen Lokomotív and Szeged Honvéd. Some clubs controlled by a town council in the form of a collective of industries adopted their town's name followed by that of Hungarian folklore heroes (ones sympathetic to the Rákosi regime of course) such as 'Dózsa' or 'Kiniszi'. Other such collectives chose names demonstrating their eagerness and ambition, such as 'Dinamo' or 'Spartacus', and the odd exceptions simply called themselves what they were, such as 'Duna-cipőgyár' and 'Kénsavgyár', meaning the Danube Shoe Factory and the Sulphuric Acid Factory respectively – the latter a name unlikely ever to be bettered.

CHAPTER 8

I felt like I was in a madhouse and that nothing and nobody made any sense.

Hungarian FA president Sándor Barcs

FEW, if any, of Hungary's football clubs appreciated the mass club and ownership changes that swept across the nation's football; but most knew that resistance, even complaining, was futile. However, the partisan support of Ferencváros was the exception.

The Fradi faithful refused outright to surrender their traditions and accept their club's new name, 'ÉDOSZ', chanting, as they always had done, 'Hajrá Fradi!' – 'Play up Fradi!' The communists had long held designs to disband Ferencváros, but plans were never followed through because of the fear of making a martyr of the club. Instead, they considered it best to have dissenters in one place, where they could be monitored and dealt with at a later date.

But the Rákosi regime did not count on the size, bravery and venom of the Fradi crowd. For a person on their own to criticise the regime would have been suicidal, but the anonymity of a football crowd, especially one as packed as Fradi's, offered the chance to vent opinions, and the club's stands became a hotbed of anti-communist catcalls and chants. And, even more gallingly for the regime, Ferencváros won the 1948/49 league title by a margin of 11 clear points, further cementing their place as the strongest team in Danubia by destroying the leading Czechoslovak club, Sparta Prague, *in* Prague.

The regime began looking for other ways to weaken Fradi. The first was to install a police chief and senior communist, Ferenc Munnich, as Ferencváros's president, but this did little to quieten the dissent. Then, under nationalisation, the club was placed under the control of the

Caterers' Union, one of the country's weaker unions. But this backfired. What the union lacked in political weight it counterbalanced by ensuring that its members were among the best-fed people in the country.

Eventually, matters came to a head when Mihály Farkas was foolish enough to attend a Fradi home game. The abuse aimed at him was so savage that the referee (wisely preserving his own future well-being) abandoned the match. Farkas immediately sought to have Ferencváros disbanded, but the wise head of Gusztáv Sebes suggested that the better solution would be to punish the club by allowing other clubs to take away their best players, with Honvéd having the first pick. Farkas agreed. As it was, he had seen it as blindingly obvious that Honvéd would conscript all of Hungary's best footballers.

Likewise, Sebes had plans to assemble Hungary's first eleven at Honvéd, and it was for this reason that he had had Jenő Kalmár replace Ferenc Puskás senior as the club coach. Sebes and Kalmár ran their eye over the Ferencváros team. The pick of the bunch were captain Ferenc Rudas, Hungary's regular right-back, and the forward quartet of Deák, Czibor, Kocsis and László Budai. But Rudas had recently broken his leg in a collision with his own goalkeeper, so that ruled him out. The unpredictable Czibor, while clearly talented, was also clearly in no way cut out for army life, and Deák's getting arrested for a drunken fight soured Sebes's already dim view of the hard-living former slaughterhouse worker.[50] This left Budai and Kocsis.

In truth, Budai wasn't quite in the same class as Kocsis – but he was his best friend, without whom Kocsis appeared lost. For a footballer, Sándor Kocsis was a particularly sensitive soul, the product of an overprotective mother. Indeed, his team-mates mocked him as a mummy's boy – all that is except Budai, who himself was a target for dressing-room ridicule: standing with a stoop and living with his mother until an age when most grown men had long fled the nest. Zoltán Czibor provided a characteristically straightforward description of the team-mate nicknamed 'hunchback':

> Budai was the type of bloke who would have money in his pocket and say, 'What shall I spend it on? I don't like coffee, I don't like wine, I don't like beer, I have a bus pass, I have a tram pass, I have two pigs at home, I have food in the cupboard, I have a place to

> live' – he lived with his mother – 'I don't know what to spend it on!' That's how he was born: 'What shall I spend it on?' He was a genuine and lovely man. Mind you, he was no genius.[51]

Budai was born László Bednarik in the Pest district of Rákospalota, where he would live his entire life. He 'Hungarianised' his Swabian surname to 'Budai', meaning a 'person of Buda', immediately after joining Ferencváros, who had spotted him playing for a local factory where he worked as an apprentice machine operator. It was in Ferencváros's youth team where Budai first met Kocsis, and quickly the pair became inseparable on and off the pitch. The two spent endless hours together alone on the training pitch – Budai making repetitive runs down the wing and crossing the ball from all angles for Kocsis. So often did the pair practise together that it reached a point where Budai, without looking up, learned to know where Kocsis would be; and Kocsis, by reading Budai's body language, could tell where the cross would be heading. Kocsis, assisted by Budai, smashed all of Hungary's youth football scoring records, and as the pair progressed to Fradi's first team, their scoring talents as a duo did not relent.

When Honvéd made to conscript the two friends, it was Budai they sent the call-up papers to first, although the army did not count upon Budai being unconcerned about obeying orders. When days later Budai still had not shown at Honvéd's training ground, Major Bozsik was despatched:

> I was lying on my bed when an army jeep pulled up outside my house. My poor mother was so scared she was shaking. When I saw it was 'Cucu' Bozsik I knew everything was alright. Bozsik asked me whether I had received my call-up papers. I said yes but I had ignored them to buy myself some time. Never eat a pudding when it is too hot! Bozsik said this would get me in trouble, but I wanted to speak to Kocsis first, so we headed off to his house. Sanyi answered his door with his call-up papers in his hand. He too had been conscripted! The next day the newspapers ran the headline 'Kocsis and Budai sign for Honvéd'. The Fradi supporters called us all the names under the sun. It really hurt me that they regarded us as traitors.[52]

At Honvéd, Budai and Kocsis joined two other new recruits, Gyula Lóránt and Gyula Grosics. The central defender Lóránt was a rarity in that he was an eager conscript, after coming from Vasas, where the club had suspended his playing licence after a falling-out over money. Unable to play, Lóránt had taken work as a clerk in a motor factory, so when Sebes appeared bearing promises and conscription papers, Lóránt agreed in an instant.

Grosics was less eager, and offered less of a choice: he was already a soldier. Grosics was the young goalkeeper who, as you may remember from Chapter 6, was arrested and banned for one year for attempting to escape from Hungary. Of the 14 banned players, Grosics was the only one to serve the entirety of his ban, refusing to demonstrate even an inkling of remorse for his actions. As a punishment for his unrepentance, Grosics was conscripted into the army and billeted to a Budapest barracks, from where once a day he was allowed out to train with his club, MATEOSZ.[53] And, as he was a serving soldier when the army took over Honvéd, he was simply ordered to play for the club, MATEOSZ receiving not a forint for their best player.

Having served his one-year ban, Grosics was recalled to the national team. In the first three matches of 1950, Hungary had won three games in a row by a five-goal margin, but it was a run that came to an end with a 5–3 defeat to Austria in Vienna. On scrutinising the loss, Sebes concluded that the goalkeeper, Géza Henni, was to blame: a goalkeeper of supposed international standard conceding five goals was inexcusable.

It was not an easy decision for Sebes to both recall Grosics and have him sent to Honvéd, for as a person Sebes disliked him immensely. Sebes was ready to accept that all goalkeepers have their quirks, but felt Grosics went overboard. He was vain, a startlingly handsome man, who knew it. He was aloof, distancing himself from his team-mates. He was stubborn, refusing to hide his Catholic beliefs, openly wearing a crucifix and crossing himself before going on to the pitch, despite being warned numerous times not to. He was a hypochondriac, unable to function normally without regular examinations and reassurance from doctors, even going so far as to cure his own 'ailments' – the most bizarre and obvious of which was his insistence on wearing a bright red beret, convinced that it would keep him from getting a brain tumour.

And Grosics was clever, a voracious reader, no fool for the communist propaganda and reciprocating of Sebes's dislike of him. But Grosics was by far and away the best goalkeeper in Hungary, and for this even Sebes was prepared to bend.

The spine of Honvéd – Grosics, Lóránt, Bozsik, Budai, Kocsis and Puskás – began to form the spine of Sebes's national team, which, following the 5–3 defeat to Austria, managed to remain unbeaten for the rest of 1950: Poland 5–2, Albania 12–0, Austria 4–3 and Bulgaria 1–1.

Sebes began plans to send more national team players to Honvéd, but these were soon scuppered by the intervention of a man that even Mihály Farkas dared not cross.

Gábor Péter, chief of the ÁVO, cared nothing for football but did care for being upstaged by Farkas and the favour that Honvéd were winning for his rival comrade in Moscow. Thus Péter had the ÁVO take control of MTK from the Textiles Workers' Union, changing the club's name to 'Budapest Bástya' ('bástya' meaning 'fortress'), and placing the players – now policemen – out of Honvéd's reach.

If the presence of Farkas had been unsettling, then Péter's was unnerving in the extreme. Péter prided himself on being the most sinister of all the leading communists. He was a small, dapper man with a pencil-thin moustache, a tailor by trade who retained a taste for bespoke suits and silk shirts. He was a sadist, regularly taking part in interrogations of those who had once been his superiors. He'd personally arrested his old comrade László Rajk, and more recently János Kádár, uncovered by Péter as a spy – arrested, tortured and sentenced to 15 years in prison.

A lesser comrade than Kádár would have faced a death sentence, but Rákosi was clever enough not to make a martyr of the wartime party leader. And whether Kádár was physically tortured during his interrogation is hard to ascertain: depending on whom he told, and when, Kádár would sometimes admit to having been beaten and that his fingernails had been pulled out and his testicles had been crushed, leaving him sterile; although on other occasions he would say that he had not been mistreated at all. Whatever the truth, the story that while Kádár lay collapsed on the floor, his bloodied mouth was prised open and pissed in by Mihály Farkas has entered Hungarian folklore.

Gábor Péter's new-found interest in football cast a shadow over the game in Hungary. It was no secret that the ÁVO had kept an eye on footballers and their comings and goings, and for the most part had let them be; but with the organisation now having a vested interest, closer scrutiny was paid.

Sándor Szűcs was a centre-half for Budapest Dózsa (Újpest) who had played 19 times for the Hungarian national team. By 1951 Szűcs was 30 years old and, while no longer in Gusztáv Sebes's plans, remained a competent league player upon whom Sebes could call if necessary.

Szűcs (pronounced 'Sootch') was a married man with two children – and a lover, Erzsi Kovács, a well-known singer. Kovács herself had a fiancé, a man with connections to the ÁVO, and a correct suspicion that his wife was having an affair with the footballer.

Szűcs was warned more than once to stay away from his lover for both their sakes – on occasion, even the Dózsa chairman, police chief Sándor Csáki, warned Szűcs. But the intrusion into his private affairs only caused Szűcs to take an even dimmer view of the regime he loathed, and he and Kovács began to make plans to leave Hungary for Italy, where he hoped to join his friend, the former Újpest star Gyula Zsengellér at Roma. The lovers' enquiries led them to dealings with a go-between people-smuggler who introduced himself as 'József Kovács'. He, for a hefty fee, agreed to smuggle them across the Austrian border and insisted that, to make it worth his while, they had to bring two more people and that Szűcs, a serving policeman, should also bring his service gun 'just in case'.

The four duly set off at the arranged time, with the smuggler Kovács driving them from Budapest to the border, where a police cordon awaited them. The four would-be dissidents were arrested, and the undercover ÁVO officer József Kovács congratulated on a job well done.

What the unfortunate Szűcs hadn't known before he embarked on his plan to flee Hungary was that weeks before a new law had been quietly passed that made it a capital offence for members of the security services to attempt to smuggle groups out of Hungary while armed. And it was the reason why the 'smuggler' Kovács had insisted on Szűcs bringing his service pistol and two civilians. From his prison cell, Szűcs managed to have a note begging for help smuggled to his best friend and Dózsa team-mate Ferenc Szusza. Szusza passed the message to Puskás, the one person he knew that could influence Mihály Farkas. Puskás, Szusza and Bozsik raced to the Defence Ministry, only for Farkas to meet them with a blithe, 'You're too late, boys – he was executed at five o'clock this morning.'

It was 40 years later that Erzsi Kovács finally spoke publicly about what happened after her and Szűcs's arrest at the border:

> Only the end result matters. Sanyi was sentenced to death for attempting to smuggle a weapon across the border. I was sentenced to four years. Originally the prosecutor wanted for me also to be given the death sentence, but because of my young age, I was reprieved. After the sentences were passed, they asked Sanyi if he wanted clemency. He replied that if they could execute someone for doing what he did, then they should execute him. That is when I became hysterical, begging them to let me speak to my lover. In total, I spent three years in prison. In 1954 when I was released, it was Feri Szusza who told me that Sanyi was dead. For so long I had hoped that he wasn't.[54]

Not long after his friend's execution, Ferenc Szusza played his last match for Hungary. The team were staying at a hotel in Moscow before a game against the Soviet Union when some high jinks resulted in a wine bottle being accidentally knocked out of an upper-floor window. The police were involved, and while the matter was smoothed over, the mortified Sebes blamed Szusza despite evidence to the contrary. Szusza was 28 years old and at the peak of his formidable scoring ability, which led him to become one of football's world record-breaking goalscorers,[55] and he never played for Hungary again all the while Sebes was in charge. Many believed Sebes knew Szusza to be innocent but used the incident to his advantage – ridding himself of a player whose grief and anger at the execution of his best friend, Szűcs, he felt was affecting the team's morale.

A further consequence of the Szűcs case was that whenever any Hungarian team travelled abroad, two or three ÁVO officers were always assigned to follow the players. There was never any mingling or idle conversation between the two. The ÁVO men kept a cold and watchful distance, while the players, sensing them in their midst, would mind their tongues. All, that is, except Puskás, who would take great delight in purposely disappearing for a few hours then suddenly returning moments before the party was due to depart – greeting the officers with a cheery, 'Go on, admit it, you thought I'd fucked off for good, didn't you?'

These visible ÁVO men were, however, more an inconvenience than a threat. The greater danger for the players lay with the 'undercover' agents – those sent by the ÁVO to spy on the players, often journalists accompanying the team or in some cases fellow footballers. What they were looking for exactly, they probably did not know themselves. They just reported everything back to their superiors, from the players' political views to their love lives.

More than 50 years later, in 2006, evidence was produced that claimed that the radio commentator György Szepesi was one such informant, working under the name 'Galambos', meaning 'pigeon'. Szepesi was so synonymous with the Magical Magyars that he was nicknamed the team's 'Twelfth Man'. He was a childhood friend of Ferenc Szusza, a friendship that got him acceptance from players, allowing him to become closer to them than certainly any other journalist. Szepesi's commentaries on Hungary's international matches enthralled millions of listeners, and even when listened to today are breathtakingly exciting. Whenever possible, Szepesi would stand with his microphone on the touchline and, at a machine-gun pace, urge, berate and praise with unabashed patriotism, referring to the players like the friends they were: 'Sanyi! Sanyi! How on earth could you miss from there???' … 'Go on, Zoli! Go on!!!' … 'Ahhhh, Öcsi, what are you doing???' But Szepesi remained silent on being accused of being an informer, although his close friend the Magical Magyar Jenő Buzánszky refused outright to believe it. However, Gyula Grosics, who knew first-hand just to what depths the ÁVO would plunge to recruit informers, kept an open mind but held no grudge.

Jenő Buzánszky was the player drafted into the team by Sebes to replace Ferenc Rudas,[56] the Ferencváros and Hungary right-back whose leg break prematurely ended his career. Sebes's search for a replacement was extensive before he finally settled upon the 25-year-old Buzánszky on the advice of József Bozsik. As the team's right-back, it was Buzánszky's responsibility to supply the right-half, Bozsik, with passes out of defence as well as cover for the pace-strapped Bozsik in cases of emergency. What Buzánszky lacked skill-wise he made up for with enthusiasm and blistering speed, and he wasn't a dirty player liable to get sent off for malicious tackling or dissent.

Buzánszky was the only one of the Magical Magyars who did not play for a Budapest club. He was a country boy, born in the small market town of Dombóvár, in south-west Hungary, and represented provincial Dorogi FC, a club where he would remain throughout his playing days, in a town where he resided for life. Over the coming years, all of Budapest's leading clubs at some time attempted to lure Buzánszky to the capital, but he turned down all offers. He saw no reason to leave Dorogi. His family was settled and the club provided him with a cushy office job at a local coal mine that allowed him to train and play as he pleased. Of course, Mihály Farkas and Sebes could have had Buzánszky conscripted into joining Honvéd at any time, but it was believed that the authorities wanted at least one member of the international first eleven to play for a provincial club. For his remaining in the provinces and his personable nature, Buzánszky's international team-mates would tease him as being a naive 'country bumpkin', yet in reality, he was as sharp as, if not sharper than, any of the city boys.

How Sebes must have yearned for all his players born in the provinces to be as well behaved as Buzánszky. The players who caused Sebes the most consternation – Grosics, Lóránt, Czibor and MTK winger Károly Sándor – were all from small country towns. Sándor was Sebes's particular bugbear. Rated as the best right-winger in Hungarian football, and for a time Europe, Sándor was enormously popular with spectators right across Hungary. Sebes hated him. Exactly why is hard to fathom. Sándor was a genial, kind-natured soul, but he was MTK coach Márton Bukovi's pet favourite, and ready to stand up for himself, as Sebes found out once when he accused Sándor of cowardice and feigning injury. It was suspected that Sebes found Sándor's social ambitions pretentious. Of all the Magical Magyars, Sándor had grown up by far the poorest, and once he became a star in Budapest, began enjoying its rewards. He developed a taste for gambling and harboured ambitions to become an actor.

Sebes preferred the more direct wing play of Budai – beat a man, straight to the byline with a burst of speed, then cross – whereas Sándor was a dribbler. Indeed it was his mazy runs that made him a crowd favourite. But Sebes saw dribbling as selfish, time-consuming and outdated. Post-war football had evolved into a game where a player in possession of the ball had little time before being surrounded, with their passing options limited. Dribbling one's way out of trouble was not considered a solution, as modern defenders had become as fast as attackers, and had also learned to hold off from lunging into tackles so as to dictate the dribbler's direction. To overcome this, the Hungarians mastered the techniques of 'feinting': shoulder dips, looking one way while passing the other, raising a leg to kick the ball but not doing so. Sándor was as adept as any other, in fact more so, but not enough for Sebes to warm to him.

Hypocritically, the traits that Sebes condemned in Sándor as not befitting of a Hungarian athlete, he tolerated in others, most notably the far more troublesome Zoltán Czibor – an argumentative, unpredictable mass of complexities who could not for the life of him hold his tongue when required. Jenő Buzánszky described Czibor as 'a law unto himself, the type of person who did not know when enough was enough', while Gyula Grosics observed that Czibor could not function without trouble in his life …

> He was uncontrollable – in fact, I could say that Zoli was uncontrollable in the extreme. On the pitch and in his private life, it was a characteristic. But I must add that he was surrounded by untruths and lies, to which he would immediately react. Speaking his mind caused him no end of difficulties. On the football pitch this was mostly tolerated, but in his private life, it brought him endless confrontations. I don't think it would be an exaggeration to say that Zoli – and this is not a criticism – was too proud a Hungarian, who always put too much emphasis on patriotism. And that type of patriot can never withhold their opinion.[57]

Czibor tells in his autobiography of his abnormal behaviour stemming from his train-driver father being violent towards him in particular because he'd wanted a daughter after already having three sons. In the same book, a misty-eyed Czibor recalls his father bursting into tears when he had to drive the train taking him and other young conscripts off to the front in the last desperate days of the Second World War. Czibor surrendered to the first American soldier he encountered, and after the war returned to his home town of Komárom to work as an apprentice train driver. While playing for the railway works team, Czibor was spotted by Ferencváros (by the same scout who'd spotted László Budai), where his team-mates gave him the nickname 'Crazy', a moniker that was explained away to the public as being based on his skills driving opponents crazy. In 1949, Czibor was one of the 18 footballers banned for a year from international football for conspiring to escape from Hungary and form a team abroad. Whether a banned player served his entire ban very much depended on his usefulness to the national team, thus Czibor served only a month of his ban before Sebes decided to hand him his international debut. However, it would be over two years before Czibor became Sebes's first-choice left-winger: Sebes held out as long as he could in searching for a winger as good as Czibor but less problematic, and none materialised – so, left with no option, Sebes was forced to select a player who annoyed and vexed him quite like no other.

Sebes would never question Czibor's dedication or determination to win, but his refusal to conform was maddening. Many assumed that his drifting from wing to wing was a pre-arranged tactic, but it was not. Czibor was wont to change wings of his own accord whenever the mood took him. Initially, coaches had screamed for him to get back to his position, but Czibor's selective hearing and potency on either wing eventually had them deciding to let him be.

When the authorities began stripping Fradi of their best players, Czibor remained. Bozsik and Puskás made it known that they did not want Czibor at Honvéd, not that Czibor was concerned for a moment – he was happy revelling in being the lone star player at Fradi, the club of the anti-communists. Until, that is, he fell out with the club management over the payment of money he felt he was due for representing the national team more than five times. It was a deal that Czibor had struck when the club was Ferencváros, but on enquiring after his money with the new owners, he had received the curt reply, 'The club is ÉDOSZ now, comrade Czibor, not Ferencváros.'

Czibor did no more, and contacted the small Pest club of Csepel SC, who a month before had approached him with an offer to join them. For the exact sum of money he believed ÉDOSZ owed him, Czibor agreed to become a Csepel player – and, free from the demands that dominated the lives of players at the leading clubs, Czibor flourished at mid-table Csepel, tolerated by the club management and left happily to his own strange devices.

Within a year, though, Czibor was at Honvéd. With Czibor it was hard to distinguish the truth from a tall story. One of his versions of his joining Honvéd was that he fell to his knees in front of Mihály Farkas and mockingly begged to be taken to Honvéd: 'Uncle Mishy, my young family will starve to death if I don't get to join.' Another version he provided was that he had no choice in joining, and that on his first day at Honvéd he stepped into the club's office to see József Bozsik looking at him: 'How did you get in here?' asked Bozsik.

'Shut the fuck up!' Czibor says he replied, helping himself to a seat. 'Your boss sent me here. Don't you recognise this uniform? I can assure you that I never wished to join this band of thieving gipsies!'[58]

And yet it was no great wonder that the country boys were the most anti-communist. Rural life in Hungary had irreversibly changed for the worse with the Soviet Union's continual unrealistic demands for produce, combined with Moscow ordering Hungary to follow the Soviet example and 'collectivise' farming. The Hungarian peasantry had initially rejoiced when the communists first introduced land reforms, seizing ownership of the land from the aristocracy and dividing it into small parcels which were given to the peasantry so that they could become their own masters. But by 1950 the peasantry themselves were the victims of land reforms, when the communist regime forced all farms to become state-owned. Known as 'collectives', the farms were extremely unpopular, as it was compulsory for the peasants to sell all their produce to a central authority (overseen by a Communist Party member) who dictated the price and the type of crop grown. The growing of private produce was strictly forbidden – it was considered a crime against the state, as were any late deliveries. Those farmers who resisted joining a collective or continued to sell their own produce privately were condemned as 'kulaks', a Russian term meaning 'rich peasants', and targeted for arrest. Kulaks were blamed for nearly all the country's shortages: if there was a shortage of bread it was because the kulaks had raised the price of flour, or if there was a shortage of meat it was because the kulaks had kept it for themselves.

The real reason, though, for the dire shortages was that Hungary was forced to export (mainly to East Germany) the vast majority of its produce and livestock, and the little that remained was of inferior quality. By 1950 Hungary, one of the most fertile countries on earth, was on the brink of starvation.

CHAPTER 9

The play of the others would range between brilliant and mediocre, but even on Puskás's very worst days his form never once dropped below an acceptable level.

Gusztáv Sebes

IN the spring of 1952, Sebes's first-team squad set out for Moscow, clutching their Communist Party membership cards (without which they would not have been allowed to enter), to play two games in four days against the Soviet Union national team. The invitation had come from the Soviets, who, like Hungary, were preparing for that summer's Olympics in Helsinki, and wanted some quality opposition against whom they could test themselves.

Hungary also needed the challenge. The previous year, 1951, they had only played three international matches, beating Poland 6–0, Czechoslovakia 2–1 and Finland 8–0. More to the point, they had yet to actually qualify for the Olympics. There remained the no small matter of a play-off qualifier against Romania, to be played in Finland a week before the tournament's start.

Both matches were played to capacity crowds at the newly refurbished Dynamo Moscow stadium, and both were hard-fought, the Saturday match ending in a 1–1 draw, and the Tuesday one in a 2–1 victory to the Soviets. Sebes took small consolation in the fact that the referee being a Russian (at the insistence of the Soviets) nullified the matches' international status, thus maintaining his team's run of eight matches without a loss. But while Sebes may have got away with his undefeated record intact, the defeat bothered him. No criticism would come from his superiors for losing in Moscow, indeed quite the reverse, but Sebes saw that his team had failed the sternest test of his two years in charge. A similar defeat at the Olympics would mean instant elimination. The tournament was fast approaching, and Sebes still hadn't decided upon his first eleven, nor a formation. A lack of real match time was one reason, but another was Sebes himself. Such was the abundance of talent at his disposal, he couldn't make up his mind. Eventually, it was Sebes's biggest coaching rival, Márton Bukovi, who settled matters. Bukovi had led MTK (or Bástya as they were officially known) to the 1951 league title, pipping Honvéd by four points, lining his team up in a 'new' 4–2–4 formation.

The 4–2–4[59] was an extension of the WM, which itself had evolved from the traditional pyramid formation.

The WM was invented by the legendary Arsenal manager Herbert Chapman. It was a more defensive formation that revolutionised English football, and at the same time led Arsenal to become the biggest club in the country. By 1940, the WM had made its way into continental Europe, brought to Hungary by a young journalist called László Feleki.

Feleki was a reporter at the 1938 World Cup Final, where he spied the watching Arsenal manager, George Allison – Chapman's successor and a coach who had adhered to the WM. Feleki asked Allison if he would allow him to spend one season training with Arsenal in the capacity of an observer for the sports newspaper for which he worked. Allison, amused as much as he was intrigued, readily agreed, and consequently Feleki moved to London, his journey and lodgings funded by the surprisingly enlightened Hungarian FA.

On his return to Hungary a year later, Feleki brought with him Arthur Rowe, a recently retired Tottenham Hotspur centre-back. With Feleki acting as translator, Rowe gave a series of lectures explaining the workings of the WM. So impressed were the Hungarians by Rowe that the Trainers' Society offered him a position as a full-time adviser, in the hope that he would become another Jimmy Hogan. But with the Second World War on the horizon and Hungary leaning ever closer to an alliance with Germany, Rowe was mindful of the accusations of treason that had been levelled at Hogan. After just three months in Hungary, Rowe regretfully headed home to England and joined the army. Ferencváros adopted the WM, and won the league twice in succession; by, 1941 all of Hungary's first-division clubs had followed suit.

By the early 1950s, though, even a three-man defence was not sufficient to stop such predatory forwards as Deák, Czibor, Kocsis, Puskás and Szusza. The obvious solution was a four-man defence, which, whenever MTK were not in possession of the ball, Márton Bukovi formed by instructing one of his two half-backs to drop back to assist in defence and his centre-forward, Nándor Hidegkuti, to retreat and fill the void in midfield: a rudimentary 4–2–4.

Such became Hidegkuti's prowess as a deep-lying centre-forward that Sebes deployed him in the same role for a friendly against Poland in Warsaw in June 1952. Poland's centre-half, Roman Kornyt, faced the same dilemma that was to befall many a fellow defender: should he follow Hidegkuti into Hungary's own half and leave his defence wide open for attack from Kocsis and Puskás, or remain in position and leave Hidegkuti to dictate the match unopposed? Hungary beat the Poles 5–1, and used the same tactic a week later in beating Finland 8–0 in Helsinki, a match arranged by Sebes so that he and his players would have some idea of what to expect at the Olympics.

Hereafter, Sebes cemented Hidegkuti as his first-choice centre-forward. At 30 years old Hidegkuti had been in and out of the national team for over a decade, appearing such a wily veteran to his younger team-mates that they nicknamed him 'Öreg' – 'Old Man'.

> I was selected because I had more brains than my predecessors, and I'll tell you why. Up until then forwards had always only ever served Puskás and Kocsis, whereas I always gave them the ball in a way that they had no option but to pass it back to me – that way I was always involved in the game. Once Puskás complained to me, 'Öreg! You always pass me the ball so that I have to give it back to you!' I replied, 'Of course. That's the point.'[60]

As it was, Hidegkuti had begun playing football relatively late in life. It wasn't until he left school that he first played football, turning out for the works team of the sewing machine factory where he worked as a clerk in his home town of Óbuda (ancient Buda). Within a year, Hidegkuti was sold to the team of a Pest gasworks for the price of a new kit and one year's free use of the gasworks' pitch. Moving up into professional football, Hidegkuti played for a series of lower division clubs, eventually joining MTK just after the war. But, despite his obvious talents as a nippy and skilful centre-forward, Hidegkuti always inexplicably ran out of steam way before the match ended. Just when Hidegkuti had resigned himself to spending his entire career as a perennial squad player, Márton Bukovi arrived at MTK. Previous coaches had just thought Hidegkuti to be 'lacking stamina' and left it at that, but Bukovi characteristically dug deeper. He had Hidegkuti medically examined, for it to be discovered that he was anaemic. Hidegkuti was placed on a strict training programme combining healthy foods, early nights and exercise. Bolstered by his second chance, Hidegkuti adhered to this advice to the point of obsession; and, full of energy, he was placed by Bukovi as the integral cog in the 4–2–4 formation, leading MTK to winning the 1951 league title and catching Sebes's eye.

But before Sebes would even consider selecting Hidegkuti, he insisted the player cover up his being the son of a Horthy regime army captain (a Swab named Kaltenbrunner), a past deemed unsuitable for a high-proflile representative of communist Hungary. Thus Hidegkuti was made to appear in a short film which showed his mother, an educated woman, working as a machine operator, with the voiceover telling how joyous she was that communism had given her and her son the opportunities to improve their lot in life. Hidegkuti and his family reluctantly went along with the charade, with the mind that those who knew them would know the film to be untrue, and besides refusal was not an option they dared entertain.

The fact that Hidegkuti's parents were of the affluent middle classes marked them in the eyes of the Rákosi regime as targets for persecution, primarily so that the government could use their properties to alleviate the chronic housing shortage that Budapest was suffering due to huge numbers of people migrating from the countryside to the capital to work in industry. Hungary's once-substantial middle classes either had their homes sub-divided up and were forced to live with workers' families, or, if they were particularly obstructive and ungrateful, were evicted outright. The evictions were carried out by the ÁVO, who would arrive with no prior warning and give the terrified families only minutes to pack their belongings. Forced to sign documents that handed the property to the state, the evictees were then separated from their children, who were placed in orphanages while the adults were transported to the countryside, where the fortunate were housed in the outbuildings of peasant farms and put to work as farmhands or used as labourers in building projects. The less fortunate (those who had once been higher up the social ladder) were placed in Educational Labour Camps. The number of evictees has never been known for sure, though it is estimated to be around 70,000.

Having beaten Finland in Helsinki, the squad returned to Hungary to spend a few nights at home with their families before gathering once again for a fortnight of intensive preparation, involving two friendly matches against the Austrian club side First Vienna, both of which they won. The fortnight was spent staying in the Red Star Hotel on Budapest's Margaret Island, within walking distance of the team's regular training pitches. The hotel, with its hot spring pools and first-class restaurant, usually catered to politicians and visiting dignitaries and was a world away from the hardships of the Olympic training camp at Tata where the rest of Hungary's athletes were preparing for the tournament. This prompted groans that the football players were receiving preferential treatment – in this communist utopia, wasn't everyone supposed to be equal?

The squad then returned to Finland to play the deciding qualifier against Romania. Never is there any love lost in a football match between Hungarians and Romanians, and so it proved in Turku, Hungary snatching a 2–1 win in a foul-tempered game that saw the ordinarily placid Sándor Kocsis sent off for the only time in his career.

It was a victory nonetheless, and one that, although it may seem insignificant at first glance, was a pivotal moment in the golden period of Hungarian football. Non-qualification for the Olympics would have spelt the end of Sebes's tenure as head coach, as well as the Rákosi government's free-spending approach towards football.

But even with his team qualified for the Olympics, Sebes remained unsatisfied. In watching the Romania match he had spotted, in left-half Imre Kovács, the team's only weakness. Sebes's problem was not with the player's ability or attitude – indeed Kovács was to MTK what József Bozsik was to Honvéd, and therein lay the problem: Kovács was too similar to Bozsik. What Sebes wanted was a midfielder to complement Bozsik, not compete with him: a left-half prepared to bow to Bozsik's superior passing ability, to do his 'dirty work' for him and place the ball at his feet. Kovács possessed too much skill to be a servile type of player; however, his MTK counterpart, József Zakariás, was prepared to undertake these necessary but lowly tasks, and it was he that Sebes decided to make Bozsik's midfield partner.

The presence of the defence-minded Zakariás perversely made Hungary a more attacking side. Bozsik, free from the constraints of having to defend, was able to push further up the field, safe in the knowledge that Zakariás was covering behind him. Hungary's defence was also bolstered by Zakariás dropping back whenever they were under attack, slipping next to Gyula Lóránt or covering for left-back Mihály Lantos's lack of speed. When Hungary were on the attack, Zakariás would push up just behind Bozsik, and in turn goalkeeper Gyula Grosics would leave his goal to stand on the edge of the centre circle, ready to repel any opposition counter-attacks. Grosics was the original 'sweeper-keeper', only ever standing on his goal line if pinned back by an attack: the rest of the time he would move up with the play. Occasionally Grosics was caught out by a well-executed counter-attack, but this was rare, and his being able to back-pedal as fast as many other footballers could sprint saw him out of trouble more often than not.

Attack began the moment Hungary had the ball under control, and at a speed which gave the opposition no time to regroup and gather their senses. Grosics was under instruction to roll the ball out to either of the full-backs, Buzánszky or Lantos; they, in turn, would quickly push it forward to Bozsik, whose options were widened by Hidegkuti, or the wingers Budai and Czibor, dropping deep into their own half to receive a pass. Once the ball was in the opposition's half, Hungary came alive. Budai, Kocsis, Hidegkuti, Puskás and Czibor – with the licence to roam as they pleased – interweaved with short passes, covered for each other and drew away opponents with dummy runs. It was a playing style that Sebes had searched for since his appointment as coach three years earlier, when he told the press, 'We need to find a new style of play and tactics, which only Hungarians can play and to which the opposition will have no answer. A hard, fast and impenetrable defence who can survey the pitch and supply an attack made up of fast wingers and goalscoring forwards.'[61]

By the time Hungary entered the Helsinki Olympics, Sebes[62] had achieved his aim, and finally settled upon a first eleven:

Grosics

Buzánszky Lóránt Lantos

Bozsik Zakariás

Hidegkuti

Budai Kocsis Puskás Czibor

In the first round, Hungary beat Italy 3–0, the first time in 27 years that Hungary had defeated the Azzurri; but in fairness, this was not the genuine Italian national team. Because Italian football was professional, the squad sent to Helsinki was made up of amateur players, whereas the countries from the Eastern bloc (Hungary, Yugoslavia and the Soviet Union) were essentially amateurs, so were able to field their full-strength national teams – 'shamateurism' as the British press called it. Still, even the hard-bitten British hacks could not deny that Hungary were something extraordinary. The correspondent for the *London Evening News*, Bernard Joy, a former Arsenal player, wrote that:

> Hungary stressed mobility and interchangeability. No man was a slave to his position but an all-rounder capable of playing almost anywhere. Although long passes were not discarded Hungary realised that short ones could be made more accurately, and so the players had to move to within reach of the man in possession. The team advanced in waves, with players gathering around the man with the ball like circles around a pebble dropped in water.[63]

In the second round, Hungary swept aside Turkey 7–1, and in the semi-final the reigning Olympic champions, Sweden, 6–1. 'Watching Hungary was like drinking a fine wine – with an aching heart I watched the clock count down, as I didn't want the performance to end,' wrote the correspondent of the highly respected West German magazine *Kicker*.[64]

Their opponents in the final were Yugoslavia – the communist nation run by dictator Josip Broz Tito, whose refusal to run his country as ordered by Moscow made him a traitor in the eyes of Stalin.

Yugoslavia had faced the Soviet Union in the first round. At half-time, the Soviets were leading by a comfortable five goals to one. At full time, the score was 5–5. Two days later at the same stadium, a replay was held, which the Yugoslavs won 3–1. A gloating Tito very publicly awarded each player the princely sum of $100.

In Hungary, Mátyás Rákosi, who never missed an opportunity to condemn Tito as a 'dog', secretly cheered Yugoslavia eliminating the Soviet Union. Had Hungary met the Soviets in the final, and won, how would the Hungarian people have celebrated – with a cheer or a sneer? How would Rákosi have been expected to celebrate?

Against Yugoslavia, though, if Hungary were to lose, the excuse existed that their opponents had also beaten the Soviets. But if Hungary were to win, Rákosi would be the toast of the Kremlin. The night before the final, Rákosi telephoned Sebes at the team's hotel and, as one old-time comrade to another, confided, 'The political situation for us is very difficult at the present moment, Comrade Sebes. You have to win.'

The final took place on an August Saturday evening in Helsinki's Olympic Stadium, packed to the gunnels with an unprecedented 60,000 spectators. The two teams began warily, both reluctant to make a mistake and offer an opening. The tentative stand-off lasted well into the first half, until Kocsis was bundled to the floor in the Yugoslavs' penalty area. Puskás stepped up to take the penalty, but shot so feebly that the Yugoslav goalkeeper only had to scoop the ball into his arms. At half-time, Sebes made a beeline for his captain … and laid a comforting arm around his shoulders. Only weeks earlier, Puskás's beloved father had died after a short illness, and the loss had hit Puskás very hard. Sebes then turned to the rest of the team and told them they were an embarrassment.

Four minutes into the second half, Kocsis seized on a Puskás through pass and scored, only for the goal to be disallowed by the English referee, Arthur Ellis, citing Czibor as offside. Feeling hard done by, Hungary stepped up their attacks, and in the 60th minute, Kocsis scored again, only for Ellis again to disallow the goal, this time judging Kocsis to have first fouled a Yugoslav defender. Ten minutes later, Puskás scored from a rebound from his own shot, a goal with which Ellis could find no fault (1–0). As the clock ticked down, the

Yugoslavs fought back. A clearance from the Hungarian half fell to Czibor. His path blocked in all directions, he searched for options as his team-mates screamed at him to launch the ball out of play to waste a few precious seconds, and more importantly prevent the Yugoslavs winning the ball and launching a counter-attack. Czibor turned and hoofed the ball towards the stands behind the Yugoslavs' goal – and as the ball arched over the flat-footed Yugoslav goalkeeper and smacked the back of the net (2–0), Czibor looked to the heavens: 'For fuck's sake! Why does nothing ever go how I want it to?'

The Hungarian football team's Olympic gold was a watershed moment in how the players were treated. Before they had been mere footballers; now they were stars (in Hungary at least). The upside was fame, money and women – the downside was being beholden to the regime who had put them there.

Once the authorities had the bright idea that a 'Golden Team' footballer should become a member of parliament, Gusztáv Sebes was ordered to produce a suitable player, so he chose József Bozsik: well behaved, the son of a worker, a settled family man and with absolutely zero interest in politics. Perfect – except that Bozsik didn't want to be a politician. He was a shy man with a dislike of talking in public. Even better, said Rákosi!

József Bozsik MP took small comfort in the fact that he was not alone in having to get involved in politics. None of his Golden Team team-mates would be immune from having to undertake political duties in some form or another, even if it was just attending ceremonies and clapping on cue.

The propaganda value for the regime of having a star footballer attend a party function, and appear to be in full agreement with what was being said, was immense.

No player was more in demand than Puskás. By 1952, Hungary's captain was rated by many to be the best footballer in the world. It was a fame that the Rákosi regime readily used to their full advantage, having Puskás introduced to all manner of influential international dignitaries safe in the knowledge that, as he spoke no language other than his native Hungarian, anything he said on Hungary's behalf had to, thankfully, go through government interpreters. Puskás may have appeared to be full of pleasant remarks to foreign ears, but to any

Hungarian speaker present, his language at times was as crude as his behaviour was infantile.

The urchin from Kispest had moved up socially, but without learning the tact and decorum required for his new status in life, and he continued to speak to everyone as if they were footballers regardless of their social standing. Puskás loved being the centre of attention and people laughing at his jokes. So if calling a particularly uptight dignitary an 'arse head' in front of everyone got a laugh, Puskás would do so, oblivious to any reason why the person was uptight in the first place.

For the butt of Puskás's humour, it was no laughing matter; these were Hungary's darkest days: cross the wrong person and arrest, torture, prison, eviction and even death could await. Puskás's team-mates and family may have known that he meant no harm, but strangers were not sure – it was, after all, no secret that Puskás was good friends with Mihály Farkas. Thus the laughter that followed Puskás's brand of humour was often of the stilted, sycophantic kind. People had to weigh up whether the butt of Puskás's jibes could one day take revenge at the slight of being laughed at, or whether Puskás himself would take offence at his joke falling flat and therefore turn his attention towards another sour-faced 'arse head'. The brunt of Puskás's tongue on more than one occasion was Sándor Barcs, the Hungarian FA president who believed that Puskás as a youth had learned his 'idiotic love of money and insufferably crude behaviour' from his Kispest team-mates. The communist Barcs felt that when football was professional in Hungary money was the sole god for both the players and profit-pursuing club owners. And at a first division club like Kispest where the players were tied to one-sided contracts that prevented them from leaving, they compensated by using their performances to blackmail the club's owners.

> They took the club owners for all the money they could get. All the time you can earn the owners money, and that you are a somebody, and can keep pace out on the pitch, the owners will pay you and whistle your tune. You should grasp every opportunity to earn as much as you can in a short career.
>
> This is the sermon that Puskás learned perfectly. He learned nothing else: he never read, nor showed any inclination to better

> himself. Actually, he would poke fun at those who wanted to better themselves, and who studied day and night to do so. Puskás covered his lack of education and knowledge with offensive, uncouth and foul-mouthed speech. Eventually, his manner of speaking became one of his characteristics, and his crudeness only added to his popularity. Because he was a somebody, he interpreted it that he was allowed to get away with more than others – nobody ever told him to behave himself. Though, I must add, his team-mates were very sympathetic towards him.
>
> No matter how low level a footballer in Hungary, if he had a problem with the authorities Puskás would help. He fought like a tiger for footballers' interests. Those acts of comradeship were not risk-free either: it meant taking sides. But ultimately Puskás was surrounded by party functionaries who bowed to his every whim. They satisfied his hunger for money, and if he asked for more, they gave it. To his rudeness, they simply closed their eyes or bore it with ill grace. When this young kid became a man, he failed to rectify these traits, and, to be honest, we made them worse, but then we never got any help in thwarting his behaviour … not even from his wife.[65]

In Puskás's defence, his crime was ignorance, not maliciousness. His talking to everyone in the same manner only endeared him to 'ordinary working people', who on meeting 'Öcsi' were always delighted to find him as salty as themselves. There exists not one story of Puskás having someone arrested, but stories of his helping team-mates and fellow soldiers who had got themselves into trouble are legion. The army, inexplicably, placed Major Puskás in charge of disciplining soldiers at his barracks. Soldiers fortunate enough to be brought up before Puskás for punishment escaped with a hearty chuckle at their exploits, and a warning to be more careful in not getting caught next time. One time, Puskás was called from his home to deal with Zoltán Czibor after the winger had returned to barracks late, drunk and covered in blood. Puskás had Czibor taken home rather than have him spend a night in a cold cell. The next morning, Mihály Farkas ordered Puskás to the Defence Ministry to have him explain why Czibor had not been more severely punished. 'Tell me then, Uncle Mishy,' replied Puskás, helping himself to a chair, 'if Czibor is confined to barracks, who will play left-wing at the weekend?'

It was because of Puskás's relationship with Farkas that in the years to come accusations would be levelled at him that he was a communist lackey. But, as captain of both Honvéd and Hungary's national team, his having to deal with Farkas was unavoidable. Farkas went out of his way to cultivate Puskás's friendship, his brash humour making a refreshing contrast to the terrified underlings who hung on his every order.

Understandably, the majority of Puskás's fellow footballers found his close relationship with Farkas at best unsavoury, but none could deny that it was the reason why footballers at Hungary's first-division clubs were able to live at a level far superior to that of an ordinary worker.

As Puskás became more comfortable in Farkas's presence, he began to push for Hungary's first-division players to be paid the same as their Western counterparts. Because Hungary's footballers were employed by whatever trade union, industry or government department owned their club, they only earned the monthly wage of a humble worker, policeman or soldier. However, this could double with win bonuses and 'calorie money' (extra money given to the nation's athletes by the government so that they could purchase more and better-quality food). Therefore in Hungary footballers were considered high earners, and that they were – in communist Hungary. But, by comparison to other European nations, Hungarian footballers were paupers. Professional footballers in England (who were restricted by a maximum wage barrier) earned a basic wage double that of their Hungarian counterparts. In Austria, footballers earned a similar amount, but it was in Italy, where clubs were largely owned by big businesses, that they earned the most.

Puskás's requests for more money were continually refused by Farkas, impatiently explaining that it was impossible in a communist country for a footballer's basic wage to be more than that of a worker. Puskás argued that pay equality was all very well and good for workers, but he and his team-mates were world-class footballers who wanted rewarding according to their worth, of which they were well aware due to the agents from mainly Italian clubs who, whenever Hungary played in the west, hung around them like bees around a honeypot. Puskás warned that sooner or later a leading Hungarian footballer was bound to succumb to temptation and defect ... but there was a way to prevent this: allow the players to earn extra money by turning a blind eye to their smuggling of black market goods *into* Hungary.

Hungary's closed borders and the Soviet Union's insistence on the Soviet bloc manufacturing its own goods meant that behind the Iron Curtain 'luxury' Western products such as whiskies, American cigarettes, perfumes, nylon stockings and gramophone records were only available to the elite.

A reluctant Farkas gave his word that the players would be unimpeded at customs when bringing in small amounts of contraband for *personal use* whenever they returned from playing in the west.

Initially, the players, rightly dubious about Farkas's word, stuck to the deal. But, as word spread of their immunity, the players became inundated with requests, which the more brazen and business-minded among them promptly turned into orders. Such became the level of orders that the players did not even have to go shopping themselves. Their contacts in Vienna would bring the goods to their hotel. All the players had to do was bring the contraband over the border, and on to Budapest. The economics graduate Gyula Lóránt dealt with more than one contact, so he would never become reliant upon one person; and in doing so, in all but name, he built up an import-export business. Czibor was characteristically unpredictable, and uncharacteristically erred on the side of caution, only dealing with soldiers and policemen. Kocsis kept his business a family affair, just dealing with his sister-in-law, who lived in Vienna, and Puskás conducted his business solely through a trusted childhood friend known as 'Ali'.

As business boomed, at times the team's train carriages were so full of goods that there was barely room to stand, let alone sit. But, despite their bravado, when it came to crossing the border, the players were always nervous – after all, Farkas was not the most trustworthy of characters, and his 'agreement' with Puskás was far from official. Border guards were sweetened with cartons of cigarettes and handshakes with the players, the most popular of whom was Puskás, who, in his own self-interest, astounded his team-mates by being polite and humble … at least, that is, until he was clear of the border.

Sebes refused to partake in the smuggling, making no pretence that he thought it corrupting, distracting and unbecoming of international athletes. But he also understood it was a necessary evil to keep his players financially happy. His one rule was that the players must only smuggle 'harmless' goods. Yet a few of the more steely-nerved players ignored this rule, and dealt with currency exchange and the smuggling of people's documents handed to them at their hotels by Hungarian émigrés who wanted to assist their relatives back home but were scared to leave a paper trail. For all parties involved, document-smuggling was the most perilous of business, fraught with danger: the ÁVO were prepared to tolerate the trafficking of nylon stockings and cigarettes, but not money and documents in sealed envelopes, and anyone rumbled could be sure of a dawn visit.

Hence, for the most part, the players smuggled readily saleable goods, although for a price they were prepared to bring in specific items. Grosics once smuggled in a clarinet for an orchestra, and Hidegkuti a suitcase full of machine parts for a factory, one that was so heavy that it had to be left in the bus's aisle, only for Sebes to complain of its presence and attempt to move it himself. 'What the devil is in this???' he asked as he strained and heaved to no avail but to plenty of tittering.

Such became the money earned by the Honvéd and national team players through smuggling that all other clubs who played abroad began to return to Hungary similarly laden with goods, to the point where professional smugglers began disguising themselves as footballers. Occasionally arrests did occur, but only ever of unknown players, and it was always Puskás who was ordered to Farkas's office to explain why a certain dick of a shit-for-brains footballer could not be a little less conspicuous in his criminal activities. Puskás would promise to reproach the player, then divert the conversation with some ribaldry and talk of an upcoming Honvéd match. Farkas was no fool and knew Puskás's game, but all the time the national team and Honvéd were winning, the authorities were willing to give the players some free rein.

The only immediate problem was the jealousy arising from the public once the players' smuggling 'licence' became common knowledge, fuelling rumours that footballers all lived in villas and travelled in chauffeur-driven cars. For the most part, though, the public did not resent the stars earning extra money on the side, especially considering that everyone else was doing the same. The Rákosi regime squeezing every last drop of sweat and forint out of the nation's workers had turned Hungary into a nation where pilfering from the state was considered the norm.

The Soviet Union's demand for goods had forced the Rákosi government to increase production. The production targets set by Moscow were without thought for the factories' capabilities, and if doubt was voiced or a target not met, the word 'sabotage' was whispered – an ugly word that was sure to draw the unwanted attention of the ÁVO. Thus the accountable government officials passed the ceaseless demands on to accountable factory managers, who dropped the full weight upon the shoulders of the accountable exhausted shop-floor workers. Soon it became evident that these series of mad production drives had caused a large increase in quantity but a lamentable drop in quality, and if there was one matter the Soviets insisted upon, it was goods being produced to an unattainably high standard – which, of course, was never reached, so they simply bought the rejects at hugely discounted prices. In turn, the factories countered the problems of rejects by enforcing fines upon workers for negligence. And so forth.

Another government ruse devised for generating money from workers was 'Peace Loans'. In the name of peace and patriotism, workers were pressured into taking out loans which were to be paid back at a high interest rate, with the government conveniently taking the repayments directly from their wage packets. 'Patriotism' was also the reason why workers were pressured to volunteer to work on national holidays. And the more national holidays there were, the more the workers could have the privilege of 'volunteering'. In 1952 alone, 11 such days were added to the Hungarian national calendar:

1 – In memory of the liberation of Hungary.
2 – In honour of 1 May.
3 – In honour of the council elections.
4 – Korea week.
5 – Constitution Day.
6 – Tenth anniversary of Rákosi's release from prison.
7 – Completion of the 1950 plan before the deadline.
8 – In memory of the introduction of local councils.

9 – Thirty-third anniversary of the Russian October Revolution.
10 – Stalin's birthday.
11 – In honour of the second Hungarian Communist Party Congress.

Workers worked under constant supervision, sanitation and healthcare facilities were at best rudimentary, pensions were non-existent, complaining was pointless and striking was a death wish. The only act of defiance left was to do their jobs to the very worst of their ability.

CHAPTER 10

When we arrived in England in 1953, we were welcomed with a friendliness that touched us deeply, but we were also left in no doubt by the press that they regarded us as England's victims.

Ferenc Puskás[66]

ON the back of their Olympic gold, Hungary's football team continued their winning ways, ending 1952 with two victories: a 4–2 win over Switzerland and 5–0 over Czechoslovakia. The following year, however, began with them being fortunate to scrape a 1–1 draw against Austria in Budapest. 'The Austrians proved that Hungary are not unbeatable,' wrote a pressman from Italy – whose team would be Hungary's next opponents.

The Italians were still smarting at their genuinely amateur team being defeated by Hungary's team of 'shamateurs' at the previous year's Olympics. So aggrieved had Italian coach Giuseppe Meazza been at Hungary's bending of the Olympic rules (and ethics) that after the match he'd confronted a grinning Sebes to tell him, 'You shouldn't forget that we could not select our best team.'

'Then we will go to Italy to face your best team,' Sebes snapped back.[67]

The match took place in Rome, the first ever in Italy's brand-new national stadium. Despite the kick-off taking place in the morning, to accommodate the later opening ceremony, the match was still attended by an 80,000 capacity crowd, who watched the honoured visitors somewhat dampen the occasion by strolling to a 3–0 victory. Such an emphatic win over a full-strength Italian team was the passing of an acid test for the Hungarians, with Puskás, in particular, being on outstanding form, scoring twice in what was his 50th international appearance. On his return to Budapest, a celebratory dinner was held in his honour, at which Mihály Farkas made a speech and awarded his 'good friend Öcsi Puskás' a small bronze statuette. 'Thanks, Uncle Mishy, but no thanks,' replied Puskás, handing the statuette back. 'You keep it. After all, a chap in your position can never know what the future might bring.'

It was a demonstration of Puskás's standing that he was awarded a celebratory dinner, and that he felt comfortable enough to tease a man as dangerous as Farkas publicly. Ordinarily, Farkas would roar with laughter at *anything* Puskás said, but this comment was too public and too close to the bone, as Farkas's stony silence proved.

Two months previously, on 5 March 1953, Josef Stalin had died. Millions across the Soviet empire perversely grieved the death of one of history's bloodiest dictators, no more so than in Hungary, where his funeral was declared a day of national mourning and a crowd of 300,000 braved wind and rain to attend a service held in Pest's City Park.[68]

Before his death, the increasingly senile Stalin, convinced that Jews were out to murder him, had demanded their purging from high government office across the Soviet bloc. The predominantly Jewish Rákosi government were terrified, and so offered up ÁVO chief Gábor Péter – arrested by his own henchmen, beaten up by them and sentenced to life imprisonment on charges of spying.[69]

Soon after, the ÁVÓ, without Péter at the helm, chose to relinquish control of MTK, handing the club back to the ownership of the Textiles Union, who changed the club name from 'Bástya' to 'Vörös Lobogó'.

But while Rákosi, Gerő and Farkas breathed a sigh of relief at Stalin's death, it also left them highly vulnerable. The tormentor had also been the protector. Rákosi's solution was to try to please the new powers in Moscow by stepping up arrests, raising export levels and winning a general election that was so undemocratic that few outside of Hungary's parliament knew it had even been held.

Then, in August, Rákosi and a number of leading fellow Muscovites were ordered to attend a meeting at the Kremlin. Awaiting the Hungarian delegation were three of the most powerful men in the Soviet Union: Georgy Malenkov, Stalin's successor; Nikita Khrushchev, the Communist Party secretary; and Lavrenty Beria, the chief of the secret police. Rákosi arrived expecting a private meeting at which he would receive praise for his recent election win and his devotion to toeing the Soviet line, and so was shocked to be made to sit at a table alongside his underlings and face a barrage of demands as to why the Hungarian economy was in such dire straits. Rákosi nervously begged to differ, providing a string of statistics that were met with scorn for the lies they were.

Khrushchev blamed the ruination of Hungary's economy on Rákosi's criminal police force and land reforms. 'The peasants will chase you away with their pitchforks!' he boomed while thumping the table. Beria, Stalin's most notorious henchman, joined in, sneering: 'Listen, Comrade Rákosi, we know that Hungary has had Habsburg emperors, Tartar khans, Polish princes, Turkish sultans, and Austrian emperors. But as far as we know she has never yet had a Jewish king, and that is what you are trying to become. You can be sure that we will never allow it.'[70]

Rákosi was as humiliated as he was dumbstruck when informed that he was forthwith being replaced as Hungary's leader by Imre Nagy, one of the Hungarian delegation present. (Mihály Farkas, also present, was stripped of his position as defence minister, demoted in all but name to the position of minister for culture and literature – although what he knew about either subject is anyone's guess).

Nagy (pronounced 'Narge') was a stark contrast to Rákosi. He was a gentile born of the peasantry, tall with a jovial manner and a love of wine and football, and considered a patriotic communist who believed that communism (not Stalinism) was the best solution to Hungary's woes. He had served as a common foot soldier during the First World War, converting to communism as a prisoner of war of the Russians, rising to become Moscow's leading expert on Hungary's agriculture.

The Soviets, in appointing Nagy as Hungary's leader, hoped that his peasant roots would earn him some empathy in the Hungarian countryside, where communism was at its most unpopular. And yet at the same time, Moscow was aware that it could not afford to sideline

Rákosi totally, for in Hungary the 'bald butcher' was nothing if not feared. Without his tyrannical presence, the Soviets were equally concerned that the Hungarian people would find the bravery to rise in rebellion (there had already been reports of riots in some villages in Hungary). The Soviets, therefore, came to the compromise of demoting Rákosi to the position of Nagy's deputy.

Nagy proved immediately to be more approachable and open-minded than Rákosi had ever been, and agreed readily to Hungary playing England in London. The idea was first mooted by Stanley Rous, the secretary of the Football Association in England. At Hungary's Olympic final victory over Yugoslavia, Rous had sat next to Hungarian FA president Sándor Barcs, and on the blow of the final whistle extended an invitation to Barcs to bring the Hungarian football team to London, offering a gentleman's handshake to settle the agreement.

With an air of embarrassment, Barcs replied that he would gladly shake Rous's hand if the decision were down to him. But alas, such matters in Hungary, Barcs explained, were decided by higher authorities than he. 'Who would that be, then?' Rous asked.

Barcs dashed to locate Hungary's sports minister, Gyula Hegyi. 'Against the imperialists in London???' Hegyi replied. 'The Soviets will never allow it.' But lest Hungary's football history forget, Hegyi may have been a communist politician, but he was a football man first and foremost and was as keen as anyone for Hungary to play at Wembley; thus he agreed to ask Mihály Farkas.

Farkas in turn agreed, but only on the grounds that Sebes, Barcs and Hegyi must accept full responsibility should the team lose or a player defect. Unsurprisingly, the three refused.

Imre Nagy, on the other hand, was less reticent about asking the Soviets for permission. Proof was evident that Hungarian football was the strongest in Europe. For alongside the first team's Olympic gold and their win away over Italy, Hungary's national youth team won that summer's FIFA Youth World Cup. Indeed the young Hungarians didn't just win the tournament, held in Belgium and featuring 15 other nations – they did so emphatically and without conceding a goal.[71] Nagy was of the mind that a similar victory over the imperialists in London could only be a good thing for world socialism. The

Soviets thought so too, and a date was agreed with the English FA: 23 November 1953.

Sebes set to work obtaining permission to undertake a reconnaissance mission to London to watch the English national team play a Rest of the World XI. The match was to celebrate the Football Association's 90th anniversary and took place at London's Empire Stadium (Wembley) in front of a 90,000 crowd. The English took the game seriously enough to give it full international status and field their first eleven, while the Rest of the World team contained top players from Yugoslavia, West Germany, Austria, Spain, Sweden and Italy, but none from Hungary. The Hungarian FA had been asked to provide Bozsik, Kocsis and Puskás, but Sebes, with the England match in mind, refused.

However, there was one Hungarian on the pitch: László Kubala. Since escaping from Hungary in 1949 and joining Barcelona the following year, the 24-year-old Kubala had come to be considered the best inside-right in world football. And, against England, Kubala demonstrated this with a customary swashbuckling performance, scoring twice in the eventual 4–4 draw. What Sebes made of Kubala he never said, neither at the time nor later, but undoubtedly he could not have failed to be impressed by the former Vasas forward, and privately rued not being able to select him. In contrast, Sebes was pleasingly unimpressed by the England team. The match had been a contest of styles: England's physical and direct approach against the Rest of the World's continental passing and movement. And, considering the visitors had never played together before, they continually managed to place England on the back foot, with only a last-minute penalty saving England's blushes.

Afterwards, Sebes asked Stanley Rous for three match balls of the kind used by the England team, and permission to return to the Empire Stadium the next day so that he could have 'a quick look around'. The next day, on the dot of three o'clock, Sebes duly stepped on to Wembley's hallowed turf with an English regulation leather football, wearing his football boots and clasping a notebook, stopwatch and measuring tape. To the amusement of the onlooking ground staff, Sebes stripped off his jacket and tie, rolled up his sleeves, and proceeded to kick the ball as high as he could up in the air, paying particular attention to the height and direction of the bounce. He then began running at various angles across the pitch, and, having caught his breath, pulled out his measuring tape and measured the length and width of the pitch, thanked the ground staff and headed back to his hotel.

Once back in Budapest, Sebes immediately had a pitch, situated in a Pest public park – Népliget – marked out with the same dimensions as Wembley (no Hungarian club had a pitch wide enough).

Hungary's meticulous preparations for the match were to be a collective effort from the whole of the nation's football. The league programme became secondary to the needs of the national team as, every day for the next four weeks, Hungary's A, B and C teams trained together on the makeshift 'Wembley' pitch. With the C team players playing the part of the English, the A and B team players tinkered with patterns of play, first without a ball and then with a ball, taking into account every conceivable situation that could develop in London.

Sebes and his coaching team primarily concentrated upon building up the players' stamina. They suspected (probably correctly) that the English had provided a winter date for the match so that a boggy pitch would hinder the Hungarians' passing game and suit their own overtly physical style of play. Sebes, in feeling that his team needed toughening up, doubled the length of their twice-weekly cross-country runs and even had them take up wrestling.

The anticipation of the match gripped the nation, and the players were constantly asked, 'How will we fare in London?' The English may have been greedy imperialists in the eyes of the Rákosi regime, but to the average Hungarian they were an upstanding nation and not one held synonymous with defeat. For while the English may not have been football's world champions (aloofly abstaining from the World Cup tournaments until 1950), as the sport's inventors, they were still considered by many – including many Hungarians – to be football's world masters. The English had brought football to Hungary and taught the Hungarians how to play it, and therefore were the yardstick for Hungary's progress. Beating Austria and Romania brought the Hungarians satisfaction, beating the Soviet Union brought revenge, but beating England would bring proof. Even Imre Nagy sought out

Sebes at a function at the Soviet embassy in Budapest to ask what the score in London will be:

> 'If my players adhere to my tactics, and the English do not realise them from the beginning, then we will win the match,' I replied.
>
> 'I must say, you are very sure of yourself, Sebes. Tell me, what are these tactics of yours?'
>
> I took Nagy upstairs to a quiet room, pulled out a coloured pencil and notebook which I always carried with me, and proceeded to explain my plan for the game.
>
> 'My wonder!' he exclaimed. 'It's like a plan of war.'
>
> 'It is, Comrade Nagy,' I said, 'only our weapon is a leather ball.'[72]

Sebes, though, could have done without having to play a full international against Sweden on the day before the squad's departure for London. Postponing the match for a later date was not an option. It was to be the Hungarian national team's inaugural match at the newly opened (but not quite finished) national sports stadium, and a sell-out crowd was expecting a barnstorming display befitting of such an occasion. And, for Sebes, therein lay the problem. On such a day, a win was a must, and he was therefore almost duty bound to select his first eleven, but was fearful of injuries – and of displaying Hungary's tactics to England manager Walter Winterbottom, who would be present at the match.

The *Népstadion* ('People's Stadium') had opened three months earlier in August 1953, five years behind schedule. In 1947 Hungary's new socialist government had grandly and somewhat optimistically announced that a national stadium that would meet Olympic specifications would be finished within a year. But the stadium's original planners grossly underestimated both the time required and financial cost of such a project, and three years later only the stadium's shell and foundations were complete. As the money began to run short, corners were cut and second-rate materials used. The workers themselves were quite unlike the patriotic Adonis images drawn up by the communist propaganda departments – instead they were an uninspired bunch, and with skilled tradesmen paid the same as labourers, neither group was under any incentive to finish the job earlier. Stealing from the site was rife, deliveries were late, and plans were altered continually to accommodate the newly reduced budgets. Furthermore, Hungary's obligation to provide the Soviet Union with steel had left itself hopelessly short of the material. It was a shortage further compounded by, at the same time as the stadium was being constructed, the Rákosi government undertaking the creation of a whole new town: *Sztalinváros*[73] (Stalin-Town), a would-be industrial and residential utopia 100km south of Budapest on the banks of the River Danube. When, in late 1951, the stadium's construction ground to a halt, Rákosi had had no choice but to direct more money to its completion, on the strict understanding that it would be finished in time for his 60th birthday celebrations to be held in the spring of 1952. Materials destined for Sztalinváros were redirected to the stadium, and as many as 1,000 workers per day were employed, but again the opening date was postponed. Rákosi's birthday celebrations had to take place in a public square. Another opening date was given, and for it the Soviet Union's national football team was invited to play Hungary – but yet again the stadium was not ready, and nor was it for another given date, with Dynamo Moscow invited to play Honvéd.

Rákosi's patience snapped once he learned of a foreign press article that had poked fun at the stadium's many postponements. He visited the site and demanded that it be completed by 20 August – a date for which the Soviet team Spartak Moscow had been invited to play Honvéd – or else. On the due day, the stadium was officially opened, although it was only two-thirds complete at best. The stands' upper tiers and a block to contain the changing rooms and offices would not be finished for another six months; it would be a further four years before the stadium's own metro station and bus terminal would be ready, and six more years before floodlights were added.

Honvéd beat Spartak 3–2 in a match at which Hungary's communist elite (minus Rákosi) watched in the comfort of what now would be classed as a VIP section, while the most important man in world sport – International Olympic Committee president Avery Brundage – was stuck out in the stands with the hoi polloi. It was an oversight that Hungary would come to regret. Brundage was the man who would have the final word on which city would host the 1960 Olympics, and he chose Rome …

Sweden were chosen as the Hungarian national team's first opponents at the new stadium, as they were considered not good enough to spoil the occasion, but also not bad enough for it to be a complete walkover. Or so the Hungarians thought. What they didn't count upon was the desperation of Sweden's English coach, George Raynor, to be acknowledged in English football.

Raynor was a coach very much in the mould of fellow countryman Jimmy Hogan: a visionary who, unwanted in his homeland, had had to move abroad to find coaching work.[74] And, knowing that influential faces from English football would be present in Budapest, Raynor went all out to catch their attention. He told anyone who'd listen that Hungary relied and capitalised upon opponents refusing (or being unable) to deviate from conventional formations and styles of play. And because their opponents adhered to this rigid mindset, Hungary were able to create exploitable spaces simply by their own players dropping out of position and coaxing their markers with them – Hidegkuti being the prime example:

> Many people have watched Hungary play and tried to spot the key man in their plan. The most popular choices are Bozsik, Puskás or Kocsis. I say that the key man is their deep-lying centre-forward Hidegkuti. Any team that wants to beat Hungary has to neutralise Hidegkuti.[75]

Come the day of the match, Raynor's Sweden neutralised not just Hidegkuti but the entire Hungarian team with a ten-man defensive wall, preventing Hungary from mustering a single shot on goal during the whole first half, much to the discontented murmurings of the home crowd. In the dressing room at half-time, Puskás asked Sebes to have the match ball changed. The one used was an English football (one Sebes had brought from London) and was slightly larger, harder and heavier than the footballs used in continental Europe. The Hungarian players complained that they had not had sufficient time to get used to the ball, the reason why they were misjudging its lesser bounce and underhitting passes (Buzánszky likened the ball to being made of wood). Sebes refused, citing that they would be using an identical ball in a week's time in London.

The builders, policemen and office clerks who made up the Swedish team had no such problems. English footballs were commonly used in the Scandinavian leagues, and 15 minutes into the second half they opened the scoring (0–1), an omen perhaps for the fortunes of future Hungarian national teams at their national stadium. The home crowd's dissatisfaction intensified minutes later when an opportunity to equalise was dashed as a pensive Puskás's penalty hit the post. The catcalls only abated when MTK forward Péter Palotás equalised soon after (1–1) and, moments later, Czibor put Hungary ahead (2–1), albeit with a suspiciously offside-looking goal. Ordinarily, once in the lead, the Hungarians held on to it – but the restless expectation of the crowd weighed heavily upon them, and the Swedes, sensing their hosts' discord, upped the tempo, and their star man, Kurt Hamrin (soon to be of Juventus), cut across from the wing and equalised (2–2). As the Swedes attacked in search of the winner, another Hamrin shot rattled Grosics's crossbar, and the home crowd once again roared its disapproval at the supposedly invincible Golden Team having to resort to desperate defending against inferior opposition. 'I was never so relieved to hear a final whistle,' Bozsik recalled.

A chorus of boos and a shower of spit crashed upon the Hungarian players as they made their way off the pitch, begging them to wonder: what would have been the reaction had they lost?

The crowd's toxic (over-) reaction was everything and nothing to do with football. The death of Stalin and the subsequent replacing of the hated Rákosi with 'the patriotic communist' Imre Nagy was perceived by Hungarians as, finally, a weakness in the Soviet Union's hard-line communist rule. Nagy's releasing of thousands of political prisoners had inadvertently propelled people to be braver, and the Hungarian team's poor display against Sweden had given the opportunity for many to voice their displeasure for the first time. Taking safety in numbers, they had unleashed their hatred of the communist regime upon the regime's underperforming favoured ones. For the shaken players, it was a dawning realisation that there was a price to pay for their privileged positions. As far as ordinary Hungarians were concerned, their subsidised apartments, high wages, soft jobs, foreign travel and licence to smuggle were the perks of being a leading communist. And if the players were willing to pocket the ups, then they should also take the downs.

It was in a sombre mood, a cloak of secrecy and a cold November rain that the squad gathered at Pest's Keleti railway station to board the evening train bound for Paris. Rather than flying direct to London, Sebes's idea was that a leisurely train ride across the Alps and two days in the French capital would give the players a much-needed lift of spirits. And indeed it was so: the gloom with which the journey began dissipated on arrival in Paris. Just being in France cheered Sebes up, and his rare show of happiness transferred to the squad. He'd loved his time there as a young man in the 1920s and always held a soft spot for the country and its people, never missing an opportunity to test (some said show off) his French. He arranged for the team to play a friendly against the works team of his former employer Renault, a light-hearted affair that Hungary won 18–1. The same evening they were guests of honour at a Parisian variety show, courtesy of the theatre's Hungarian owner. The cries of 'Puskás!' that continually interrupted the performance had Öcsi beaming in delight and the performers wondering just who the audience had come to see.

A similarly warm greeting awaited the party's ferry as it docked at the English port of Dover, as did another on their arrival at London's Victoria railway station. The crowds were driven by curiosity, wanting to see in the flesh these mysterious football-playing communist soldiers who hadn't been defeated in three years. Likewise, the Hungarians were just as curious about the English. What they had expected was a reserved nation of bowler hats and afternoon tea parties – what they saw instead was geniality, flat caps and warm beer. Even the ordinarily stand-offish FA went out of their way to be welcoming. Conscious of the world's spotlight being upon the match, the FA went all out and arranged for the Hungarians to stay in one of London's most exclusive hotels – the Cumberland, next to Marble Arch. But alas, while the luxurious rooms and views over Hyde Park brought no complaint, the food was a different matter. Just one meal in the hotel's restaurant was enough to convince the Hungarian players that English food was not to their liking. Diet being an integral component of the team's preparation, Sebes went to the effort of searching for a

Hungarian chef in the vicinity, eventually finding one who worked at a nearby Czech restaurant, to where, for the duration of their three-day stay, the Hungarian players would troop en masse every evening for their goulash.

On their first morning, some of the players went for a stroll, ending up in Hyde Park, drawn by the gathered crowds at Speakers' Corner, a corner of the park where members of the public can get on a soapbox and voice an opinion on any subject they so wish. No such thing existed in Hungary, so naturally the players were curious as to what was being said – but they had to rely on their interpreter, who predictably explained that every speaker was cheering the virtues of socialism. The players did not believe it for a moment. At the same time, Sebes was also in the park. He'd accepted an invitation from the editor of Britain's communist newspaper the *Daily Worker* to meet there for an interview; but before the meeting got underway, the interviewer and his photographer, on learning that a member of the royal family was nearby, made their apologies and raced off. The paper's editor attempted to make amends by taking Sebes later the same day to meet a group of Hungarian émigré workers at a factory in the suburb of Croydon, to whom Sebes recounted his being stood up for royalty. 'I suppose that's the type of communists they have here,' he grumbled.

CHAPTER 11

Best team I ever played against?
Hungary in 1953.

Stanley Matthews

THE day before their match against England, the Hungarians paid a visit to Wembley Stadium, professing much amusement at the greyhound racing track that circumnavigated the pitch, admiration for the turf and disappointment that they were not allowed to train on it: forbidden by the FA to even their own national team. Instead, it was arranged for the Hungarians to train at the west London club Fulham's ground, Craven Cottage, watched by, among others, the former Arsenal player turned journalist Bernard Joy …

> A coach kept throwing the ball high to the centre-half, in front of whom stood the centre-forward, mainly to harass his colleague. Suddenly the coach would throw a short low ball and the centre-half had to be on his toes to round his opponent after it. At the other end of the field, another coach was 'feeding' Puskás, their top goalscorer, with a supply of balls which Puskás had to hit first time at goal, at whatever height, speed or angle they came. The backs hit long, low and accurate passes to one another, always without steadying the ball first. Another coach supervised the right wing triangle, which acted as a unit, inter-passing along the touchline. The interrelation of all departments was constantly emphasized. It was the earnestness of the preparations which impressed me the most. From this training on the eve of a match, the players may not learn anything technically. But the purposeful note keyed them up tremendously because they felt they were doing something of

> practical benefit. Even when the other players were slackening off their special exercises, Puskás, a lonely figure at the other end of the goalmouth, continued his shooting practice. Plainly he'd had enough. He was breathing hard and his accuracy had dropped appreciably, but he carried on, hitting first-time balls thrown at him.[76]

The England manager, Walter Winterbottom, had seen Hungary play both at the 1952 Olympics and in Budapest against Sweden just over a week earlier. He had also met in Budapest with the Sweden coach, George Raynor, who reiterated the need to contain Hidegkuti, preferably with two different players – one in the first half and another, fresher one in the second. There was also another Englishman ready to provide Winterbottom with information: Arthur Rowe, manager of Tottenham Hotspur. In 1939, Rowe, who had recently been a Tottenham defender, had spent three months in Hungary – primarily giving lectures on the WM formation, but also gleaning what he could from Hungarian football. When, a decade later in 1949, Rowe became manager of Tottenham, he introduced a style of play that he had first observed in Hungary. He had his charges push short, fast and incisive passes into the path of a team-mate, and then themselves race into open space for a return pass. The English called it 'push and run', and with it, Rowe, in his first season at Tottenham, led the club to the Second Division title and the following season to the First Division title.

In contrast, Gusztáv Sebes had no such luxury. Because no Hungarian residing in Hungary dared to keep open contact with anyone in the West, Sebes was very limited in what he could learn about the England team. He may have known their results and the names of the players, but as to *how* they played he was almost clueless. The only way Sebes could see of overcoming this lack of insight was to take the *Népsport* journalist László Feleki to London, who, as you may remember from Chapter 9, in 1938 had spent a season with Arsenal and subsequently brought back to Hungary Arthur Rowe[77] and the WM formation.

It may have been 15 years since Feleki had last been in England, but this didn't stop Sebes deeming him the English football expert and assigning him to find information on the England team. And what Feleki reported back astonished Sebes. He'd assumed that, like Hungary, the English had been in preparation for the match for weeks. But no: for the match to be held on Wednesday the 23rd, the English squad had met up for the first time on Monday the 21st, with each player having played for their respective league clubs on Saturday the 19th.

The root of England's insufficient preparation stemmed from the team being controlled by an eight-man, self-elected committee made up solely of league club chairmen. Known contemptuously throughout English football as the 'blazer brigade', the board's members were for the most part well-intentioned, but were inclined to place their own clubs' interests before those of the national team. The very notion of postponing a weekend's lucrative domestic football or allowing players time off to train with England was never even considered. Their grip was unshakeable and very much to the detriment of English football. Team selection, for example, was made via a voting system along the lines of: 'Now, gentlemen, we shall accept nominations for the position of left-back.' Favouritisms or rewarding a player for long service to a club were reason enough for selection; and, of course, the system worked in reverse, with players ignored because of personal dislikes or petty rivalries between the board's members. In some cases, players were nominated without the board ever having seen them play.

Hence by the 1950s England, once the sport's masters, were long into the process of being overtaken by the pupils, trailing years behind other leading football nations regarding training methods, tactics, injury prevention and players' diets. The last (and first) major competition England had entered had been the 1950 World Cup in Brazil, where they'd crashed out in the first round, humiliatingly beaten 1–0 by a United States team made up solely of second-rate amateurs – 'The worst performance ever by an English team' being the view of one pissed-off English reporter. England's isolation was not lost, however, on FA chairman Stanley Rous. A former international referee, Rous, in 1946, set up a national coaching scheme, appointing as the director of coaching a man of similar ambition: Walter Winterbottom, a former Manchester United centre-half whose career had been cut short by injury. It was a role that evolved into Winterbottom becoming the first manager of the English national team, but he was never to be his own man. He was hindered and undermined by the suffocating restrictions placed upon him by his superiors' archaic system of team selection. Any attempt by Winterbottom to formulate a team of his own was always nipped in the bud by the 'blazer brigade', well aware that by giving away this 'duty' they would be making themselves quite redundant.

And despite this, the overwhelming opinion throughout English football was that they would see off the Hungarians with ease. After all, every team has its hiccups, and it remained true that England were a match for any team in the world, their winning being the accepted norm and losing a newsworthy rarity. Furthermore, they possessed three of the world's best players: Billy Wright, Tom Finney and Stanley Matthews; the 'Wing Wizard' Matthews, in particular, was considered more than a match for this Puskás chap (although Winterbottom was less enamoured, thinking his dribbling selfish and outdated). Newspapers were equally optimistic: 'England can beat Hungary within ten minutes' – 'Hard tackling the way to beat Hungary!' – 'Hungary's fancy stuff won't beat England'. Even Britain's communist newspaper the *Daily Worker* ran with the headline 'England will win' – but, as Sebes had already pointed out, England did seem to possess a strange kind of communist …

However, the small number of Englishmen who had actually *seen* the Hungarians play weren't so full of blind optimism, the most notable being Chelsea chairman Joe Mears, head of the England Selectors' Board. While in Budapest, Mears had candidly admitted to Sweden manager George Raynor that he didn't think England's players were skilful enough to cope with Hungary's style of play. Another more public view was that of Geoffrey Green, the highly respected football correspondent for *The Times*, then Britain's most-read daily broadsheet. Green had perhaps seen Sebes's Hungarian team play more times than any other Englishman, and had long been scathing of English football's failure to move with the times, predicting 'One of these days we shall wake up and find six goals in the back of our net.'[78]

On the morning of the match, the Hungarian party peered out of their London hotel to see a dense green fog enveloping the surrounding streets. The smoke and fumes from factories, vehicles and households caused smog in all of Europe's capital cities, but London's was particularly thick and putrid. Sebes was worried that this would mean a postponement of the match, but was cheerily informed by the hotel receptionist that a 'pea-souper' rarely led to football matches being cancelled. The English sporting public wanted their sport in all weathers, even if it meant not being able to see the goings-on.

The news, though, failed to cheer Sebes. He had hardly slept through anxiety. It was as if, through the night, he had grasped the magnitude of the task. In the two days that the team had been in their hotel, they had received 8,000 goodwill telegrams from Hungarians all over the world, and incessant telephone calls – including one from Mátyás Rákosi reiterating, in his inimitable way, that the hopes of communism in Hungary were upon Sebes's shoulders. Sebes's nervousness was conveyed in his team talk, which he held straight after breakfast. Standing at the back of the hotel's meeting room was the Hungarian FA president, Sándor Barcs:

> My good lord – Sebes went on for two hours! If I had been a player in that team and someone had asked me what the tactical team talk at the Cumberland Hotel was about, I wouldn't have been able to tell them. The whole talk was pure gobbledy-gook.[79]

In fairness to Sebes, he and Barcs rarely saw eye to eye; another observer, radio commentator György Szepesi, was a tad more understanding:

> Sebes just wanted to be thorough. I am sure his tactical talk could have been shorter, but he wanted to make his point at any price. It's a fact, though, that whatever tactics were discussed, they meant nothing to Puskás – he would do whatever Puskás wanted to do.[80]

The crux of Sebes's instructions (noted word for word by László Feleki) was for Hungary to nullify England's major threat, that of Stanley Matthews, by strangling the source of his supply from Billy Wright. Sebes also gave instructions to begin the game defensively, so as to give themselves time to find their composure. Hidegkuti was told to remain high up the pitch until at least 15 minutes had gone, then to confuse the English by dropping back into a deep-lying playmaker role. But the most interesting insight is the absolute acceptance of Puskás's constant interruptions:

Sebes – Buzánszky, remember the pitch is very wide: make sure you position yourself inside more.

Puskás – And don't dribble!

Sebes – The same goes for you, Lantos. If the play is on Buzánszky's side of the pitch, you are to come inside and Matthews is to be picked up by Czibor. Czibor, you have two further duties: move around the pitch a lot and don't be slow in crossing the ball.

Puskás – And don't cross the ball to my head. What am I supposed to do with that?

Sebes – Any free kicks on the right hand side, Bozsik is to take them. I myself don't understand why a player who can aim a ball as wonderfully as Comrade Bozsik doesn't choose to take more free kicks.

Bozsik – What can I do? By the time I get there, Öcsi has always already taken it.

Puskás – What should I do? Wait for you? You're so slow that by the time you'd get there the referee would have blown the full-time whistle!

[Laughter][81]

Once at Wembley, Sebes declined an invitation from the English to have a pre-match walk around the pitch, but did ask for his players to be allowed to warm up on a small patch of grass that he had spied in the stadium's shadows. Unbeknown to Sebes, the spot was where the dogs were kept on greyhound racing days; he'd assumed it was where visiting teams warmed up. What Sebes further didn't know was that rigorous warming-up as the Hungarians knew it – with limbering exercises (designed primarily to prevent injury) – was alien to English football. The novelty of the Hungarians not only going through their exercises of star jumps and squat-thrusts as one but in a shit-ridden dog pen quickly collected a small crowd of inquisitive spectators, two of whom were West Ham United footballers Jimmy Andrews and Malcolm Allison. Andrews (a Scotsman) pointed out Puskás: 'Look at the size of his belly! He must be a stone overweight. England are going to murder this lot.' Allison, who 20 years later would become one of English football's most colourful and innovative coaches, wasn't so sure. 'They ain't a bad team, you know ...,' he replied, impressed that in such a confined space the Hungarians were comfortable zipping the ball to one other with such speed, accuracy and swagger. [82]

ENGLAND v HUNGARY
23 November 1953, Empire Stadium, London

ENGLAND: 1 Gil Merrick (Birmingham City), 2 Alf Ramsey (Tottenham Hotspur), 3 Bill Eckersley (Blackburn Rovers), 4 Billy Wright (Wolves), 5 Harry Johnston (Blackpool), 6 Jimmy Dickinson (Portsmouth), 7 Stanley Matthews (Blackpool), 8 Ernie Taylor (Blackpool), 9 Jackie Sewell (Sheffield Wednesday), 10 Stan Mortensen (Blackpool), 11 George Robb (Tottenham Hotspur)

HUNGARY: 1 Gyula Grosics (Honvéd), 2 Jenő Buzánszky (Dorogi Bányász), 3 Gyula Lóránt (Honvéd), 4 Mihály Lantos (Vörös Lobogó), 5 József Bozsik (Honvéd), 6 József Zakariás (Vörös Lobogó), 7 László Budai (Honvéd), 8 Sándor Kocsis (Honvéd), 9 Nándor Hidegkuti (Vörös Lobogó), 10 Ferenc Puskás (Honvéd), 11 Zoltán Czibor (Honvéd)

The very first time the two sets of players laid eyes on each other in the flesh was minutes before the match, in the tunnel, preparing to walk out on to the pitch. It was here that the England captain, Billy Wright, pointed out the Hungarians' low-cut boots to team-mate Stan Mortensen and whispered the immortal line: 'We should be all right here, Stan – they haven't even got a proper kit.'[83] Puskás, looking at the England players looking at him, nodded towards their diminutive inside-forward Ernie Taylor: 'No problems here, lads! Look at him – he's even more of a shortarse than I am!'

The sheer weight of the occasion, combined with the palpable anticipation of the partisan Wembley crowd, put Hungary's captain at his cocksure best. At the captains' handshake and pennant swap, he broke protocol, juggling the pristine match ball while flashing his counterpart Wright a cheeky grin, one the England captain interpreted as 'Just you wait until you see the rest of my tricks.' His duties done and the toss won in his favour, Puskás returned to the ball and continued juggling, flicking it on to Czibor, who did the same. Grabbing a feel of the match ball was common practice in Hungary, but not in England, and the Hungarians' juggling came across as showing off. It was also not the only sight baffling the English. Neither had they ever before seen a team line up with the centre-back (Lóránt) wearing the number 3 shirt, the left-back (Lantos) wearing the number 4 and the right-half (Bozsik) wearing 5. It took the perception of BBC commentator Kenneth Wolstenholme to explain: 'You might be mystified by some of the Hungarian numbers. The reason is they number their players rather logically with the centre-back as 3, and the full-backs as 2 and 4.' It was not to be the first time that afternoon that England were to witness something new.

On the blow of Dutch referee Leo Horn's whistle, Hungary moved the ball out to the right wing, winning a throw-in that was taken in an instant by the nearest player – Budai. This caught the English on the hop, for teams in England always had designated players on either side of the pitch, usually the full-backs, who would take the throw-ins, ambling up to the ball, giving both attackers and defenders time to get into position. The idea that any player could take a throw-in did not seem right: why would a winger take a throw-in when his role was to be on the wing, attacking? And yet here was Hungary's right-winger, Budai, taking a throw-in – a foul throw that the referee handed to the English, whose poor throw landed at the feet of Bozsik. 'The number 5 who is not a centre-half' accelerated forward, threading a pass to Hidegkuti. England's manager, Walter Winterbottom, had decided against George Raynor's advice to man-mark Hidegkuti, instead choosing to keep a defensive line which would only get tight to the Hungarian number 9 whenever he was within shooting distance of goal. 'Too proud to learn from little Sweden,' Raynor would later remark. The unmarked Hidegkuti had the time to weigh up, dummy and sidestep England's centre-half, Harry Johnston, before firing a shot into Merrick's goal that stunned the Wembley crowd into an abrupt silence (0–1). Hungary were ahead and not even a minute had passed.

Johnston was quick to make amends by intercepting a Hungarian attack, moving up to the halfway line and releasing the ball to Mortensen. The Blackpool forward deftly pulled Lantos and Lóránt out of position, then sent a through ball to the unmarked centre-forward, Jackie Sewell. 'It must be a goal,' gasped Wolstenholme. And it was (1–1). The Wembley crowd breathed a sigh of relief that things had reverted to how they should be. For an awful ten minutes, they had actually begun to think that England might lose.

It was relief that was short-lived. Five minutes later, Puskás fell in the England penalty area, but as he did so he managed to raise a leg and flick the ball towards Hidegkuti (1–2). Next came one of the greatest goals ever seen at Wembley. Puskás broke free just to the right of the England goalmouth, but with Wright close behind he had no space to either turn or shoot, so he waited until the England captain launched his tackle before dragging the ball backwards with his left heel, leaving Wright lunging into thin air ('like a fire engine rushing to the wrong fire', wrote *The Times*'s Geoffrey Green). With only Merrick to beat, Puskás made it 3–1 to Hungary. It was the first time a British crowd had ever seen a 'drag back', and they applauded accordingly. In Hungary it was nothing new: Puskás himself had learned it as a small boy on the Kispest 'grunds', and had merely implemented it at Wembley instinctively to avoid getting clattered by Wright.[84]

Soon after, Puskás extended Hungary's lead when a Bozsik free kick was deflected off his heel (1–4). With half-time nearing the Hungarians eased their pace, at which England upped theirs. The in-form Mortensen brought the score to 2–4, and in the half's dying seconds England nearly added a third when a header from debutant George Robb[85] forced a fingertip save from Grosics. 'Bravo Gyula!' yelled György Szepesi. 'Bravooooo!!!'

In the England dressing room at half-time, Harry Johnston asked what he should do about Hidegkuti: 'If I follow him into midfield, then I leave myself exposed at the back, but if I stay where I am, he is unmarked to do as he damn well pleases! I am bloody helpless!' Matthews argued that Wright should do more to pick up the Hungarian number 9. Wright replied that he was busy trying to shake off Zakariás while at the same time trying to contain Bozsik; perhaps Matthews might like to help out in defence? No, Matthews could not! He was also busy trying to overcome his three man-markers, and besides, how could he backtrack and mark Czibor when the blasted chap kept changing wings? The only solution Winterbottom could see was for his players to play the way they knew best: hard, fast and full-blooded.

Alas, the 'soft continentals with no stomach for proper football' did not wilt in the face of the English onslaught. Sebes's focus on building up his players' strength paid dividends, and it was the home team who came off second best, Wright going down after firing over a low cross, from which Mortensen knocked himself semi-conscious colliding with the sea of Hungarian shins. As Mortensen lay in a crumpled heap, Grosics and Lóránt carted him off the pitch, one by the arms, one by the legs. With England's two best players receiving treatment on the touchline, Bozsik was free to race forward unchallenged. Making his way to the right wing he crossed low to Puskás, Öcsi turned and flicked the ball up for Kocsis whose header smashed against the post. England cleared the rebound but only as far as Bozsik, who now stood on the edge of the penalty area, to fire back a shot that rocketed high into the England goal (2-5). Straight after that, Hidegkuti had his hat-trick denied when Leo Horn declared his perfectly good goal offside. 'Referee! How can that not be a goal???' exclaimed Szepesi. 'Never mind, listeners, there will be others.' And there was another: Hidegkuti, in the 56th minute, scoring his third and Hungary's sixth goal with a volley from a lobbed Puskás cross (2–6).

The England players, understanding that the game was now out of their reach, began to put the emphasis on limiting the scoreline and their own embarrassment; and ironically, with this defensive mindset, produced their most attacking football of the game, resulting in their winning a penalty after Buzánszky tripped Robb – a penalty which full-back Alf Ramsey fired past Grosics (3–6). The moment play resumed, Grosics signalled to referee Horn that he had injured his wrist and could no longer continue. In the football of the time, the only players who could be substituted were goalkeepers, and they had to be injured. The Dutchman was sceptical of Grosics's claim: after all, only minutes before he had been doing cartwheels celebrating

Hidegkuti's sixth goal, but Grosics certainly looked in pain, so Horn agreed to Hungary's reserve goalkeeper, Sándor Gellér, coming on as a replacement.[86] In truth, there was little wrong with Grosics that he couldn't have withstood until the end of the match, but he wanted to give his closest friend in the team a small role in history, for which Gellér would be eternally grateful. Minutes later, Horn blew the final whistle, and as the ecstatic Szepesi bellowed joyously into his microphone, a cut-glass English accent called over his shoulder: 'Bravo Hungária! Bravo.'

The immediate aftermath of Hungary's victory was, for them, rather an anti-climax. There was no section of Hungarian spectators cheering their team's win for the players to wave at, and the terraces emptied as, with nothing to celebrate, the crowd rushed for the exits. Likewise, the England players, once they had offered their sporting congratulations, slipped swiftly from the field. To this eerie silence, the Hungarian team sat quietly in their dressing room, attempting to comprehend the enormity of their achievement. Sebes congratulated each player individually with a handshake and a heartfelt thank-you, while the sport minister, Gyula Hegyi (who had made his way to London en route to the Modern Pentathlon World Championships in Chile), took a phone call from Mihály Farkas, who merely warned: 'Just make sure they all come home.'

Only that evening, in their 'local' Czech restaurant with the Hungarian chef, did the Hungarian party have the opportunity to celebrate. Yet the lack of money in their pockets and the cost of alcohol in London's West End prevented them from going overboard in their celebrating, so they retired early to bed: all, that is, except Buzánszky and Czibor. The two were recognised by a pair of Scotsmen, who invited them to a wee dram (or two) in the hotel's bar as a reward for beating the English. Buzánszky couldn't keep pace and soon called it a night, whereas Czibor was made of sterner stuff, outlasting his Scottish hosts and continuing until daybreak, serenading the hotel's night staff with his vast repertoire of Hungarian folk songs.

While Czibor collapsed into bed, his team-mates awoke to the rare sound of the English press munching on humble pie. Newspaper headlines acknowledged not just the historical significance of the Hungarians' win, but also the breathtaking way in which they had gone about it, with a display of teamwork, passing and movement that left the Wembley crowd spellbound – why else the 'Magical Magyars'?

Frank Cole, sportswriter for the *Daily Telegraph*, called the Hungarians' performance 'the most brilliant display of football ever seen in this country. The mantle of masters rests gracefully on their shoulders.'[87]

Stanley Matthews admitted, 'To my mind, the result did not truly reflect the Hungarians' overall superiority,'[88] and winger Tom Finney, injured for the match and who'd watched from the bench, said, 'They were almost too brilliant for words, brilliant both individually and collectively. Their brand of football was revolutionary.'[89]

At a packed press conference in a hall on Park Lane, the Hungarians were inundated with questions, the most burning of which was 'How did they do it?' Puskás reiterated the observations of many: 'We demonstrated the golden rule of modern football, and that is: the good player keeps playing even without the ball.'[90] Others lay the root of their win on one of England's own …

> Gusztáv Sebes – We played football as Jimmy Hogan taught us. When our football history is told, his name should be written in gold letters.
>
> József Bozsik – Without Jimmy Hogan's influence on Hungarian football our victory would never have happened.'
>
> Sándor Barcs – Am I rude if I say England could use some of the hints that Hogan gave to us? He taught us everything we know about football.[91]

The English pressmen were amazed. Those that knew of Hogan remembered him as (in the words of Stanley Rous) a ball-juggling showman, more famous for his treachery during the First World War than any achievements in coaching. They quickly tracked Hogan down, finding him a spry 70-year-old still very much involved in football, working as coach of Aston Villa's youth team. He had attended the match with a number of his young charges, having convinced the Villa management to fork out for tickets so the youths could see something 'out of the ordinary'.

> Although I received numerous congratulations at the end of the game, I was very sad. After all, I am a British coach – and during my twenty-one years' teaching experience on the Continent of Europe, I have always fought hard for the prestige of British football. Though I was glad to see my old pupils the Hungarians give such a grand display, it came as a shock to see England defeated.[92]

The Hungarians, for their part, assumed that Hogan was as respected in his homeland as he was in Hungary, and had been at the match in the VIP section and would be a guest of honour at that evening's post-match function. Sebes, especially, was looking forward to meeting with 'Jimmy Bacsi'. Hastily the FA despatched a belated invitation to Hogan. 'I won't be going,' he said, handing the invite straight back. 'I coach the junior team on Thursday evenings.' Sebes therefore had to make do with sitting next to Stanley Rous. Despite all the evidence to the contrary, England's FA secretary put down England's loss as an off-day, and asked the Hungarians for the chance for the team to redeem themselves, in Budapest. The Hungarians readily agreed, settling on a date for May …

CHAPTER 12

In amongst the 105,000 people watching the match at Wembley were steelworkers, Bond Street shop assistants, Piccadilly artists, Hampstead bricklayers, engineers, fair ladies, off-duty policemen, readers of the London broadsheets and listeners of the BBC. And they all asked themselves just one question: 'Is it really possible that in Hungary, a country capable of producing such wonder, life is as bad as we are always told?'

Peace & Freedom, 6 December 1953[93]

THE Hungarians' return train ride to Hungary from London was a total contrast to the pensive journey that they had undertaken just a week before. Arriving in Paris, they were welcomed by a large crowd of émigré Hungarians, one of whom, a wealthy banker called Andre Kosztolányi, rewarded the entire party by paying for them to stay in the Hotel Louvre, one of Paris's finest hotels.

After two days of living in the lap of luxury, the well-oiled party crossed the Alps to Vienna, home to the largest population of Hungarians outside of Hungary, where an even bigger crowd and a lavish liquid dinner awaited. But it was as the train crossed back into Hungary that the celebrations really began. At the border town of Hegyeshálom, the sheer size of the welcoming party meant that it spilt on to the tracks, delaying the train's arrival and departure – a scene repeated at every single station on the 170km journey from the border to Budapest.

The train finally arrived at Budapest's Keleti station five hours behind schedule, and to a crowd of an estimated 100,000 people. A military band piped up the national anthem as the train pulled in, and as the players disembarked, they were lost in a sea of handshakes and backslaps, only wrestling their way through the crowd with the assistance of the police. It took Puskás six hours to reach his home on nearby Rökk Szilárd Street, ordinarily a ten-minute walk from the station. Even once they reached their homes, the congratulations showering the players did not end. Crowds were waiting for them on their streets, and even once indoors a constant stream of well-intentioned friends, neighbours and strangers arrived throughout the following days and nights to drink a toast to the greatest sporting achievement in Hungary's history.

For the team, the reception brought a dawning realisation of the meaning of their win to the Hungarian public. The world was talking about Hungary! Hungary still existed! The players had known that it was important, but not this much. Their wages, food, transport and housing all being taken care of by the regime had had them recently living sequestered lives – nothing like the pampered existence of today's footballers, but they certainly did not have to deal with the harsh realities facing the ordinary folks cheering them from lamp posts and rooftops.

The intrusion into the players' everyday lives hereafter was new to most of the team, and something that they would have to learn to live with. Puskás was the exception: gregarious by nature, he had long got used to being recognised by the general public, but the rest had all gone about their lives mostly unobstructed. Their victory over England, though, had made them all household names, with their pictures on the front pages of the nation's newspapers. In a land starved of film stars and musicians whom the public could choose to like of their *own* accord, the triumphant, handsome and wholesome footballers became the nation's idols. If free drinks, party invitations and female attention had been plentiful for the 'Golden Team' before victory in London, post-London they were positively inundated. Life became a little finer than it was already. Restaurants began giving them free food and the best tables just for their presence, politicians curried their favour, actors and actresses pushed to be seen with them, taxi rides were free, queues were jumped and bars were kept opened late. The players' wives (and in some cases lovers) began enjoying lifestyles equalled only by the wives of the most senior government officials. Sándor Kocsis's wife, Alíz, remembered just how well they lived compared with 'ordinary' women:

> In the 1950s we did not live like queens – we lived better! The difference between us and ordinary women was greater than that between rich and poor. Only we wore the latest Western fashions, Western stockings, and if we went to a café, bar or restaurant we were treated like prima donnas – we were treated the same as our husbands. For us nothing was unobtainable, whereas for other women everything was unobtainable.[94]

Unsurprisingly Sebes, a coach who refrained from drinking and swearing in front of his players, was of the mind that the 'good life' was the road to ruin. Thus, faced with a three-month winter break from domestic football after their return from London, Sebes ordered the players to attend daily training sessions on Margaret Island, so that they would not succumb to temptations and would remain in prime condition for the visit of England in May and the World Cup beginning in June.

When a number of the squad questioned having to train in sub-zero temperatures for a mid-summer tournament, Sebes chided them, pointing out that workers from a nearby boatyard were voluntarily clearing the snow off the training pitch before every session. Yet Sebes was also in agreement that the weather conditions were not ideal, and so accepted an invitation from the Egyptian ambassador in Hungary to play against the Egyptian national team in Cairo.

Sebes had hoped that, besides the mild weather, Egypt would offer his players some degree of anonymity, but quickly realised he was mistaken. The country was in the midst of a desperate struggle to obtain independence from British rule, and with anti-British sentiment running high the film of Hungary's 6–3 win was packing out Egyptian cinemas night after night. Not that the players minded – the sun was shining, and Egypt was one of the few countries where Hungarian currency went a long away. After three weeks of sunbathing, donning fezzes, riding camels and visiting the cinema to see themselves on the silver screen, the Hungarians repaid their hosts by beating their national team 3–0.

The trip was a resounding success, and the players arrived home tanned and in peak condition for the visit of England. Beforehand, though, Sebes had to fulfil an obligation to play Austria in Vienna. It was a match that Sebes could have done without – the Austrians always seemed to up their game whenever they faced Hungary. And so it proved, a full-strength Golden Team being fortunate to claw a win via an Austrian own goal. It was a win nonetheless and took Hungary's unbeaten run to 28 matches in just under four years.

Sebes had his players greet the England party when they arrived at Ferihegy Airport. Exactly why is hard to ascertain – it wasn't standard practice. Maybe Sebes was reciprocating the warm welcome his own team had received in London, or perhaps he wanted his players to weigh up the English before the match. If it was the latter, they would have spied a lot of unknown faces. Only four of the England squad that had lost at Wembley were selected to travel to Budapest. One of them was the captain, Billy Wright, who, on his first trip to Hungary, offered an outsider's perception as to why Hungary's football team was so successful:

> In Hungary, football and the success of the national team has become a means of expression. It is interesting to examine the number of players compared to pre-War. In 1939 Hungary had 15,000 registered players. Now in 1954, there are 100,000 plus the youth and schoolboy players who are registered with the Hungarian FA. They also have 900 qualified coaches travelling the country passing on valuable hints to the youngsters. It must be borne in mind too, that the mania for football in Hungary is largely due to their being offered much fewer forms of entertainment than we have in the Western world. Television, radio and cinemas do not take from the playing fields youngsters in the number these entertainments do in Britain. Hungary, in fact, resembles Britain from 1920 until about 1936. Everywhere you go you see small boys

> kicking a ball about. This soccer fever, let me repeat, is the basis of Hungary's success. Another feature of Hungary's soccer power has been their willingness to test the skill of their cherry-shirted stars against anyone. They'll play a works team – even a very junior side – if it means giving Puskás and co a hard work-out, for their belief, and an accurate one, is that the only way to keep on top, and on your toes, is by playing plenty of football.[95]

The clamour to see the Hungary versus England match was unprecedented. Never before or since has a sporting event, indeed any entertainment event, in Hungary generated such public interest. On the January day when tickets had gone on sale, an estimated 500,000 people (5 per cent of the population!) had braved the bitter cold and converged upon the Népstadion for the 90,000 tickets that were available to the public. Children were not permitted to buy tickets, nor were they allowed entry to the stadium on the day of the match. Tickets were also limited to two per person, to prevent people buying them in bulk and then selling them on the black market.

The bulk of the tickets allocated for dignitaries went to Hungarian government officials and their cronies, with only around 100 being divided between diplomats and foreign journalists. The latter, however, may have been small in number but were well treated. The Hungarian government desperately wanted to show that communism had bettered the country, and what better demonstration was there than the splendour of the brand new Népstadion? The press box was the most modern in the world, with a first-class view of the pitch, cushioned chairs, and telephones and typewriters on every desk. The dressing rooms were so sumptuous that England goalkeeper Gil Merrick recalled that when the England team first entered theirs, they did a double-take, thinking that they'd 'accidentally walked into someone's castle'.

The Hungarian government also wanted to give their visitors the impression that Hungary was a democracy, and that the journalists were free to go wherever they wanted and to speak to whomever they chose. To this end, the ÁVO arranged for the entire press party to arrive in Hungary as one, by train from Vienna, and to be transported directly to Budapest's most luxurious hotel, the Palace Hotel. The

ÁVO's hope was that if the journalists' every whim was catered for, this would be enough to prevent them wanting to leave the hotel. It wasn't.. The journalists indulged in both the enticements and the opportunity to go walkabout and speak to whomever they chose. But what they found was a wall of silence. The Hungarian public were not stupid enough to give their real opinion of communist Hungary to a foreigner, especially one who was so clearly being tailed by the ÁVO.

One visitor, however, was neither a journalist, a diplomat nor a concern for the ÁVO: Jimmy Hogan. Unable to meet with the Hungarian team while they were in London, Hogan accepted an invitation from the Hungarian FA to be a guest of honour in Budapest.

It was 38 years since Hogan had last been in Hungary, and, although shocked and saddened by the scars of war and obvious oppression caused by the Soviets' occupation, he was overjoyed by the welcome he received from his old friends and colleagues. The pinnacle was a dinner held in his honour the evening before the match, at which Sebes ended his speech by asking for all gathered to give a tearful Hogan a standing ovation.

At the very same dinner, Puskás made an appearance – his entrance, one West German journalist noting (his phone call tapped and documented by the ÁVO), 'causing a commotion that would make a country's leader envious'. Puskás, conscious that he was being watched and would be playing the next day, declined any food and drink (until he got home, at least), but did work the room like the dab hand he'd become, shaking hands and cracking jokes that tested the skills, and patience, of the interpreters. But it was a joviality that masked an ugly argument that had broken out that afternoon at the Hungarian team's training ground …

The sports minister, Gyula Hegyi, had called the players one by one into an office, handing them, in a sealed envelope, their financial reward for the victory in London. The players were rewarded in three separate groups: Puskás and Bozsik receiving the most – 300,000ft each which is worth £20,000 in 2019 values; Budai, Czibor and Kocsis receiving the least – 10,000ft each (£700), The rest of the team each received 50,000ft, (£3,500).

It is hard to imagine what the team management's thinking in giving the players such disparate amounts was – as to whether they believed that the players would keep their amounts secret from each other, or they wanted the players to each know their worth. Either way, on discovering that he was one of the three to have been rewarded the least, Zoltán Czibor retired to his room to spend a sleepless night trying to work out why he, Budai and Kocsis were being treated so shamelessly:

> The conclusion I came to was that all three of us had played for Ferencváros at the time when the club was banned for having fascists among their supporters. Thereafter, the national team's management always referred to us as the 'three fascists'. Can you understand that? If someone had said 'Mussolini' to Kocsis, he would ahve asked what team he played for. And Budai? Well, he was just a normal bloke… like me. They should have sat us down and explained their reasons. And if I hadn't liked the explanations then I could have gone back to train driving. Because there for sure I would have been treated with more respect.[96]

As never before, the team was divided, and irreversibly so. Some of the players were simply grateful for any reward and did not want to be causing trouble, especially on the eve of facing England. Czibor and Grosics, though, felt that it would have been fair for every player to receive the same amount. The situation wasn't helped by Puskás's refusal to be anything other than boastfully unrepentant in accepting a sum that would help him to buy a new home for his family.[97] In comparison, the humble Bozsik felt deeply embarrassed about the whole scenario. Although he would never side against Puskás, he was understanding of the anger of those of his team-mates who returned to confront Hegyi demanding an explanation, and, when one was unforthcoming, refused to play against England.

On Sebes's being told that the team were arguing over bonus payments, he was taken aback that money was an issue for an argument. Surely they were *all* looked after handsomely? Reminding himself that at this particular moment he needed the players more than they needed him, Sebes first went for tact: 'Come on now, lads, enough is enough, you've made your point.' When this did not have the desired effect, he tried shaming: 'You will be letting your nation down' – but again it was to no avail, so he turned to rage, notably at Grosics: 'If there is ever any trouble, it is always you who is the instigator, and now you are involving three-quarters of the team!'[98] Rage morphed to threats of life bans, but it was still to no effect: the players held the upper hand and Sebes knew it. Finally, undermined and humiliated, he turned to his last resort and sent for Mihály Farkas.

Delegating was never part of communist politics, which was just as well for Farkas, for neither was it a part of his make-up. He stormed into the Red Star hotel's foyer, then – for the first time showing the players his true colours – eyed them menacingly and snarled, 'Whoever of you wants to can fuck off now, but believe you me, you won't reach home.'[99] Grosics was not alone in remembering that his blood ran cold:

> I swear those were Farkas's exact words. He didn't start the meeting with 'What's the matter, comrades? Sit down and we can discuss it.' No, instead he instantly threatened us, making it crystal clear that we only had one choice – to play. No one dared leave, not even me. To have done so would have been suicidal.[100]

The abashed would-be rebels returned to their rooms, but over the coming weeks the sense of injustice did not dissipate, and it would ultimately split the team into two different cliques. The sad irony of the whole sorry episode was that it happened on the eve of the most 'perfect' day in Hungarian football history. Budapest was awash with brilliant sunshine; Népstadion, gleaming in all its newness, was packed with the largest attendance ever at a football match in Hungary; and the 'Golden Team' produced, in front of their own people, a display of football at its absolute finest.

HUNGARY v ENGLAND
23 May 1954, Népstadion, Budapest

HUNGARY: 1 Gyula Grosics (Honvéd), 2 Jenő Buzánszky (Dorogi Bányász), 3 Gyula Lóránt (Honvéd), 4 Mihály Lantos (Vörös Lobogó), 5 József Bozsik (Honvéd), 6 József Zakariás (Vörös Lobogó), 7 József Tóth (Csepeli Vasas), 8 Sándor Kocsis (Honvéd), 9 Nándor Hidegkuti (Vörös Lobogó), 10 Ferenc Puskás (Honvéd), 11 Zoltán Czibor (Honvéd)

ENGLAND: 1 Gil Merrick (Birmingham City), 2 Ron Staniforth (Huddersfield Town), 3 Roger Byrne (Manchester United), 4 Billy Wright (Wolves), 5 Syd Owen (Luton Town), 6 Jimmy Dickinson (Portsmouth), 7 Peter Harris (Portsmouth), 8 Jackie Sewell (Sheffield Wednesday), 9 Bedford Jezzard (Fulham), 10 Ivor Broadis (Newcastle United), 11 Tom Finney (Preston North End)

Perversely, the one player who had accepted his lesser money without so much as a murmur of dissatisfaction, László Budai, Sebes dropped from the team for the match against England. Sebes may have disliked Czibor and Grosics's defiance, but secretly he admired their mettle in standing up for themselves, whereas Budai, who had received the equal lowest payment, had been as docile as ever. More discouraging for Budai was that Sebes replaced him with a debutant, József Tóth. The Csepel winger had long been in Sebes's plans, and would have accompanied the squad to London had he been eligible for a passport to travel outside the Soviet bloc, but his mother having once lived in England and an aunt who lived in the United States had put paid to that.

Sebes sent his players out with instructions to begin with caution until they had worked out England's tactics and formation. Sebes was convinced that Walter Winterbottom would be playing a more defensive game, placing an extra player in defence to deal with Kocsis and Puskás, and having Hidegkuti picked up whenever he drifted into midfield. But, beside the England selectors having made some strange selections (Peter Harris hadn't played for England for five years, and Bedford Jezzard was a debutant) it also quickly became apparent that England were adhering to the same game plan that had seen them get thrashed in London.

Once Bozsik and Hungary's forward line realised that England's centre-half, Syd Owen, was at the same loss that his dropped predecessor Harry Johnston had been at in the Wembley match, they pushed forward and interchanged with confidence, exploiting the spaces created by Owen's indecision. After just eight minutes, a long-range piledriver of a free kick from Mihály Lantos (taken from so far out that England had seen no need to form a wall) placed Hungary in front (1–0). In the 18th minute, a Kocsis cross was cleared directly into the path of Puskás (2–0), and just over ten minutes later a Puskás cross fell to Kocsis (3–0).

The first half ended with commentator György Szepesi noting that Czibor was playing at nowhere near his usual standard. In fact, Szepesi's words were an understatement: Czibor barely touched the ball, a lack of effort and non-contribution that had gone unnoticed in the midst of Hungary's three goals. Instead of being his usual hyperactive self, Czibor, much to Sebes's fury and England right-back Ron Staniforth's relief, had spent the entire first half standing on the wing moping:

> I didn't notice any of the crowd, I didn't hear any of the team announcements. I was in a daze. The only thing that came into my head was whenever Puskás was giving it his usual 'Put it here, put it there' I was thinking, 'How is he worth so much more than me?' I was just standing about. It was a surprise that the crowd didn't start whistling me. For the second half I pulled myself together. I was suddenly overcome with a strength that I had never felt before. I said to myself, 'Zoltán Czibor you will show Sebes, Puskás, the nation, everybody, what you are worth!' Well, whenever the ball came to me I ran with it like a lunatic. Of course, it is very possible that I wasn't right in the head. But then again it didn't matter shit because everything came together. Everything just clicked. [101]

Czibor, tearing at the English defence like a man possessed, had a role in each of Hungary's next three goals, which all came within the space of just six bewildering minutes through Kocsis (4–0), József Tóth (5–0) and Hidegkuti (6–0). 'We want seven!' roared the crowd. In the 68th minute, England salvaged a smidgen of pride when their inside-left, Ivor Broadis, seized upon a Grosics parry (6–1); but it was far too little far too late, and five minutes later a Hidegkuti pass found Puskás unmarked (7–1).

On the final whistle, the England team offered only the most cursory of handshakes before dashing from the field. 'We were just glad the ordeal was over and to get off the pitch before the score reached double figures,' explained Billy Wright. The result remains the biggest defeat in the history of the England football team, and was summed up in Britain with the next day's headline: 'Disaster on the Danube'.

In contrast, the Hungarian players remained on the pitch long after the match's end to soak up the cheers from the ecstatic crowd, now convinced that Hungary would be winning the World Cup. Even a watching Mátyás Rákosi forced a grin.

CHAPTER 13

'The Battle of Berne'

Hungary v Brazil 1954

HUNGARY'S qualification for the 1954 World Cup had come via a bye – their would-be qualifying opponents, Poland, abstaining from the tournament, along with East Germany and the Soviet Union, for 'political reasons'. In other words, their respective governments felt that their nation's teams were so mediocre that at some point a humiliating heavy defeat was inevitable – the worst-case scenario being a defeat to West Germany. Hungary, at 6/4 favourites to win the tournament, held no such fears.

FIFA's decision to hold the 1954 tournament in Europe was made in 1946, with Switzerland, the least damaged and contentious of the war-torn continent's nations, chosen as the host country.

The 16 qualifying teams were placed into four groups of four, each containing two seeded and two unseeded sides. A group's two seeded teams did not play each other, and instead played once against each of the two unseeded ones. The group leader then went straight through to the quarter-final, while the second- and third-placed teams contested a play-off.

Group 1 – Brazil, France, Mexico, Yugoslavia

Group 2 – **Hungary**, South Korea, Turkey, West Germany

Group 3 – Austria, Czechoslovakia, Scotland, Uruguay

Group 4 – Belgium, England, Italy, Switzerland

Hungary 1954 World Cup Squad:

Goalkeepers – Gyula Grosics (Honvéd), Sándor Gellér (Vörös Lobogó), Géza Gulyás (Kiniszi).[102]

Defenders – Jenő Buzánszky (Dorogi Bányász), Gyula Lóránt (Honvéd), Mihály Lantos (Vörös Lobogó), Béla Kárpáti (Győr ETO), Pál Várhidi (Budapesti Dózsa).

Midfielders – József Bozsik (Honvéd), József Zakariás (Vörös Lobogó), Imre Kovács (Vörös Lobogó), Antal Kotász (Salgótarjáni BTC).

Forwards – Zoltán Czibor (Honvéd), Sándor Kocsis (Honvéd), Nándor Hidegkuti (Vörös Lobogó), Ferenc Puskás (Honvéd), László Budai (Honvéd), József Tóth (Csepeli Vasas), Ferenc Machos (Honvéd), Lajos Csordás (Vasas), Péter Palotás (Vörös Lobogó), Mihály Tóth (Budapesti Dózsa).

The Hungarians based themselves in the small, picturesque town of Solothurn, 40km north of the capital, Berne. The hotel was within walking distance of Solothurn FC's ground, where the team would train daily, as well as being large enough to accommodate the Hungarians' entire party – by far the largest at the tournament. Sebes had insisted upon the bringing of too many[103] rather than too few, so, along with the usual gaggle of administrators, journalists and ÁVO officers, there were doctors, masseurs, chefs, a dietician and an expanded coaching staff including Márton Bukovi. Sebes, as ever, kept his rival away from the training ground and players, but made use of Bukovi's expertise by placing him in charge of scouting opponents. The Hungarians also arrived a week earlier than any other squad, time in which Sebes had them play three friendly matches against local league clubs. The first was a 17–1 win against Solothurn FC. Two days later, Hungary faced slightly harder opposition in a 9–0 win over the Swiss first-division side Young Boys, a Berne-based club whose home ground was the Wankdorf Stadium, the planned venue for the World Cup Final – this is why Sebes went to great lengths to have them as opponents. And lastly, two days before the tournament began, a full-strength Hungary thrashed another Swiss first-division club, FC Servette, 8–2.

The tournament opened on 15 June with the reigning champions, Uruguay, beating Czechoslovakia 2–0. Two days later, Hungary played their opener, facing South Korea in Zurich, a match that was no more arduous for Hungary than a stroll-out against a works team. The South Koreans, playing in their first-ever World Cup, had only arrived in Switzerland two days before the match after a six-day journey from their homeland by boat, train and bus. The full-time 9–0 scoreline would have been higher had the second half not been continually interrupted by the exhausted South Koreans collapsing one after the other to require treatment for cramp. Against such second-rate opposition, Sebes had expected nothing less than an easy victory. Indeed, his greater interest was in the progress of Hungary's next unseeded opponents, West Germany, who the same afternoon had played Turkey and won 4–1.

The 1954 World Cup was West Germany's first since Germany had been partitioned. In the aftermath of the Second World War, the then (united) German national team was banned indefinitely from international football. It was only in 1949, when the east of Germany, under Soviet governance, became the 'German Democratic Republic', and the west became the 'Federal Republic of Germany', that the two new entities of East and West Germany were permitted to play internationally.

But the new West German national team were not the most welcome of visitors, and they struggled to find opponents willing to play them. And whenever they did play abroad, protests and endless abuse usually awaited them. Yet the hindrance of not playing against the very best nations was counterbalanced by the fact that the team remained a largely unknown entity in international football circles, as Jenő Buzánszky remembered:

> We hardly knew anything about the West Germans. The press in Hungary never travelled further than the border. Against those teams we'd never met before, we hadn't any idea who they were – who Fritz Walter was, who Helmut Rahn was. We didn't even know if they wore glasses or had wooden legs.[104]

The West German coach, Sepp Herberger, had been the coach of the German national team at the time when it was banned in 1945. Likewise, he too was banned from all involvement in football because of his membership of the Nazi Party. But in 1950 when the West

Germany national football team was formed (the country was formed a year earlier), Herberger was forgiven and (re-)appointed as team coach.

For Sebes, the very thought of losing to a former Nazi Party member was enough to give him sleepless nights. He went overboard in gathering information on the West Germans, and selected his strongest eleven for the match, laying heavy emphasis on the importance of a solid win. He was therefore taken by surprise when he learned, on being given the West German team sheet, that Herberger was fielding a weakened team – six reserve players and a debutant goalkeeper. As perplexed as the Hungarians were, they decided to take the initiative and test the young West German goalkeeper from the off. Hungary's attack flew at the West German defence. Kocsis opened the scoring in just the second minute, and by half-time they were leading 3–1. The second half continued in the same vein, with Hidegkuti scoring twice in succession early on. It was all too easy … and then an incident happened that changed the entire direction of Hungary's World Cup.

In the 60th minute, with the score at 5–1, Puskás was upended from behind in the penalty box by the West German full-back Werner Liebrich. The Hungarian calls for a penalty were waved away by English referee Bill Ling; and as play continued, Puskás remained on the ground, clasping his right ankle and calling to the bench, 'It's gone!'

Substitutes would not be allowed in World Cup matches for another 16 years, so when Puskás was carried from the pitch, Hungary remained for the last 30 minutes with just ten men. And they still managed to win 8–3.

Puskás was rushed separately back to the team's hotel, into the care of Hungary's own medical team, who diagnosed a severely twisted ankle that, in their opinion, would prevent him from playing for at least a fortnight.

Sebes was incensed, adamant (forever so) that Herberger had had Puskás deliberately nobbled. Just the sort of thing a Nazi would do! The Hungarian players on the field were, however, of the belief that Liebrich had acted of his own accord, targeting Puskás after his fellow defender Jupp Posipal (whose mother was Hungarian) had translated for him exactly what Puskás was saying. Puskás himself would remain of an open mind, and, in Liebrich's defence, there was no evidence before or after to suggest that he was the type of player who would stoop so low as to deliberately injure an opposing player – apart from kicking Puskás out of Hungary's World Cup, that is.

The absence of Puskás highlighted a flaw in Sebes's management. So reliant was he on his captain, and so rarely injured was Puskás, that it had not occurred to Sebes to select a replacement inside-left in his 22-man squad.

There did, however, exist in Hungarian football a more than adequate replacement inside-left in Újpest's Ferenc Szusza, but Sebes had refused to select the record-breaking goalscorer since 1952. His similar refusal to select the equally popular MTK winger Károly Sándor further brought into question his judgement. A country the size of Hungary could ill afford to ignore players of Szusza and Sándor's calibre for a World Cup, and it was all because Sebes was unable/unwilling to rise above his own petty personal grievances.

Sándor had actually accompanied the squad to Switzerland in the belief that he was playing – only for Sebes to inform him at the very last minute that he was surplus to requirements. In his autobiography, Sebes praised the 'patriotic' manner in which Sándor accepted the news and agreed to remain and assist the squad. Sándor, in his book, tells quite a different version. His remaining with the squad wasn't an act of patriotism: he just didn't have the means to get home alone.

Thus for the quarter-final clash with Brazil Sebes had to make do with placing Czibor in Puskás's inside-left position, and on the left wing a young and inexperienced Újpest right-winger called Mihály Tóth. 'Does this mean I now get the same money as Puskás?' Czibor asked.

The Hungary–Brazil quarter-final was one of the most eagerly anticipated matches of the tournament. The two nations had never met, but did have a history. Dori Kürschner, as you may remember from chapters 1 and 2, was the former MTK player and assistant of Jimmy Hogan during the Englishman's first spell at the club in 1915. From Hungary, Kürschner's travels took him to Switzerland, where he spent a fruitful decade, before in 1937 he was lured to Brazil by the president of the leading Brazilian club Flamengo after the club had toured Switzerland. Brazilian football, at the time of Kürschner's arrival, was the same as that played on the streets and beaches, with an emphasis on attack and flair rather than on maintaining any tactical formation. At Flamengo, Kürschner immediately implemented some discipline and a three-man defence, but left after just one season. His successor, Flávio Costa, retained a three-man defence, extending it to a formation called the *diagonal*. Instead of Flamengo's two half-backs and inside-forwards standing square to each other, Costa had them stand in a diagonal formation. So if the opposition attacked down the right, Flamengo's left-half would drop into defence, and the inside-left into midfield: a very basic 4–2–4. It was a formula that was quickly adopted by the Brazilian national team, and for which Kürschner was heralded as the forefather of tactical football in Brazil – praise that, alas, was posthumous, for he died from a mystery virus in 1941.

With Europe enveloped in war, it was Brazil and their 'diagonal' that became the dominant force in world football, and when the World Cup was resumed in 1950, the nation was duly chosen as the host. The Brazil World Cup was different from others in that the four nations who made it through to what would ordinarily be the semi-finals played each other once in a league system. So the 'final' – Brazil versus Uruguay – was not the final, rather the last of a series of pool matches, and one in which Brazil needed only a draw to win the tournament. Convinced of their superiority over their tiny opponents, Brazil were showboating their way to victory when halfway through the second-half Uruguay clawed an equaliser, followed in the 80th minute by the winner. Brazilians treated the defeat as a national catastrophe, and the coach, Flávio Costa, was sacked. Hence for the 1954 tournament they were determined not to make the same mistake and took a more cautious approach by appointing Zezé Moreira, a defensive-minded coach said to be the inventor of zonal marking. Moreira took with him to Switzerland a less flamboyant squad of players, containing just one player from the team that had lost to Uruguay. Clad for the first time in their now iconic bright yellow shirts, they progressed to the quarter-finals by topping the group with a 5–0 win over Mexico and a hard-fought 1–1 draw with Yugoslavia.

As had become their tactic in recent matches, Hungary launched into attack from the off, laying siege to the Brazilian goal five times in the first three minutes. On the sixth attempt, a Czibor shot rebounded off Brazil's goalkeeper to the feet of Hidegkuti (1–0 to Hungary).

Five minutes later, Hungary added a second: Czibor, whose refusal to remain in the inside-left position vexed the Brazilian defence (and Sebes), charged down the wing and crossed perfectly for Kocsis (2–0). It was at this point that the match, which by rights should have been a celebration of football at its finest, degenerated into what *The Times* declared to be the 'Battle of Berne'.

The Brazilians were the initial perpetrators: elbowing, tripping, stamping. Whether it was a deliberate tactic to thwart the Hungarians or born of frustration is not known. Either way, the Hungarians replied in kind. And as fouls exploded all over the pitch, the English referee, Arthur Ellis, struggled to maintain control. He remembered the match as the most savage he'd ever refereed in his long and distinguished career,[105] and was convinced that it was a battle of religion and politics – Catholicism versus communism – with him, as neither, stuck in the middle.

In the 17th minute, Buzánszky and Lóránt combined to hack down Brazil's centre-forward, Índio. The subsequent penalty was duly converted by Djalma Santos (2–1). As Indio received treatment, Brandaozinho sought revenge: steaming so viciously into József Tóth that the damage caused to the Csepel winger's leg would leave him playing no further matches in the World Cup. Hungary were essentially down to ten men, as no substitutes were allowed, forcing Tóth to remain valiantly but lamely on the pitch, hobbling, harassing and cursing his assailant.

Sebes and Moreira's half-time calls for restraint obviously had some effect, for the second half began a tad calmer – that is until Pinheiro used his hand to slap away Czibor's cross, allowing Mihály Lantos to score from the penalty (3–1). The sight of the Hungarians celebrating was a red rag to the Brazilians, and again they resumed their provocation. Sebes's frantic yells for his players to turn the other cheek fell on deaf ears, and surprisingly it was Bozsik, supposedly the most placid of the Hungarians, who was the first to lose his temper, retaliating to being punched by Nilson Santos by giving the Brazilian a 'Kispest sandwich' straight back.

The sight of two players swapping punches finally snapped the patience of referee Ellis. Kicking and elbowing the Englishman would take, but chaps punching just wasn't on! Throughout his long career

Ellis had never once had to send a player off in an international match, and now he dismissed two: first Santos, who walked without a second glance, then Bozsik, who stood gawping with a mixture of disbelief and shame, seemingly unable to comprehend that he was being ordered off for the only time in his entire career. 'He's sent you off, Cucu,' said Hidegkuti, gently taking his captain by the arm.

With Hungary's lynchpin gone (maybe that was the plan?), the Brazilians produced their best attacking football of the match. Their speedy right-winger Julinho dodged past Lantos, cut inside Zakariás, flat-footed Lóránt and smashed a shot past Grosics (3–2). With an equaliser so tantalising close, the Brazilians threw everything into attack. But it was a dangerous game to play against a team as potent in counter-attacking as the Hungarians, and sure enough, with two minutes of the match remaining, the inside-left, Czibor, standing on the right wing (possibly avoiding his marker, Djalma Santos, who was seeking blood after Czibor had spat at him), collected a clearance from Hidegkuti and crossed for Kocsis (4–2). The Brazilians, realising that a two-goal deficit was almost impossible to close within such a short time, and aware that the Hungarians dare not retaliate for fear of getting sent off, set about them with a new vigour; the last kick of the match literally being their inside-right Humberto running his boot down Lantos's thigh. The dismissal of the Brazilian was his last act of the match … or so he thought. As the two teams left the pitch, a brawl erupted between them, one that took the police with batons drawn to bring to an end. Who actually started it and what happened is now, as it was then, impossible to ascertain, but perhaps the best, if somewhat characteristically embellished version, belonged to Zoltán Czibor …

> Mihály Tóth was the first down the tunnel, and as he went down a Brazilian smashed him in the face with a pair of boots. He didn't knock Mishy out – thank God – but he certainly flattened him. I was last down the tunnel because I was always last out on to the pitch and last back off – always. As I went down I saw Sebes bleeding, deathly pale and gibbering like a goose: 'They attacked me!' He was like a six-year-old kid. Gyula Hegyi was there also, he had come down from the comfort of the stands to congratulate himself, but got a smack instead. I armed myself

> with three big water bottles that were on the massage table. I had two in each hand and one under my arm. I then turned off all the lights and: 'Come on!' There was blood and fists everywhere – a little war![106]

The Brazilian version of events was, of course, entirely different. They claimed that as they came off the pitch Czibor offered his hand for left-winger Maurinho, then pulled it away as the Brazilian went to shake it. Maurinho replied by punching Czibor in the stomach. Coach Zezé Moreira intervened, for which he received an eyeful of spit (culprit unknown), and in the ensuing melee Puskás (even with his sprained ankle) tooled himself with a glass bottle and whacked it over the head of centre-half Pinheiro.

An investigation into the post-match brawl by the World Cup Disciplinary Committee came to the tepid conclusion that both teams had been as bad as each other. Despite it being a disciplinary committee, it proved not to be inclined towards dishing out discipline, leaving punishment to the respective teams' own governing bodies, who in turn refused to punish their own players.

The Committee did, though, overturn Bozsik's one-match ban (which would have kept him out of Hungary's semi-final match against Uruguay) on the grounds that he had a hitherto impeccable disciplinary record, and that referee Arthur Ellis admitted that he had maybe been a tad harsh in sending him off. Many years later, the then retired Ellis fell into conversation with Bozsik at a function and enquired discreetly if, as a member of parliament, he was punished in any way for his punching an opponent. 'No,' replied Bozsik in all seriousness, 'in Hungary politicians aren't punished for things like that.'

'You'll have more of the same against those Uruguayans,' was one Brazilian pressman's parting warning. And that was what Sebes feared. The last thing he needed, with a place in the final just one win away, was another player getting sent off, or injuries to add to those suffered by Puskás and József Tóth.

But, on closer inspection, it was clear that the Uruguayans would also be reluctant to have a bloodbath – they were a nation proud of their renown for free-flowing football; and besides, a needless injury or suspension of a first-team player could be catastrophic to a team from a country with a population of 2.3 million (1954).

And it was so. And what followed was the complete opposite of the depressing debacle against Brazil. The Welsh referee Mervyn Griffiths's stamping hard on the game's opening foul had the desired effect, and from there on in his involvement was that of a spectator to what was one of the finest games of football ever played at a World Cup.

With so much at stake, both teams began tentatively, and it wasn't until the 14th minute that Hungary launched their first serious attack. A Czibor volley – hit more in hope than aim – took a deflection and flat-footed the Uruguayan goalkeeper (1–0 to Hungary). They hung on to their lead into the second half, probing with short passes, long passes, backwards, sideways, forwards, until eventually an opening appeared. A low Budai cross flicked up off a defender's outstretched leg, and as the ball looped into the six-yard box, Hidegkuti flung himself head first, seizing on the Uruguayans' hesitation (2–0).

The world champions, fearing a third goal, pushed forward with more adventure. In the 76th minute, a slip of concentration by the Hungarian defence allowed Juan Hohberg a free run at Grosics (2–1). Sensing the Hungarians' creeping nervousness, Uruguay pushed even harder forward, and with four minutes remaining Hohberg collected a throw-in, rounded Buzánszky and let fly a shot that Grosics could only parry, Hohberg won the scramble for the rebound (2–2). Hohberg fainted before he could celebrate his goal, as nearly did the Hungarians when minutes later Juan Schiaffino smashed a shot against the post.

In extra time, Hidegkuti sent Budai down the right wing. Budai looked for Kocsis, whipped over a cross, and Kocsis rose to score (3–2). The Hungarians' recapturing of the lead lifted them and visibly deflated the flagging Uruguayans. As the game drew to an end, Kocsis's marker, Victor Andrade, collapsed with cramp; and Bozsik, seeing Kocsis finally alone, launched a long, high ball towards him that he met with a thumping header (4–2). Hungary were in the World Cup Final.

MTK circa 1916. Jimmy Hogan stands on the back row, far right. Imre Schlosser – the first star of Hungarian football – stands two to Hogan's right. (MTVA/MTI Photo)

A new conqueror. Russian troops march through central Pest, 1945. (Fortepan)

'Stalin's Best Pupil'. Mátyás Rákosi, 1949. (Fortepan – Rádio és Televizió Újság)

A new face in the crowd. Rákosi looks down upon Hungary v Italy, 1949. (Fortepan – Ernő Márton Kovács)

The genius. The Messi, Maradona, Zidane, Pelé of his day. Ferenc Puskás, playing for Kispest in 1949. (Fortepan – Ernő Márton Kovács)

The masterminds. Gyula Mándi, Gusztáv Sebes and team doctor László Kreisz. (Hungarian Olympic and Sports Museum)

Commentator György Szepesi interviews the Hungarian players after an 8-2 win over Poland in 1949. Waiting third in line stands a 20-year-old Puskás. (Fortepan – Ernő Márton Kovács)

Zoltán Czibor accepts his reward. To his right stands Jozséf Bozsik. (Fortepan – Ernő Márton Kovács)

Ferenc Szusza and Károly Sándor keep their distance behind Sebes, as well they might. Sebes fell out with both players, outcasting them despite their being two of the very best forwards in European football. (Fortepan – Ernő Márton Kovács)

Ferenc Deák – another to meet Comrade Sebes's disapproval. In Sebes's eyes, the former slaughterhouse worker's notoriety for hard living overshadowed his record-breaking goal feats. (Fortepan – Ernő Márton Kovács)

A teenage Sándor Kocsis. (Fortepan – Ernő Márton Kovács)

The VIP section – Újpest, 1949. János Kádár sits far left, FA president István Ries in the middle and to his left the defence minister Mihály Farkas. In time each would be purged by the regime they served. Kádár and Farkas would be imprisoned, while Ries would be beaten to death during his interrogation. (Fortepan – Ernő Márton Kovács)

'A gift to the Hungarian nation'. The eight-metre high bronze statue of Stalin, erected in Pest's City Park in December 1951. (Fortepan)

'The Golden Team!' – Olympic champions, Helsinki 1952. (Fortepan – József Kovács)

'The Magical Magyars' – Back row: Lóránt, Buzánszky, Hidegkuti, Kocsis, Zakariás, Czibor, Bozsik, Budai. Front row: Lantos, Puskás, Grosics. (Fortepan – Tibor Erky-Nagy)

Note, top right, that the Hungarian badge is adorned not with the hammer and sickle of communist Hungary but the Kossuth Coat of Arms. An ancient Hungarian symbol, the 'Kossuth' was seen as a sign of defiance against the Stalin regime. A simple oversight or a purposeful act? (Author)

'They haven't got the proper kit'. Captains Puskás and Billy Wright lead out their respective teams at Wembley, 1953, for the 'Match of the Century'. (Getty)

The body language of the England players says it all as Puskás wheels away after scoring Hungary's seventh goal in their 7-1 drubbing of England in Budapest, 1954. The 'Disaster on the Danube' still remains the England national team's biggest defeat. (Hungarian Olympic and Sports Museum)

'Do that again and you're in trouble!' Gyula Lóránt gives the West German forward Helmut Rahn a word of advice during Hungary's first round 8-3 win at the 1954 World Cup. The referee calling for calm is Englishman Bill Ling, also the referee of the final between the two nations. (Hungarian Olympic and Sports Museum)

'The Battle of Berne'. The most violent match ever to take place at a World Cup – Hungary v Brazil 1954. Brazil's goalkeeper Castilho thwarts an attack by Czibor. Far right of the picture looking on is József Tóth. (Hungarian Olympic and Sports Museum)

'The Miracle of Berne' – the World Cup Final 1954. According to the defeated Hungarians, it was a miracle that the West Germans won. A dejected Gyula Grosics (far right) looks on with unbridled envy as the West German captain Fritz Walter walks off clasping the Jules Rimet trophy. (Hungarian Olympic and Sports Museum)

'The Battle of the Champions'. Wolves v Honvéd, December 1955. For a third time, captains Billy Wright and Puskás lead out their respective teams, though this time Wright would not walk off humiliated. Note the Wolves players' shirts – purposely made of extra shiny satin so as to sparkle fluorescently under the club's brand new floodlights.(Hungarian Olympic and Sports Museum)

Revolution! October 1956. Civilians look on at a Russian tank disabled by the revolution's ragtag army of freedom fighters – an army whose tactics wrote the textbook on guerilla warfare. The tank's crew lay dead in the street. Hungarians refused to bury the Soviet dead; however, their own dead (numbering more than 2,000) were given heroes' burials. (Fortepan – Gyula Nagy)

The despised bronze statue of Stalin is dismantled in a Pest side street. Note the disabled Russian tank in the background.
(Fortepan – Gyula Nagy)

The corpses of lynched ÁVO officers rot in a Pest square. However, once the Soviet army returned to quash the revolution the ÁVO would wreak revenge of their own.
(Fortepan – Gyula Nagy)

Eleven worried men. The Honvéd team in Italy, December 1956, preparing to face Roma in a friendly match. Note the black armbands. It would be decades before Kocsis, Czibor and Puskás returned to Hungary. (Fortepan – József Kovács)

One exile and two soon-will-bes. Béla Guttmann, Kocsis and Puskás, in Lisbon 1956. (Hungarian Olympic and Sports Museum)

'The Three Amigos'. Kocsis, Kubala and Czibor at Barcelona. (Hungarian Olympic and Sports Museum)

June 1981. Puskás back in Hungary for the first time in just under 25 years. (Fortepan – Tamás Urbán)

CHAPTER 14

It is not possible to stop the Hungarian attack but theirs is a defence that lets in goals.

Sepp Herberger

AS a reward for the players reaching the World Cup Final, their wives and fiancées were permitted to travel to Switzerland. Their arrival was the result of a drunken promise fulfilled to Puskás by Mihály Farkas, who, at the dinner to celebrate Hungary's 7–1 win over England had, in his euphoric state, agreed to Puskás's request that the players' wives and fiancées could travel to the World Cup. Sebes disliked the idea from the start, fearing that the ladies' presence (including that of his own wife) would provide nothing but an unnecessary distraction from the serious business of football. But, not wanting to upset either Farkas or Puskás, Sebes reached upon a compromise that the ladies could visit if Hungary got to the final – but could only see their men for the first time once the match was over.

For the majority of the women, the trip to Switzerland was their first time out of Hungary and became a crucial turning point in many of their mindsets. Compared with other women in Hungary, the footballers' wives were by no means poor, but that did not mean they were well off either, and the sight of plush Alpine towns and the luxurious comfort of their Swiss hotel opened their eyes to another world. It was a lifestyle they knew could be easily attainable should at any time their husbands accept an offer to play abroad.

Back in Budapest, Mihály Farkas was so assured of Hungary beating West Germany that he ordered the printing of 2.5 million postage stamps with the design of a giant football and a giant Hungarian flag (complete with hammer and sickle) overshadowing a map of the world. Farkas also saw that all the players would be rewarded with bonuses of 50,000 forints (worth £13,500 in 2019 money), and Gusztáv Sebes and Gyula Hegyi would be awarded the 'Red Flag Workers Decoration': a prestigious honour given only to an elite few socialist heroes.[107] He then telephoned his fellow member of parliament József Bozsik at the team's hotel:

> Farkas – Where shall we hold the celebration banquet?
>
> Bozsik – We haven't played the match yet.
>
> Farkas – Is Puskás playing?
>
> Bozsik – Maybe.

Farkas's blind optimism that Hungary winning was a foregone conclusion was a reflection of the nation's as a whole. After all, the papers were reporting that Puskás would be fit for the final, and hadn't they already beaten West Germany 8–3?

However, in Switzerland, Gusztáv Sebes and his team of coaches were not so assured. Sebes learned from Márton Bukovi's reports on the West Germans that their coach, Sepp Herberger, had fielded a weakened team against Hungary in the group stage, so as to save the bulk of his first-team players for the later games.

After losing to Hungary, Herberger had begun to field what was essentially his first eleven; their pool play-off opponents Turkey were swept aside 7–2, they beat quarter-finalists Yugoslavia 2–0, and in the semi-final, Austria were destroyed 6–1. Clearly, for Hungary to contain a full-strength West German team would require a full-strength Hungarian team, and that posed Sebes the most critical decision of his time as coach – should Puskás play in the final?

Hungary's captain had declared his right ankle strong enough to allow him to play in the semi-final against Uruguay, but Sebes, on the advice of the team doctors, had refused to select him. For the final, Puskás was even more vocal in expressing his desperation to play, but Sebes was not sure whether his captain was genuinely fit or hiding the truth in his understandable – and, in Sebes's eyes, admirable – desire to be the Hungarian who would lift the Jules Rimet trophy.

Quite out of character, Sebes (possibly with one eye on a backlash should Puskás have to come off, reducing Hungary to ten men) referred to his coaching team for a collective decision on whether Puskás should play. The answer was that it was possible that Puskás was hiding his injury, but a Hungarian team with a lame Puskás was better than a Hungarian team with no Puskás at all.

Öcsi's grin told his team-mates he was back.

On the afternoon of the day before the final, the Hungarian team couldn't help but notice that a huge stage was being assembled on the square outside their hotel. Sebes located the hotel's manager to ask what was going on. 'The annual Swiss boys' orchestra festival,' came the reply. 'It happens in Solothurn every year at this time. Didn't you know it was on when you booked the hotel?' Sebes had not known, and wasn't too happy about it, but decided nonetheless to enjoy the music – after all, what better way to distract and relax his players than an evening spent listening to the soothing tones of live orchestras?

As midnight passed and the band showed no sign of slowing their tempo nor the party its swing, Sebes collared the festival organiser. He was a man obviously indifferent to football, for he curtly informed Sebes that the music would cease at the same time it did every year … at dawn. Sebes couldn't believe it! How had such a thing been overlooked? Who could he blame? No one: the decision to stay at the hotel had been made by him. He had even made a pre-tournament visit to Solothurn to check out the town and hotel facilities!

Unable to sleep, Sebes sat in the hotel foyer … from where he spied a group of players sneaking back to their rooms. Kocsis, Budai and some reserve team players weren't drunk, but they had disobeyed a strict and precise instruction to remain in their rooms and rest. 'We couldn't sleep, Uncle Guszti, so we nipped out for some fresh air,' they replied, as shocked to see Sebes as he had been to see them. 'Get to bed!' he barked. Sebes then set out on patrol to see how many others had just 'nipped out'. One was missing! 'Where's Zakariás?'

The discovery that József Zakariás had spent the night with a chambermaid hurt Sebes more than it angered him. Of all the squad players, Zakariás was the one whom Sebes considered himself the closest to, even more so than Puskás and Bozsik. It was a favouritism that many believed stemmed from Sebes seeing himself as a player in Zakariás: compensating for a lack of skill with an overabundance of enthusiasm and obedience. Equal to this was Sebes's friendship with Zakariás's father – a director of Budafok FC in the Buda district, where Sebes lived, who after the war had been secretary of the local Communist Party, a branch of which several of the Zakariás family were members.

The minimum Sebes expected for his loyalty was for Zakariás to set an example. And yet here he was on the eve of a World Cup final, disobeying an order to remain in his room to spend the night with a chambermaid. And he was a married man! It was all too much for Sebes, and after the final Zakariás never played for Hungary again.

By the time the whole team were up and breakfasting, Sebes had made his mind up to punish Budai as well. Sebes did not want to be seen letting his and Kocsis's disobedience go unpunished, but Kocsis, as the tournament's leading scorer, was indispensable, and so was let off with a stern talking-to. Budai was dispensable, and therefore was dropped for the World Cup Final. As it was, Budai already had, albeit unwittingly, peeved Sebes in the match against Uruguay. Afterwards, Sebes had demanded an explanation as to why Budai had not made an effort to get himself on the end of a particular cross, to which Budai, in his amicable way, replied that he had been too tired. 'What can you say to that?' the still incredulous Sebes would write many years later.

In Budai's place on the right wing Sebes placed Czibor, who, although naturally right-footed, had not played on the right wing in over a decade. On the left wing, Sebes selected Czibor's understudy, Újpest's Mihály Tóth, a selection that baffled no one more so than Czibor:

> I really loved that Mihály Tóth. If he was here now I would give him a great big cuddle, I really would. You know why? Because like me he too was a Komárom boy. But please excuse me the world, he wasn't in any way an international footballer. He wasn't even a first division footballer. He didn't belong in our team![108]

On the journey from the hotel to the Wankdorf Stadium, Kocsis smouldered at the mistreatment of his best friend. Mihály Tóth nervously wondered if he was not just a bit out of his depth. Grosics complained of nausea, and indeed would vomit once in the dressing room. Puskás agonised over whether his ankle would last the match. And Zakariás, who would ordinarily lead a sing-song, sat silent, aware of his betrayal of Sebes's trust and also possibly fearful that word of his indiscretion would reach the ears of his wife, also making her way to the final.

The West Germans had no such problems. They stayed at a quiet, secluded hotel on the shores of Lake Thurnen, a world away from the noise and intrusion of a bustling Saturday night town square. The Hungarians had had to rely on their ambassador in Switzerland to locate for them a hotel, training facilities and transport – a man who, in fairness, probably had other pressing matters at hand and was a complete stranger to Sebes. In contrast, the West Germans' arrangements were organised by a compatriot of theirs, Karl Sing, who had close ties with Swiss football and was trusted implicitly by Sepp Herberger. Sing had played for the Swiss club Young Boys during the 1920s, and after his playing days ended, continued coaching in Switzerland.

When German football was resumed in 1949, Sing, because of his residing in Switzerland, was appointed the German Football Association's representative at the Zurich-based FIFA. Sing was therefore in a position to ensure that the West German team at the World Cup stayed at the very best hotel and had access to the very best training facilities. He was even able to gain Herberger access to Berne's Wankdorf Stadium the day before the final, so that the West German coach could inspect the pitch, and on the day of the match arranged for the West German team bus to park right next to the dressing rooms' entrance door.

Maybe the West Germans' blocking of the car park was unintentional, or maybe it was all part of Herberger's psychology to make things difficult for the Hungarians – either way, it meant that the Hungarian team had to disembark outside the stadium and make their way on foot through a heaving crush of curious onlookers. Nearby soldiers, thinking that the gate was being rushed, blocked the entrance. Sebes barged his way to the front and, in his best French, demanded to be let through: didn't the soldiers recognise them? They didn't, and one proved he didn't by giving Sebes a clump with his rifle butt. They recognised Puskás, though, mumbled an apology, and let the Hungarians through the gate and to their fate.

HUNGARY v WEST GERMANY
World Cup Final, 4 July 1954, Wankdorf Stadium, Berne

HUNGARY: 1 Gyula Grosics (Honvéd), 2 Jenő Buzánszky (Dorogi Bányász), 3 Gyula Lóránt (Honvéd), 4 Mihály Lantos (Vörös Lobogó), 5 József Bozsik (Honvéd), 6 József Zakariás (Vörös Lobogó), 7 Mihály Tóth (Dózsa), 8 Sándor Kocsis (Honvéd), 9 Nándor Hidegkuti (Vörös Lobogó), 10 Ferenc Puskás (Honvéd), 11 Zoltán Czibor (Honvéd)

WEST GERMANY: 1 Toni Turek (Fortuna Düsseldorf), 2 Jupp Posipal (Hamburger SV), 3 Werner Kohlmeyer (FC Kaiserslautern), 4 Horst Eckel (FC Kaiserslautern), 5 Werner Liebrich (FC Kaiserslautern), 6 Karl Mai (SpVgg Fürth), 7 Helmut Rahn (Rot-Weiss Essen), 8 Max Morlock (FC Nürnberg), 9 Ottmar Walter (FC Kaiserslautern), 10 Fritz Walter (FC Kaiserslautern), 11 Hans Schäfer (FC Köln)

The night before the match, Herberger had had his players twice watch a film of Hungary's 6–3 win over England. During the first showing, the players had been enthralled by the Hungarians' mastery, whereas the second time they began to see weaknesses in their final opponents as Herberger pointed out that Hungary had become so used to attacking that they neglected the art of defence.

Straight away the West Germans set out to clip the roots of Hungary's creativity. Bozsik was never given a moment's peace, shadowed at all times by at least one of three West German players instructed to mark him out of the game. And Hidegkuti was tightly man-marked by Horst Eckl and tracked all over the pitch. In the first five minutes, while the Hungarians adjusted, the West Germans had three shots at Grosics's goal, but against the run of play Kocsis broke. His shot smacked against the back of a West German defender and rebounded to the feet of Puskás (1–0 to Hungary). The Hungarian nation rejoiced – Puskás was fine!!! Minutes later, fortune again favoured Hungary. Under pressure, West Germany goalkeeper Toni Turek fumbled a back pass, and Czibor pounced (2–0). Two goals ahead with only ten minutes gone, the millions of Hungarians listening to György Szepesi's commentary cheered the inevitable victory – but to the Hungarian players on the pitch, it was evident that the scoreline flattered them. Even with such a short time gone, it was apparent that the West German team fielded was quite a different proposition from the one they had thrashed in the group stage.

Two minutes after Hungary had gone two goals ahead, Max Morlock sneaked behind the flailing Zakariás to score from a low, whipped cross (2–1). The next ten minutes were nothing but a sustained West German attack that was eventually rewarded with a goal. A Fritz Walter corner, West Germany's third in a row, dipped into Hungary's penalty area. Their left-winger, Hans Schäfer, following instructions to deliberately obstruct Grosics whenever his team had a corner, lay an arm on Grosics's shoulder as they jumped together; Grosics flapped and the ball sailed straight to Helmut Rahn (2–2).

The Hungarians came back swinging, but the posts, bar, goal-line clearances and goalkeeping heroics kept them from regaining the lead. Midway through the second half, they were clearly flagging. A combination of lack of sleep, the exertion of the bruising quarter-final against Brazil and having to play extra time in the semi-final against Uruguay began to take its toll.

The West Germans, on the other hand, were still fresh: not only had theirs been an easier route to the final, but at half-time Sepp Herberger had allegedly arranged for the players to be given injections of some sort, to boost their energy levels. Herberger had also had his players change the studs on their boots to longer ones to suit the pitch's ever-increasing muddy condition.

The removable studs were a new invention by one Adi Dassler,[109] a sports shoe manufacturer whose company, adidas, supplied the West German team with boots, and who was sitting, pride of place, on the West German bench.

Having withstood the frantic bombardment of their goal, the West Germans began to regain the initiative. In the 84th minute, Bozsik was caught in possession just inside his own half by Schäfer. Racing from the tangle, Schäfer lofted the ball into the Hungarians' goal area. Lantos intercepted with a header that dropped into the path of Helmut Rahn, who feinted to his right, inducing Lóránt to lunge, before switching to his left and unleashing a powerful shot past the rigid Grosics (2–3). 'Let me live!!!' yelled Rahn as he struggled to free himself from the crush of his celebrating team-mates.

With only five minutes left and the World Cup slipping from their grasp, the Hungarians threw caution to the wind and piled forward en masse. Czibor missed an open goal, Hidegkuti hit the post, and an outstanding save from Toni Turek prevented Kocsis from scoring. 'Turek, you are a football god!' yelled the West German commentator.[110] The Hungarians thought otherwise.

Eventually, with only two minutes remaining, Hungary found a way through the wall of West German defenders; Hidegkuti's swift through ball was picked up by Puskás, who wrong-footed Turek to put the ball into the net. Hungary erupted as Szepesi bellowed:

> Öcsi has done it!!!!! How wrong were they to doubt Puskás! …Oh, no, wait a second – the linesman is waving his flag …

Having given the goal, referee Bill Ling was on his way back to the centre circle when the West Germans brought to his attention the flag-waving linesman Mervyn Griffiths. Ling's predicament was not an enviable one – he very much knew the enormity of any change of decision. From his viewpoint, Puskás had been onside. But Griffiths had had a better viewpoint right across the forward line, and was adamant that Hungary's captain had moved before Hidegkuti's pass. Allowing himself to be overruled, Ling disallowed the goal, pointing instead for a free kick to the West Germans.

It is admirable, and a sign of the football of the times, that the Hungarians did not surround and harangue the officials – but their disbelief was very real and remained so for a lifetime. 'That was a perfectly good goal. I can never forgive him,' the usually diplomatic and much-mellowed Puskás would still say of Griffiths many years later. Griffiths, for his part, remembered Puskás shooting him a murderous look and snarling something in Hungarian, something the Welshman got the general gist of.

The disallowed goal would prove to be a pivotal moment in both of the nations' football histories. When, moments later, Ling called full time, the victorious West Germans would grow to become a football superpower, while Hungary would never come so close again and would slowly disappear into footballing anonymity. The millions listening in Hungary were stunned by György Szepesi's words:

> The end, my dear listeners. The end. The end. We need to accept second place. It was a very sporting match. We were leading 2–0, and from our grasp gave away victory. These things happen from time to time. It's the end of the match. The West Germans are the world champions. Dear listeners, believe me, it is difficult for me even to speak. I cannot find the words. But we have to acknowledge that the West German team won fairly; they are worthy victors. What is true, is true. We lost that match. A West German team won 3–2. They won the World Cup. For four years we were unbeaten. And now we've lost.[111]

The pain of having to watch the West Germans accept the Jules Rimet trophy over, the Hungarian team trudged back to their dressing room. Some sat openly crying, others just silently brooding to the background noise of the West Germans celebrating next door. Sebes could find nothing to say. Only the news that their wives were waiting outside the stadium lifted the players from their stupor. The women had a more pragmatic approach to the defeat: their men had done the best they could – people back home would understand that.

From the stadium, the players only wanted to return to their hotel, but first were maddeningly obliged to attend a post-match 'victory' function at the Hungarian Embassy in Berne. Such had been the Hungarian ambassador's belief that Hungary would win that he'd arranged the function, inviting a host of dignitaries from Swiss politics and the Swiss-based FIFA. Gyula Grosics spent the entire evening hiding in a toilet cubicle, and the band, specially brought over from Hungary, were told not even to bother unpacking their instruments. Even the ambassador, who had been so keen throughout the tournament to integrate himself with the players, kept his distance. Mind, he was privy to information coming from Budapest that suggested distancing oneself from the team was probably a wise decision for the future.

CHAPTER 15

'Traitors!'

IN Hungary, the defeat was greeted with a sense of total disbelief. As György Szepesi signed off his commentary in a flood of tears, the millions who had been glued to the radio found themselves at a loss. They had been expecting an afternoon of delirious celebration, but now were left with nothing. And they were sick of having nothing. Since the communists took power, ordinary people had been fed an endless stream of propaganda: unfulfilled promises of better living conditions, better working conditions, education, health. Instead, the reality was that the shops were empty and life was no better than it had been under fascism – in fact, it was worse. One of the few morsels of comfort had been the belief that the Hungarian football team was the best in the world – which now, in the wake of defeat, was clearly not the case.

In Budapest, the authorities had, foolishly in hindsight, permitted people to gather at the Népstadion to listen to the match on loudspeakers. As the crowd left, a rumour spread that the players had sold the final in return for brand-new Mercedes cars, cars that had in the previous weeks been spotted in and around Budapest.[112] As they spilt out on to the surrounding streets, their ire was fuelled further by the sight of workers at the nearby Keleti railway station hastily stripping from the building's facade bunting and two giant flags (the Hungarian national flag and the communist red flag) which had decked the station in anticipation of the team's triumphant return.[113] On Rákóczi Road – the main street in front of the station – a tram was overturned and shop windows displaying photographs of the Golden Team smashed. A crowd of around 2,000 then broke off and made towards the offices of the newspaper *Nép Szabad* (Freedom Nation), a regular meeting and focal point for football followers because the paper's building was the place in Hungary where football results were first received and straight away chalked up on a board for the public to see. At the offices, stones were lobbed and windows broken until eventually some police arrived; but they were desperately outnumbered and unprepared – arresting terrified citizens in their homes for 'crimes against the state' was one thing, confronting an angry mob numbering thousands was quite another. However, people were still very much afraid of the consequences of being arrested, so once the police gathered themselves and grabbed a few who *appeared* to be ringleaders, the others moved on and away before they too found themselves in the grasp of the ÁVO.

But while the crowds may have dispersed, the broken windows quickly repaired and a handful of arrested dealt with, the authorities had for a brief moment been scared – and everyone present, for a euphoric moment, had sensed it.

In the meantime, the Hungarian squad on their train back to Hungary remained oblivious to the happenings in Budapest. A night's rest, and their mood had changed from despondency to grudging acceptance, and a want to go home. All agreed that they had lost due to misfortune rather than incompetence: a shooting ratio in their favour of 26 shots on target to West Germany's seven proved their dominance. Their goal tally of 27 was the most scored at the tournament, and Kocsis, with 11 goals, was its overall top scorer. And then there was the small matter of Hungary's run of 32 matches unbeaten, a new world record.[114]

Thoughts turned to the 1958 World Cup: by that time, the likes of Puskás, Grosics, Kocsis and Czibor would still be at their peak, leading a new team of primed and readied young players. Yes, despite the loss, the future still looked rosy, and as their train passed through Vienna, the Hungarian team witnessed crowds of Austrians lining station platforms, waiting to cheer their own returning team – who had finished third. The second-placed Hungarians sat back and looked forward to their own adoring crowds.

Indeed, there was a welcoming party of sorts at the border town of Hegyeshálom: a large number of police, a small number of pressmen and the senior Muscovite Zoltán Vas.

Nonplussed by the absence of the general public, Sebes asked Vas what was happening and asked, 'Why exactly have *you* come to meet us?'

Vas explained that he had been despatched personally by Mátyás Rákosi to ensure that the players, instead of going to Budapest, were to have their train carriages detached and coupled to an empty train that was to speed to the nearby town of Tata, and the Hungarian Olympic training headquarters, where Rákosi himself was waiting …

Had the team won, the original plan was to go directly to the Parliament Building, from where they would have, on the vast square outside, stood side by side with the country's leaders and basked in the love of the adoring nation. Instead, they had to endure Rákosi at a spartan former monastery. But at least the deputy president was in good cheer, and remained so throughout the evening, as if somehow he was pleased about the defeat, which he may well have been. After all, the riots hadn't happened when he had been president.

At dinner, Rákosi held court at the head of a long U-shaped table (Mihály Farkas was also present, but, according to his new lowly status in the party, was placed lower down the table, where he kept his silence), and ended the evening with a short speech along the lines of 'You can be proud, you did your best, now we can continue to build socialism together.'

The players relaxed: if the most feared man in the country was so apathetic about the defeat, maybe that reflected the mood of the nation. Then the interior minister, László Piros, a former butcher, yelled across to Sebes: 'You needn't worry, Comrade Sebes – everything is under control. We have policemen posted outside your apartment.'

Sebes paled. 'Why do I need policemen outside my apartment?'

It was now that the team were informed that their bonuses for the tournament were to be significantly reduced, Honvéd and MTK's planned lucrative post-World Cup tours of Brazil were going to be cancelled and a commission to make statues[115] of the 11 players who had played in the final scrapped … Oh, and for their own safety, they were to be held at Tata for a further three nights, until things quietened down.

Things? What things? Riots? What riots? Were their families okay? Were their houses still standing? How on earth were they responsible for riots? It was only a football match! Not a war. Surely the public should be applauding their achievement, not gathering in lynch mobs!

The recriminations began immediately. Three days of isolation gave the players plenty of time to examine the defeat. The dropped Károly Sándor blamed Sebes's selection of the inexperienced Mihály Tóth, deriding Sebes as a coach who wanted to be eternally renowned as a tactical genius. Czibor blamed Puskás for playing when only half-fit. 'You selfish bastard – you only wanted the world to see you lift the World Cup!'

'Fuck you, Crazy! You'd have done the same!' retorted Puskás.

Others, aware that Sebes (along with Puskás) was still in charge, chose to blame the match officials, claiming that referee Ling and linesman Griffiths were part of a conspiracy ensuring that a Western nation won the World Cup and not a communist one. Why else did only Britons referee all six of Hungary's tournament matches? Although, in defence of Ling and Griffiths – men whose reputations elsewhere were beyond reproach – with them both having served in the forces during the war, it is unlikely that they would have had a soft spot for the Germans.

And then there lay the subject of the West Germans injecting themselves at half-time with 'something', as witnessed by a member of the Hungarian party. Interestingly the West Germans never denied injecting their players for the final, but they did deny that there was anything untoward in the syringes, claiming they had had vitamin injections only. The Hungarians weren't convinced. Their scepticism would be the cause of friction between the two football associations for many years to come.

Circa 1954, there were no rules preventing players from taking performance-enhancing substances. Not that the Hungarians knew of their existence. A decade later, it would be a different scenario, when sport in the Soviet bloc was riddled with such drugs. But, in the 1950s, all the Hungarians had to sustain themselves was God's fresh air and the occasional swig of palinka.

Finally, on the third night, a fleet of black ÁVO cars arrived, and one by one departed every ten minutes carrying a player to his home, were they were instructed to remain indoors for a week, during which time police officers were posted outside their doors. Then, as now, the authorities' reaction did seem a tad extreme – but they were not protecting the players, they were protecting themselves. The players, by their association with Rákosi and Farkas, had, whether they liked it or not, become part of the regime. Hence an attack on a 'Golden Team' member would be akin to an attack on a leading party member (which, of course, Sebes was), and that had to be prevented at all costs.

To appease public anger, an inquiry was held to find a reason (scapegoat) for the team's failure. The inquiry was, like most inquiries under the communists, a mere showpiece where nothing of any real relevance was solved. The actual happenings on the pitch became a side issue. Sebes was told off for the choice of hotel and failing to warn his team against the English referee Bill Ling's well-known bias against socialist nations(!). Mihály Farkas was criticised for allowing the players to become distracted by giving them carte blanche to live off illegal earnings; thus an abrupt end was placed on athletes being 'allowed' to bring goods in from abroad. Meanwhile, Hungary's sporting press was held accountable for 'overexciting the nation'. László Feleki was sacked from his post as editor of the nation's sports newspaper, *Népsport*, and György Szepesi suspended from commentating on football matches – until, that is, Mihály Farkas listened to his replacement: 'What is this shit? Bring back Szepesi!'

Sebes too was very much of the mind that the press was responsible for the welcome he and the team had received on their return to Hungary, being overheard at Tata barking at Szepesi: 'It's your lot's fault that we are in this mess!' Feleki also fell foul of Sebes after writing a front-page article titled 'Why We Lost', in which he dared to question Sebes's selection decisions.

But while Sebes's sidelining of Szepesi and Feleki did show that he was still in control, it did little to abate the public's anger at the team's failure to win the World Cup. If anything, the suspending of the country's two most popular football journalists only had the effect of inciting further anger, the public asking themselves: how could two journalists be remotely responsible for what had happened on the pitch? Surely the blame lay with Sebes the coach and Puskás the captain!

All of the players who played in the World Cup Final team were abused as 'traitors' at some point or another. But away from football stadiums, bar the occasional yell on the street, they were able to go about their daily lives as normal. Most people remained friendly and inquisitive, overjoyed to have met a member of the Golden Team.

For Sebes and Puskás, however, the abuse they faced was at another level, bordering on cruel. Sebes's having a baying mob outside his apartment on the night of the final had frayed both his and his family's nerves – not helped by the daily pile of hate mail he received, and his son being so badly beaten up at school that he had to change schools. So disenchanted did Sebes become that he seriously considered his wife's pleas to tender his resignation as head coach. And so desperate did he become that he accepted an invite from the arch-survivor himself, Mátyás Rákosi, to accompany him to the opera: 'Come now, Comrade Sebes, you have to show yourself some time!' What the pair knew or cared about opera, or indeed each other, was irrelevant: Rákosi was in desperate need of comrades to support him in his plot to oust Imre Nagy, while Sebes hoped that his being seen as a close comrade of Rákosi's would send a sign that he was still a man not to be trifled with.

Puskás, on the other hand, was finding that his powerful friend was no longer powerful. The only fear Mihály Farkas generated was the fear of being seen with him. Farkas was a comrade on his own. In the battle for power between Nagy's 'reformists' and Rákosi's 'Stalinists', Farkas had hedged his bets with Nagy – resulting in Nagy distrusting him, and Rákosi despising him, more than he had done already.

Puskás, without Farkas's protection, was suddenly vulnerable and unprepared for his plummet from hero to villain. For all his bravado and big mouth, at heart Puskás was a gentle soul. He had no grasp of hate mail or threatening people's families – all he had ever known on his journey from Kispest to world star was being (for the most part) overwhelmingly liked.

Unlike Sebes, who could pick and choose matches, Puskás had no choice but to run the gauntlet of football crowds every weekend. Bozsik tried to direct his friend to ignore the provocation. But that was easy for Bozsik: he was never one to display emotion, and with no reaction forthcoming, the abuse towards him faded away. But Puskás was retaliatory by nature, unable to restrain himself. To begin with, he attempted to react with humour, pretending to conduct the crowd whenever they whistled him, and smiling and winking at yellers.

But these attempts only had the effect of inflaming feelings. Puskás's relationship with the leading communists had rendered him a traitor in the eyes of the public, and they were in no mood to be condescended to by a lackey who lived in a luxury villa and had sold the World Cup out for a car.

Realising the futility of trying to win the abusers over, Puskás began responding in kind, with lots of eyeballing, fuck-offs and even on one occasion showing his contempt by dropping his shorts to bare his arse. Eventually, the abuse began to affect his form, and thereafter his mood. And the tetchier Puskás became, the more his falling out with Czibor took on a spiteful edge.

Ever since Czibor's berating of Puskás for playing in the World Cup Final 'injured', the two had begun goading and openly arguing during matches. Puskás would make to pass the ball to Czibor by yelling 'Go!', to which Czibor would duly race off, only for Puskás to pass the ball to someone else and then complete his sentence with 'and fuck yourself!' Czibor's retorts were loud and long, and usually referred to Puskás's weight and the rumour that he was an ÁVO informer (not true).

Their beef began to affect Honvéd: even an ÁVO officer reporting on the team felt the need to inform his superiors that 'the two mutually hate each other'. Honvéd's coach, Jenő Kalmár, was at a loss as to how to deal with the pair. As coach of a club that was essentially a military battalion, it was not as straightforward a matter for Kalmár to transfer a player as it was at an ordinary league club.

For Sebes, however, the matter was very straightforward. He could not allow the two's arguing to disrupt the national team, and nor was he ever going to go against his beloved Puskás. Czibor learned he was dropped via an article in *Népsport*:

> Czibor's skill as a footballer is not in any doubt, but his behaviour as a man is. He is a wonderful footballer who has played a huge part in the success of the national team, but now he is dropped for disciplinary reasons – those being that he continually speaks out of turn and is forever provoking arguments with his teammates.[116]

Hungary's first game after the World Cup was a 5–1 win against Romania at a full-to-capacity Népstadion, Sebes replacing Zakariás and Czibor with two young debutants, Antal Kotász and Máte Fenyvesi, respectively.

Sebes's dropping of two of the Golden Team's stalwarts was further justified throughout the autumn of 1954, with Hungary drawing with the Soviet Union in Moscow (1–1) and beating, at home, Switzerland (3–0), Czechoslovakia (4–1) and Austria (4–1).

For the match against the Austrians, Sebes had relented and recalled Czibor to the first team, but only in the absence of Puskás (who was serving a one-match international ban for walking off the pitch during a recent Honvéd match). Czibor only lasted just over 30 minutes before Sebes replaced him, a substitution that Czibor was adamant was made to humiliate him.

Sebes, in his biography, recalled Czibor sitting next to him at the match and pointing to his replacement, Fenyvesi, to ask why Sebes thought him a better player. Sebes recalled his reply as: 'He is not a better player, Czibor, but he is a superior person. And later you will see how important that is in life as well as on the football pitch.'

Alongside Zakariás and Czibor, the next to fall from grace was Gyula Grosics: banned indefinitely for the heinous crime of smuggling … hairpins.

The ending of a blind eye being turned to footballers bringing goods back into Hungary had been adhered to for as long as it took for the storm of losing the World Cup Final to blow over. Too many people, from border guards to high-ranking party officials, had been making too much money for the smuggling to stop entirely.

Grosics, for one, married with two children, had missed the extra income. He arranged to have fellow goalkeeper Sándor Gellér send back from Vienna some boxes of hairpins for an associate's business venture.

Gellér, in Vienna with his club, Vörös Lobogó, so as to fly onward to Turkey for a match, passed the money and order on to a Hungarian smuggler called Sándor Schwarz, who acted as an agent for many of the players, saving them the effort of shopping and packing goods themselves. Schwarz duly placed the hairpins on the Vörös Lobogó bus returning to Hungary.

On crossing the border into Hungary, the bus was searched by customs.

The arrested driver 'confessed' to having three accomplices – Schwarz, who was out of reach in Vienna; Gellér, who was in Turkey; and Grosics, who was in Hungary and oblivious to what awaited him.

Telephone calls were made to the Sports Ministry, and a decision was made to withdraw Grosics's playing licence with immediate effect.

He was preparing for a Honvéd match against Vasas when he was tapped on the shoulder by Jenő Kalmár. 'I've been ordered not to select you.'

'That's not funny, Uncle Jenő.'

'You know that I would never joke about that, Gyula. Go home and wait.'

For the next month, Grosics existed in limbo until eventually he was ordered to the Defence Ministry to face a disciplinary panel led by General Sándor Nógrádi, president of Honvéd and a hard-line communist. Nógrádi held a strong and long dislike of Grosics and his slovenly approach to soldiering. Once he had declared Grosics guilty, Nógrádi gleefully informed him that he could expect a hefty prison term or possibly even the death sentence!

But Grosics, a veteran of being arrested, was not so easily bluffed. As frightened as he was, he knew very well that if this were the case, then at that moment he would be in prison, and not ordered to return a week later to the Sports Ministry, where he was to learn his fate.

Confronted this time by the less fearsome duo of Gyula Hegyi and Sándor Barcs, Grosics sat sullenly to hear that he and his understudy, Sándor Gellér, were to be banned for one year from football entirely. Barcs was too ashamed to meet Grosics's eyes throughout the meeting. All he could offer were attempted words of comfort. 'I want nothing from you two,' spat Grosics, rising to his feet and slamming the door.

'Where once doors used to open for me, now they were closed,' was how Grosics described his year as a *persona non grata*. Avoided by family, friends, neighbours and associates, and unable to work, Grosics spent most of the year cooped up indoors, leaving only twice a week: once to collect his wages from the barracks, and the other when an ÁVO car came to take him for questioning at the secret police's new headquarters on Buda's Fő Street. The ÁVO were keen to learn of Grosics's smuggling contacts abroad and in Hungary. To his eternal credit, Grosics never once divulged any information, which, of course, only worsened his situation. However, belated praise from an unlikely source came many years later when the officer who interrogated Grosics was traced by a journalist and spoke of his surprise at the time of being ordered to interrogate the Golden Team's goalkeeper, also praising his refusal to name names: 'Believe you me, in those years in that building, those that did not break were made from very hard wood.'

But why, of all the smuggling sportsmen, was Grosics targeted? Well, Sándor Barcs, for one, was eternally convinced that the hand of Sebes lay behind the whole episode. Sebes was planning for the future and wanted neither Grosics nor smuggling to be a part of it. The rest of the Golden Team's 'problem' players had been dealt with: Gyula Lóránt, aged 33, was released by Honvéd to join lower league Budapest Spartacus, Czibor was dropped, Zakariás disgraced, Sándor and Szusza long ignored, while only Grosics had remained.

Sebes, the cunning old commie, was having a purge.

CHAPTER 16

After the Wolves v Honvéd match we held a post-match dinner. At the end of the main meal, Puskás was still going strong. I watched fascinated as he ate a dozen biscuits laden with butter and Danish blue cheese. I caught his eye as biscuit followed biscuit, pointed to my waistline and shook my head warningly. Puskás just smiled – and carried on eating.

Billy Wright[117]

CIRCA 1954, the idea of a European-wide cup competition to prove beyond doubt the best league club on the continent had been bounced around for decades, but to no avail. Distances, politics and wars had always kept such a cup from becoming a reality. There had been, however, the Challenge Cup, a knockout competition featuring the top clubs from Vienna, Budapest and Prague. The cup was the invention of Englishman John Gramlick, founder of Vienna Cricket and Football Club, and lasted from 1887 until 1911, when bickering between the nations' associations forced the competition's abolishment.

It wasn't until 1927 that another similar competition was formed: the Mitropa Cup, the idea of the Wunderteam mastermind, Hugo Meisl. It was a knockout competition for central Europe's leading clubs, and lasted up until the outbreak of the Second World War.[118]

But by the mid-1950s, despite Europe not having been at war for over a decade, there was still no competition to answer the question:

just who were the best club in Europe? It was a question that the French newspaper *Le Soir* sought to answer. In October 1954, they organised, in Belgium, the 'Festival de Football', setting the team considered the best, Honvéd, against the English FA Cup winners, West Bromwich Albion.

West Brom were managed by a former Tottenham Hotspur player called Vic Buckingham,[119] a protégé of Tottenham manager Arthur Rowe, the man responsible for bringing 'push and run' to English football from Hungary. At West Brom, Buckingham combined 'push and run' with long-ball tactics, winning the 1953 FA Cup – still the club's only major trophy.

The Honvéd–West Brom match took place in Brussels's Heysel Stadium in front of the now customary sell-out crowd for any Honvéd match. The Hungarians took the lead through Puskás, but were quickly placed on the back foot by West Brom's direct play, and at half-time were 3–1 behind. There was no small amount of patriotic pride in West Brom's game: Hungary's two thrashings of England had damaged English football's reputation, and Buckingham wanted his team to be the one to restore some prestige. Likewise, once the Honvéd players gathered their senses, they realised that Hungary had thrashed England twice: they saw no reason why they couldn't give the nation's supposed best club a lesson too, and so it was. Once Honvéd began playing their own style of passing and movement football, they had the beating of West Brom and cruised to a 5–3 win.

In England, the 'club match of the century' had been followed with huge interest, and nowhere more so than at West Brom's bitter local rivals Wolverhampton Wanderers. As the English league champions,[120] Wolves had been peeved to see their mere FA Cup-winning neighbours represent English football on the European stage. Wolves' invitation to Honvéd to come to play the 'battle of the champions' at their home stadium, Molineux, was readily accepted by Honvéd, or rather by the Hungarian FA.

On accepting the invite, the Hungarian FA then decided to use the trip to kill three birds with one stone. Hungarian football's winter break from late November to late February was enforced not for the players' or spectators' well being but because the pitches in Hungary were too frozen to play upon. It was always a lean time for Hungarian football as a whole. So, seeing as the bulk of the national team would be at a loose end, and made up of Honvéd and Vörös Lobogó players, it was arranged for the Hungarian national team to play Scotland in Glasgow on 8 December, Honvéd to play Wolves on the 13th, and Vörös Lobogó to play Chelsea[121] on the 15th.

The three teams all travelled in one group, staying in London at the Cumberland, the very same hotel where the national team had stayed the previous year. The return to England was just the tonic for many of the players – a much-needed respite from the repressive atmosphere in Hungary. Wherever the players went in both England and Scotland, huge crowds gathered, with Puskás's autograph being by far the most sought after. It was a reminder to Öcsi of just how popular he was outside of Hungary.

A delegation from the Scottish FA met the Hungarian party on their arrival in Glasgow by train. One elderly member gave a short speech referring to the Hungarians as the 'Austro-Hungarians'. Once he was done, Sebes collared the man to point out his error – Hungary was now 'The People's Democratic Republic of Hungary'.

'Och, it's the same thing,' replied the Scotsman.

The match against Scotland was a sell-out, no mean feat considering it was held on a Thursday afternoon and in sub-zero temperatures. Indeed, so bitterly cold was it that straw covered the pitch until an hour before kick-off and was heaped to the touchline as the game got underway. There was not a glove or legging in sight as Hungary won 4–2.

Honvéd's visit to Wolverhampton was the first by a Hungarian club to England since their national team had beaten England 6–3. For English football, the defeat, and the following 7–1 loss in Budapest, had brought a realisation that their football belonged to a bygone era, and that if they were to achieve the Hungarians' level of mastery with the ball and tactical superiority, then change was a must.

But this is not to say that all Englishmen were convinced of the Hungarians' superiority. Alf Ramsey, England's right-back for the defeat at Wembley (incidentally his last appearance for England), believed poor goalkeeping and a failure to stick tightly to the Hungarians had been the reasons for England's downfall. At the time, Ramsey's opinion was considered sour grapes, and it was only some

13 years later, when he himself as England manager (he succeeded Winterbottom) led England to World Cup victory in 1966, that his gripes were given any credence.

A far less well-known doubter of the Magical Magyars' superiority, but one whose influence would have a more immediate effect, was an RAF commander by the name of Charles Reep.

Reep was possibly football's first-ever data analyser, attending hundreds of English league games, where he would document every kick of the ball. His studies informed him (rather obviously) that the longer the ball was in the opposition's penalty area, the more chance there was of scoring. He concluded that the most sure-fire way to score goals was to get the ball into the opposition's penalty area as quickly and often as possible with direct long balls.

Reep got to practise what he preached with the team of his RAF base, and their subsequent success with 'route-one football' gave him the courage to offer his services to the local professional club – Wolves. Fortunately for Reep, Wolves were managed by Stan Cullis, legendary for his uncompromising, authoritarian approach to coaching. The 'Iron Manager' was duly impressed by Reep's military standing and statistics, and recruited him into the Wolves coaching fold.

Cullis began utilising Reep's findings, developing for Wolves a style of play that had the players forgoing dribbling and long chains of passes (too susceptible to mistakes and interceptions), to have them instead launch the ball as quickly as possible into the opposition's penalty box.

It was football at its ugliest, but remarkably effective, leading Wolves to their first-ever league title but earning Cullis more critics than praise. Cullis, though, was unconcerned: his answer was that he was making the most of what he had at his disposal; besides, 'nice football' had seen England humiliated by Hungary.

But time would tell that the criticism was unjustified, and that Cullis was a far more astute coach than given credit for. He was one of the first coaches in Britain, if not the first, to foresee the onset of television, evening matches and regular competitive games between top European clubs.

So that Wolves would be prepared for the inevitable, Cullis had floodlights installed at Molineux, among the first in British football.

He also tested Wolves against a host of top foreign clubs, starting with the Argentinian champions, Racing Club, followed by the Soviet clubs Dynamo and Spartak Moscow. Wolves' 'route-one' football defeated them all.

The visit of Major Puskás and the Mighty Magyars, though, was the icing on the cake: proof that Wolves were worthy of hosting Europe's very best. The BBC thought likewise and agreed to televise the second-half live – the first-ever midweek televised[122] match in Britain as well as the first between an English club and foreign opponents.

Cullis and Reep got their heads together to formulate a plan. Reep's statistics from Hungary's 6–3 'proved' that they had won simply because they had been quicker at getting the ball to their forwards in the England penalty area. Armed with this information, Cullis decided the way to stop the Hungarians was to stop them passing the ball. Thus three hours before kick-off he ordered the Wolves apprentices to wheel out the hosepipes and flood the Molineux pitch until it resembled a bog.

Cullis also counted upon Wolves' notoriously partisan support intimidating the visitors. The occasion was, and remains, the biggest night in Wolves' history. One Wolves apprentice, the future Manchester United manager Ron Atkinson, described the atmosphere as one he would never forget …

> What I also remember is the noise of the crowd – it was quite phenomenal, and I don't think I've heard a noise quite like it in a football match in all my time in the game at Manchester United and other clubs, or even working as a TV commentator. It was quite awesome.[123]

It was a cauldron, though, which failed to faze the Honvéd players. By now they were old hands at playing in front of packed away crowds; and besides, only five days earlier the national team players among them had played before 115,000 Scots – double the size of the Wolves crowd. Molineux was a church choir compared with the Hampden Roar.

In the tenth minute, Kocsis rose above the Wolves defence to meet a floated Puskás free kick from the edge of the penalty area (0–1). Four minutes later, Honvéd extended their lead. Kocsis, deep in midfield, threaded a neat pass through the Wolves defence for the sprinting Ferenc Machos to latch on to (0–2). 'The best football I have ever seen,' was Ron Atkinson's memory of Honvéd's first half.

At half-time, while Honvéd sipped their coffee and quietly congratulated themselves, Cullis tore into his players for what he perceived as their lack of effort. Even the ordinarily polite and placid Wolves captain, Billy Wright, ripped into his team-mates. As captain of England, Wright had taken the brunt of the criticism for the team's two losses to Hungary, despite being England's sole outstanding player on both occasions. At Wolves he was a club hero – locally born and a club player for the entirety of his career, the club's greatest player of all time. Billy Wright was not willing to lie down and let the Hungarians humiliate him again, and certainly not in front of his own people.

Wolves came out fighting for the second half and quickly forced Honvéd to give away a sloppy penalty, which they converted (1–2). With the scoreline reduced and the mud thickening, Wolves began to thump an endless stream of long balls into the Honvéd goalmouth. Geoffrey Green of *The Times* wrote:

> Bit by bit Wolves began to tighten the screws. Their shirts of old-gold, trimmed with black at the edges and specially treated with luminous effect for night matches, began to fill the dark field. They seemed to double in number and swarm everywhere. The pitch, more and more churned up, resembled thick glue. And the Molineux crowd surged, tossed and roared like a hurricane at sea, and called for the kill.[124]

With 15 minutes to go, Honvéd finally buckled. Wolves centre-forward Roy Swinbourne slipped free to head the equaliser (2–2), and then two minutes later he hit a low, hard winner past Lajos Faragó (3–2).

'Wolves have licked the greatest club side in the world!' bellowed the BBC commentator.

'Cullis' Kings of the World!' ran the next morning's *Daily Mail* headline. And indeed the man himself was of similar pretension, boasting that Wolves were now the 'world champions'.

It was, however, a boast treated with scorn on the continent. The highly respected Austrian journalist Willy Meisl, younger brother of Hugo, pointed out that Red Star Belgrade had beaten Honvéd a month earlier by the same scoreline and no one was calling the Yugoslav club the world champions. Not even Red Star themselves. Meisl further remarked that world championship matches were not usually contested on quagmires.

Similarly Gabriel Hanot, former French international and editor of the influential French sports newspaper *L'Equipe* wrote:

> We had better wait until Wolves travel to Budapest and Moscow before proclaiming their invincibility. There are other clubs of international prowess like AC Milan and Real Madrid. If the English are so sure of their hegemony then this is the time to create a European tournament.[125]

The English press's gloating prompted Hanot to contact all of Europe's football associations with the proposal of forming a knockout cup competition, with home and away legs all the way to the final. The result was, in April 1955, 18 of Europe's leading clubs meeting in Paris to finalise plans to begin the competition the following season. The clubs that gathered were not all current domestic league champions, but had been invited by Hanot on the basis of their popularity and past achievements, although this would change a year later when only league champions, plus the holders, would be allowed to enter the competition.

FIFA gave the competition the go-ahead and placed it under the jurisdiction of UEFA (Union of European Football Associations), an association founded in June 1954 to serve the interests of European football. In September 1955, the European Cup began,[126] culminating in a thrilling final – Real Madrid defeating the French club Stade de Reims 4–3 in Paris.

Unlike the modern Champions League, where teams can afford to lose a game or two in the qualifying stages, the European Cup offered only one chance of redemption, with matches being over two legs – one at home, one away. Referees were bribed, honey traps were laid in hotels, foreign countries really were alien lands, the playing styles of the nations were visibly different and the second legs knife-edge affairs.

Europeans loved it.

In January 1955, the Soviet premier Georgy Malenkov – Stalin's successors – was removed from office by the Kremlin old guard, disturbed by the speed and radicalness of his reforms.

Malenkov was replaced by the very comrade who had plotted his removal: Nikita Khrushchev. Khrushchev was a hard-line traditionalist, and one of his contentions with Malenkov was his leniency towards Hungary, where the Imre Nagy government had begun to adopt a form of communism that was pro-Hungarian.

Hungary under Nagy was still very much a Soviet state, but everyday life for ordinary Hungarians had improved, certainly in contrast to the dark years they had endured under Stalin and Rákosi. Goods such as coffee and sugar reappeared, basic medical supplies became available, a blind eye was turned to people doing their own private work, and in the countryside the deeply unpopular forcing of peasants to join collectives was ceased.

But an offshoot of the slight relaxing of the hold over people's daily lives was that it inadvertently caused opponents of communism to become more outspoken and braver in defiance, best demonstrated in the protests that marked Hungary's defeat in the World Cup.

Such defiance had Khrushchev believing that Nagy was going too far with his reforms; so he had the Hungarian leader hauled to Moscow. Khrushchev accused Nagy of 'rightist deviation', and gave him one month to rectify the situation as well as exercise 'self-criticism' – i.e. publicly admit his mistakes. Nagy, in feeling that he had no mistakes to admit, remained silent, but the stress of defying Moscow caused him to suffer a mild heart attack, giving Khrushchev the perfect excuse to dismiss him from his presidential post and reappoint Mátyás Rákosi as leader. Why Khrushchev chose Rákosi is not entirely clear, for he certainly never liked or trusted him – but the general opinion is that Khrushchev believed Hungary, at that time, needed a leader the people feared: Mátyás Rákosi.

For some Hungarians, the return of 'Stalin's Best Pupil' was all too much. At Easter 1955, while the national team were returning from a triumphant tour of Scandinavia (where they had beaten Norway

5–0, Sweden 7–3, Denmark 6–0 and Finland 9–1), one squad player, Csepel's Pál Csernai, disappeared as the homeward-bound party crossed West Germany. Csernai's[127] defection was Hungarian football's first in four years, since 1951 and the execution of the Újpest centre-half Sándor Szűcs.

Sebes, who'd given the 23-year-old Csernai his debut for the tour, was quick to condemn the player as a traitor, but among his fellow footballers Csernai was the target of much admiration. He had merely answered the question that most of them were asking themselves – did they want to live in a country ruled by Rákosi when the world outside was their oyster?

CHAPTER 17

Two friends are sitting in a bar. 'Tell me,' one says to the other, 'what do you think of Rákosi?' 'I can't tell you in here,' says the other. 'Let's go outside.'

Out on the street, his friend asks him again, 'So now tell me: what do you think of Rákosi?'

'No, not here, it's too busy, let's walk.'

So they keep on walking until the edge of town. 'Can you tell me now?'

'No, not here, somewhere quieter – let's go to the countryside.'

Eventually, in the middle of an empty field, his friend asks, 'Now can you can tell me what you think of Rákosi?'

The other looks around furtively before answering in a whisper, 'To tell you the truth … I quite like him.'

Old Hungarian joke

WITHOUT the licence to smuggle, Hungary's footballers were finding it hard to make ends meet. The high-profile one-year ban of Gyula Grosics (and Sándor Gellér) had had their fellow footballers ceasing their own black market activities with great reluctance. Having built up profitable businesses from the selling of smuggled goods, footballers had become used to a high standard of living, one which they could no longer maintain simply on the pittance that was the weekly wage from their clubs. Equally, the embarrassment of travelling abroad to wealthier countries with empty pockets and frayed clothes was becoming tiresome, especially since all the while they knew that western European clubs were ever ready to offer them wages which would be a tenfold increase on what they earned at home.

And nor would escaping Hungary be difficult for a footballer: no need for them to dodge armed border guards or pick through barbed wire in the dead of night – a footballer could simply slip away while on a trip abroad. As had Pál Csernai.

The players' concern over depleting incomes was exacerbated further by people's notion that footballers were rich. All people saw were the cars, villas and women[128] – how could footballers not have money? It was a problem summed up by Czibor's argument in a bar with a waitress who called him a 'smuggler':

> I said, 'Lady, we can't all earn our money like you – lying on our back.'
>
> She jumped up and screamed, 'You fascist!'
>
> 'Fascist?' I said. 'Better that than a Bolshevik whore!'
>
> Then, of course, I had to pay the bill, but I didn't have any money on me! Can you imagine! I don't know why – I must have left my wallet in another set of clothes. 'What – all that smuggling and you have no money? You expect me to believe that? Shame on you!' she sneered. So I jumped in a taxi to take me home to Buda so I could get some money.
>
> Once I was indoors, the devil possessed me. I drank a glass of something or other that I had brought back from Sweden, and my lord was it strong stuff! I was as drunk as a sack, yet I swear I only drank one glass. I went straight back to the bar and threw the money in her face. 'With that money, you can pay a man to fuck you, because you are as ugly as communism.'[129]

The next morning, Czibor was arrested by the military police (he'd been in army uniform). The hotel bar staff's version of events was that Czibor had turned up drunk and was the instigator of the argument and the ensuing scuffle with the hotel doormen (or ÁVO informers, as Czibor described them). This was probably the case, and for Sebes it was the final straw. Of late, Czibor's drinking had begun to get increasingly out of control and his behaviour more and more unpredictable, not to say insulting – like the time at a recent function when he had pointed out to a senior Communist Party dignitary that his trouser zip was undone, saying loudly, 'Careful, grandad, we don't want that old worm falling out.' As amusing as such stories were in creating an image of Czibor as a rebel, in reality they only made people want to avoid being in his company.

Czibor was banned from playing all football for a year, with the hope it would give him time to learn his lesson. Only time would tell.

If Puskás was relieved at having Czibor temporarily removed from Honvéd, it was just a fleeting tranquillity, quickly replaced by tension between himself and Kocsis. There had always been an undercurrent of jealousy between the two, engineered by Puskás, with Kocsis – out of shyness – initially holding his tongue … but then starting to come out of his shell after marrying a headstrong older woman: Alíz, the sister of his smuggling contact in Vienna:

> I noticed that footballers were surrounded by girls – and not just the floozie types – desperate to sleep with them just so they could boast that they'd been with Kocsis, Czibor. But I wasn't like that. I had no interest in football and no clue who Sándor Kocsis was. But once I did, I found it really strange that this person who was so famous was totally hapless and so in need of direction. He was like a big kid. Mind you it wasn't a surprise – because of football Sanyi always got everything given to him on a plate. His family wanted to keep him at home, they wanted nothing to do with me – a married older woman. They had even chosen a fiancée for him. But he was in love with me. He left her, and I divorced my husband to become Mrs Sándor Kocsis.[130,131]

Kocsis's new wife instilled in him a sense of self-respect that hadn't existed all the time he'd remained tied to his mother's apron strings. Alíz Kocsis opened her new husband's eyes to his worth, dumping his dowdy clothes for the latest Western fashions and having him buy a home in the most exclusive part of Buda. Hitherto Kocsis had lived with his parents in Ferencváros.

Kocsis's mother was aghast at the change in her son. If it wasn't bad enough that he was dumping his fiancée for a married woman (who had a child!), he was now living on the other side of the city, as if he was ashamed of his upbringing. To try to win her son back, Kocsis's mother took to showing that she cared for him the most, even going so far as to meet with the sports minister, Gyula Hegyi, to ask why her Sándor got less money than Puskás. It was all perfect ammunition for Puskás's training ground banter, but the married Kocsis was not the shy Kocsis of old: 'Fuck off, Öcsi, it's a fair question. I was the top scorer at the World Cup, not you!'

Remarkably, even with all the tension and conflict besetting the national team, Hungary remained unbeaten throughout 1955 – Austria (2–2), Scotland (3–1), Switzerland (5–4), Soviet Union (1–1), Czechoslovakia (3–1), Austria (6–1), Italy (2–0) and Sweden (4–2).

But the players were tired. Alongside the international matches and a full domestic season, Hungary's top four clubs, capitalising on lucrative invites from far and wide, undertook more friendly matches in 1955 than any other previous season – friendly matches in which the opposition always stepped up their game for the feted Magical Magyars.

Honvéd's solution was, at the 1955 season's end, to send the team on a three-week, nine-game tour of Egypt and Sudan. The players returned suntanned and exhausted, to rest for a week before the internationals among them were packed off with the national team for a tour of the Middle East to take on the Turkish and Lebanese national teams, also playing four more matches against city and regional teams.

The Hungarian party landed in Istanbul and into one of the worst Turkish winters in living memory. The snow caused havoc to the playing schedule and travel plans, and instead of Hungary playing Turkey first, as scheduled, they played two matches (as Budapest) against Ankara and Istanbul, then faced the Turkish national team. For the Turks, the match was the equivalent of a World Cup final, and they played accordingly, outfighting the fatigued Hungarians to win 3–1.

From Turkey, the Hungary squad travelled by train to Syria and Lebanon, and, as 'Budapest', beat their respective national sides. But these victories were inconsequential back in Hungary, where news of the defeat to Turkey had been met with derision. The Hungarian public had no notion of the conditions the team faced, nor cared that it was Hungary's first defeat in 12 matches. All they saw was the result: Sebes's team had lost to a nation they had thrashed four years earlier at the 1952 Olympics. Surely the players were too busy shopping and sunning themselves to be concerned with national pride.

But it wasn't just the failings of the 'once great' Golden Team pissing Hungarians off – everything was. The whole country was enveloped in a cloud of despair – three years had gone by since Stalin's death and little, if anything, had changed, proof being that the arsehead Rákosi was back in power. And then a glimmer of hope ... In February 1956, the Soviet leader, Nikita Khrushchev, gave a speech in Moscow in which he admitted that Stalin had made some serious 'errors'. The speech, published in full in the next day's Hungarian newspapers, wasn't an apology, but it was an explosive admission that sent shockwaves across the Soviet bloc – the Soviet leader admitting that Stalin wasn't a god!

In Hungary, Mátyás Rákosi was unsure as to how to react. His survival tactic had been simple: follow Stalin's example of leadership to the letter. It was a devotion that had seen Rákosi imprison and murder more of his own people, percentage-wise, than any other Soviet satellite dictator. It was an 'achievement' of which Rákosi had been openly boastful: that was, at least, until that coal-mining oaf Khrushchev began saving his own skin and condemning Stalinism.

Rákosi's having to ease off on the arrests and show trials couldn't have come at a worse time. Imre Nagy releasing tens of thousands of political prisoners meant that Hungary was awash with embittered, vengeful opponents, men and women that Rákosi rued not having murdered. How he knew his merciful ways would come back to haunt him!

Initially, the returning prisoners had, on pain of re-arrest, remained silent about what they had witnessed and endured in the prison camps. But as the number of the released grew, many did begin to talk, and the public learned of the beatings, tortures and murders of law-abiding citizens: patriots who had been falsely imprisoned as saboteurs, spies and traitors.

The defiance against Rákosi began with the nation's writers, which again left him facing a conundrum. For years the communist regime had praised and celebrated writers who had been loyal to the party, so when those very writers began to criticise Rákosi, it was impossible for the government to claim their writings were suddenly nonsense. Books, pamphlets and newspapers were still the most popular media through which political opinion was spread, and the illustrious names of famous writers condemning Rákosi simply fuelled wider readership.

Because the writers were neither arrested nor even condemned, soon the defiance spread to other aspects of daily life. Hungarians, having had many masters over history, had long learned the art of civil disobedience, and under Soviet rule it became an act of patriotic duty to somehow thwart or hinder the authorities in any small way – bending the rules and wearing the system down. Countless different and ingenious ways were found to hinder the system: telephone wires were cut, police called to false alarms, parts omitted from machinery in factories, papers in government offices wrongly filed, wrong goods loaded on to the wrong wagons, anti-Soviet graffiti left unremoved a little longer than usual.

Sabotage was still, however, a deadly game to play: the ÁVO were still present and feared, and everyone knew that if Khrushchev gave the word, then Rákosi would resume the arrests and hangings without hesitation. But it was a risk many Hungarians believed was worth taking, and the defiance slowly grew.

Two months later, it was Khrushchev himself who inadvertently gave Rákosi's opponents the sword with which to strike. In April 1956, the Soviet leader made a visit to Yugoslavia to meet with the country's dictator, Josip Tito. Tito had fallen foul of Stalin by daring to form his own brand of communism, independent of rule from Moscow. Khrushchev wanted to rekindle economic ties with Yugoslavia to make use of the country's vast resources, and so made peace with Tito with a speech that admitted that the Yugoslav leader had been innocent of all the accusations that had been levelled against him by Stalin.

It was a speech that was printed in full in the next day's Hungarian press, begging the question: if Tito was innocent, what of all the people Rákosi had executed for 'Titoism'? What of the László Rajk case, where the former interior minister and his associates were hanged on evidence that they were 'Titoists'? Surely it must have all been an entire pack of lies.

Rákosi scrambled to make amends. He had released Rajk's wife Julia (sentenced to six years at the time of her husband's execution) from prison, as well as reuniting her with her infant son László junior, who had spent the duration of his mother's imprisonment in a state orphanage under a different name.

Julia Rajk, herself a former high-ranking Communist Party member, repaid Rákosi by giving a speech immediately after her release to a crowd of 1,500 people:

> I stand before you deeply moved after five years of prison and humiliation. Let me tell you this: so far as prisons are concerned, Horthy's jails were far better, even for communists, that Rákosi's prisons. Not only was my husband killed, but my little baby was torn from me. For years I received no letters and no information about the fate of my little son. These criminals have not only murdered László Rajk. They have trampled underfoot all sentiment and honesty in this country. Murderers should not be criticised. They should be punished. I shall never rest until those who have ruined this country, corrupted the party, destroyed thousands and driven millions into despair receive their punishment. Comrades, help me in this struggle![132]

Buoyed by the fact that Julia Rajk was still walking free (Rákosi did not have the nerve to arrest her), the next day a crowd of 6,000 crammed into a Pest meeting hall for a debate on 'press freedom'. A series of Hungary's most prominent writers took to the stage, and one speaker after the other condemned the Rákosi regime. The meeting lasted an astonishing nine hours: no one left – people had waited 11 years for this moment and revelled in the opportunity to speak their mind.

Ideally those present would have liked to have no communist government at all, and knew that ridding Hungary of the Soviets would be a slow and difficult process; but where better to start than to rid themselves of Rákosi? And therefore who better to support than Rákosi's rival, Imre Nagy – who, although a communist, did at least have Hungary's best interests at heart. 'Long live Imre Nagy!

Long live Imre Nagy!' cheered the crowd as the meeting finally drew to a close.

In the following days, Rákosi plotted Nagy's arrest. He was in full flow at a meeting of the Hungarian politburo, condemning Nagy as a traitor, when in burst Khrushchev's deputy, Anastas Mikoyan. 'You want to arrest Imre Nagy? A good communist for whom the people cheer?' Mikoyan had been despatched by Khrushchev to sack Rákosi, preferably in front of the entire politburo for maximum humiliation. Informed that he was no longer leader, the paling Rákosi could do nothing but mumble a few words about mistakes and forces beyond his control. The very next morning, he was flown straight to the Soviet Union, never to return to Hungary.

To prevent Hungarians dancing in the streets, Khrushchev immediately replaced Rákosi with an equally hard-line Stalinist: Ernő Gerő, a skeletal, severe-faced man with stomach ulcers that gave him both halitosis and a short temper. It was an appointment Hungarians greeted with disappointment – all the Soviets had done was swap a fat, smelly Stalinist for a thin, smelly Stalinist! But at least it was a start ...

In the aftermath of Rákosi's sudden departure, those comrades who were considered loyal to him, or at least had enjoyed some protection under him, suddenly found themselves highly vulnerable. One such was Comrade Sebes.

While Sebes's wife and family loved him dearly, and ordinary people who met him were always pleasantly surprised by his having time for them, Sebes was gruff and dismissive with those he held in low regard. Unfortunately for Sebes, two such men, who had long borne the brunt of his high-handed approach, were now the two who held his future in their hands: sports minister Gyula Hegyi and FA president Sándor Barcs.

Hegyi, in particular, had long dreamed of his old foe Sebes's downfall, and seized the opportunity to strike the moment Sebes's Hungary hit a poor run of form. After returning from their defeat to Turkey, Sebes's team struggled to a draw against Yugoslavia and then lost 4–2 at home to Czechoslovakia. 'Some people acted like it was the end of the world,' said Sebes of Hegyi's reaction to the defeat, which was Hungary's first at home in 13 years and the first ever at the Népstadion.

Hegyi had demanded an explanation for the poor run of form, but did not offer Sebes the dignity of a personal meeting; instead he had one of his underlings, one Imre Terényi, confront Sebes with accusations that he was opposing 'the development of sport and the ethical and political education of the youth'. Sebes wasn't sure what he resented most: being accused of such nonsense or having it said to him by a non-footballing bureaucrat.

Hegyi was all for sacking Sebes immediately, but Barcs warned against such rashness. Sebes was (and remains) by far the most successful coach in the history of the Hungarian national team, and to sack him because of one dip in form may have resulted in a backlash against themselves. Therefore the two agreed to give Sebes another month in charge, to see how Hungary fared in upcoming matches against Belgium and Portugal.

Alas, against the Belgians in Brussels, Hungary lost 5–4. The referee, Leo Horn, who had refereed Hungary's historic win over England at Wembley, couldn't help but notice that 'the Hungarian team then and now are not comparable'. Six days later against Portugal in Lisbon, Hungary could only draw 2–2.

Sebes took his sacking with dignity and his head held high, as well he might – his record (69 matches, won 50, drew 12, lost 7, 278 goals for and 98 against) is unlikely ever to be bettered. It was more of a humiliation than a surprise. Since the demise of Rákosi he had sensed Hegyi's readying to pounce, but had half-hoped that he would remain in charge until at least the 1958 World Cup.

He was, though, still respected enough to remain vice-president of Hungary's Olympic Committee as well as the nation's FIFA representative. They were roles , however, that Sebes carried out only through a sense of duty – they never remotely compared to the thrill and pride of being Hungary's national team coach. But Sebes's wife, Erzsebet, for one, was happy – at least they weren't going to get any more hate mail, nuisance phone calls … but then again neither was she going to have the president seeking her husband's opinion …

A week after Sebes was sacked, Márton Bukovi was appointed as his replacement, vindicating in Sebes's eyes his years of fear that his so-called 'assistant' was after his job. The truth, though, was that Bukovi, having seen the toll the job took on Sebes, had had to be convinced into taking it. He himself had his own recent health problems, quitting MTK in 1954 with nervous exhaustion, the cost of coaching a club run by the ÁVO. Bukovi spent a year recuperating before returning to football as coach of Dózsa, where he stayed for a season until being appointed as Sebes's replacement.

Mindful of his recent illness, Bukovi was reluctant to take the position, but relented on being allowed to have full control over the team, and being assured that Sebes would have no part in national team matters. Bukovi was his own man, with his own ideas. His first move was to dismiss Sebes's loyal assistants Gyula Mándi and Pál Titkos and replace them with his own coaching team. Similarly, for his first match in charge, a 4–1 win against Poland in Budapest, Bukovi dropped two of Sebes's most loyal servants, Mihály Lantos and Jenő Buzánszky (Buzánszky never playing for Hungary again), while recalling Ferenc Szusza for his first international match in four years.

For his next match, a 3–1 win over Yugoslavia, Bukovi recalled Károly Sándor and Gyula Grosics, having arranged for Grosics's ban from international football to be lifted. Grosics had actually returned to league football at the beginning of the year with Tatabányai Banyász after the club's president had approached Mátyás Rákosi (when the then leader visited the town) and asked for Grosics's ban to be lifted so that he could play for the town's club. Rákosi referred the matter to Gyula Hegyi, who, always looking to oppose Sebes, called Grosics into the Sports Ministry and told him that – whether he liked it or not – he was now a Tatabányai Banyász player. 'The happiest days of my life,' remembered Grosics.

Zoltán Czibor too was returned to the team by Bukovi, to fittingly score the vital goal in a 1–0 win over the Soviet Union in Moscow. 'We beat the communist bastards in their own yard!' sang Czibor while dancing a jig on a dressing room bench.

From Moscow, the team flew directly to Paris, where they beat France 2–1, before beating Austria 2–0 in Vienna on their way home. There was no time for rest, though: from Austria the team returned to Hungary and straight to the Olympic training facilities at Tata to prepare for a home match against Sweden the following week.

This time around, the players didn't mind being at Tata: one more week away from their families was a price worth paying to rekindle the love of the public. Under Bukovi, the future was looking bright. Five wins from five matches against quality opponents was better than anyone could have hoped for. Bukovi had strengthened the defence, returned Grosics, Czibor, Sándor and Szusza to the team, and enticed Bozsik and Puskás back to form. All agreed that the 'Golden Team' under Bukovi was more than capable of winning the 1958 World Cup. And then a revolution happened.

CHAPTER 18

Had Hungary won the 1954 World Cup there wouldn't have been a revolution.

Gusztáv Sebes[133]

ON THE evening of 22 October 1956, 5,000 students attended a meeting at Budapest's Technical University. Their question was simple: 'How to remove the Soviets from Hungary?'

It was immensely brave, foolish even, but then again, as they asked themselves: what other option was there?

Between them they drew up a manifesto, the main points of which were that: Soviet troops leave Hungarian soil; Imre Nagy replace Ernő Gerő as leader; those associated with the crimes of the Rákosi regime be immediately removed from government; a public inquiry be held into the crimes of Mihály Farkas; the statue of Stalin in central Pest be replaced with a monument to the martyrs of the Hungarian 1848 revolution; the Hungarian army revert to their traditional uniforms; trade and export deals that exploit Hungary cease; democratic elections are restored.

The students also declared a solidarity with the workers and students of Poland, where similar anti-Soviet protests had broken out in the summer. For this reason, it was agreed that the next day they would march to the statue in Buda of General Josef Bem, a Polish general who had fought and died on the side of the Hungarians in their 1848 revolution against Austrian rule.

President Ernő Gerő made moves to ban the march, but was convinced otherwise by the Budapest police chief, Sándor Kopácsi, who saw the consequences of trying to stop 5,000 people from marching. Kopácsi promised Gerő that the march leaders would be monitored for later arrest.

At three o'clock the following afternoon the students set off, yelling slogans such as 'Friendship with Poland!' and 'Poland shows the way!' The sight of such a large procession encouraged 'ordinary people' to join in, and as the numbers swelled, so did the marchers' courage, and the chants began to take on a more rebellious tone – 'Throw Gerő in the Danube!' and 'Russians go home!'

Some residents along the route dusted off their Hungarian flags and hung them from their windows and balconies – one, in particular, cutting out the hated communist 'hammer-and-sickle' emblem, leaving a Hungarian flag with a hole in the centre. This simple act would become the symbol of the revolution.

By the time the march reached Bem Square two hours later, it had mushroomed to an astonishing 25,000 people. But the square provided nothing that the marchers could focus their ire upon – so when cries of 'To the Parliament!' went up, the entire crowd headed back across the Danube for the 2km walk to the heart of the government.

News of the protest whipped throughout Budapest, and as dusk fell a quarter of a million people had descended upon the streets around the Parliament Building. Chants for Imre Nagy to make a speech began.

Instead, however, the crowd received the wisdom of Ernő Gerő. Sneering and snarling like the Stalinist dinosaur he was, Gerő berated the demonstrators as 'unpatriotic' and 'a mere mob looking to cause trouble'. One young reporter present, Mátyás Sárközi, noted: 'The mood changed as soon as Gerő had finished. You could feel it at once. That speech was the fuse that lit the revolution.'[134]

Around 6,000 of the crowd broke off and headed for the nearby Hungarian Radio building. Whether the crowd intended to protest outside what was the primary broadcaster of Soviet propaganda or to take control of the transmitters, no one is sure. But what is sure is that once they arrived, the sight of the armed ÁVO guards who protected the building day and night provoked the crowd into throwing bricks and cobblestones at the windows, to which the ÁVO inside replied with live gunfire, killing two students.

A nearby military unit arrived under orders to clear the crowd, but, vastly outnumbered, the soldiers were easily convinced by the demonstrators to hand over their weapons – in fact they willingly did so. The demonstrators became insurgents. And the revolution truly began.

By the break of dawn on 24 October, Soviet tanks, stationed in Budapest, had taken to the streets to try to quell the unrest. The mighty Soviet army was expecting to crush the ungrateful Hungarians with ease, but immediately found that it was dealing with a determined and highly inventive enemy that was also unexpectedly heavily armed – during the night, Budapest's police chief, Sándor Kopácsi, had changed sides to the rebels, taking almost his entire police force with him and opening up police weapon stores for the rebels. A day later, the vast majority of the Hungarian military would follow suit, ignoring an order to impose martial law and siding with the rebels instead.

The most senior military leader, Colonel Pál Maléter, would come to be considered, by the Soviets at least, as the leader of the rebels; but, in truth, there was no defined leader. The Hungarian freedom fighters were a mixture of everyday folk: workers, housewives, students and in some cases children, all with one common aim.

Their spontaneous street-fighting tactics became a textbook on how to fight an inner-city guerrilla war against a superior foe. To compensate for being outgunned, the rebels devised countless inventive ways to stop the Russian tanks, which had been sent ahead to clear the way for their infantry behind. It was quickly discovered that the easiest way to thwart a tank was by placing in its path objects that looked like anti-tank mines, such as dustbin lids or dinner plates. When the tanks stopped, they were bombarded with petrol bombs, and as the crews clambered out of their burning vehicles, they were set upon with gunfire and stones. The captured tanks then made excellent barricades.

The Soviets felt humiliated at their tanks being repelled by what essentially was a rag-tag group of armed civilians; and while Khrushchev knew that he could crush the rebellion by sending more troops, it was a path that he was reluctant to go down for fear of the certain massacre of Hungarian civilians causing harm to Russia's newly repaired, post-Stalin international status.

Therefore Khrushchev sought a political solution, sacking Gerő and replacing him with János Kádár, who, you may remember, was the leader of the Hungarian communists during the Second World War. Kádár had been imprisoned by Rákosi in 1951 on treason charges, and released by Imre Nagy in 1954, giving him a minuscule amount of kudos with the rebels, even if he was still a communist.

But the news that Gerő had been sacked was not broadcast in time to prevent a crowd of 5,000 people marching upon Parliament to demand his dismissal. As the crowd gathered in front of the Parliament Building, it was fired upon by the combined forces of Soviet troops and ÁVO officers, under orders to liquidate the protest. In total, 75 people were killed and 282 wounded. Hungarians were convinced (and many remain so) that the ÁVO purposely herded the demonstrators into the square so that they could be gunned down. The massacre[135] turned the mood of the insurgents from rebellious to murderous. Revenge was in the air.

The tension across Hungary was so palpable that even the national team, isolated deep in the countryside, knew there was something amiss. But their only line of communication with the events unfolding in Budapest was the radio. Gyula Grosics was asked by his team-mates to locate on his wireless set Radio Free Europe, a banned station that was broadcast from Vienna by Hungarians. It was via Radio Free Europe that the team learned that their match against Sweden was to be cancelled.

Coach Bukovi wanted the players to remain at Tata to see how things panned out, but not one wanted to do so. All were desperate to check upon their families. The next day, 25 October, strings were pulled, and the players returned to Budapest on a specially chartered train. However, because of the barricades that the insurgents had thrown up across the city centre, the players had to disembark at a distant suburban station – Kelenföld – and make their way home on foot. With gunshots ringing out in the not-too-far distance, the players' first strides were tentative. The more famous among them were fearful of revenge attacks for having done very well out of the communist regime, but the fears evaporated as people, surprised to see the Golden Team walking down the road, cheered and clapped. People were especially pleased to see Puskás, whom they heard had been killed in the fighting.[136] 'Not yet, comrades!' replied Öcsi.

Puskás's bravado was just that. All but one of the players adhered to the order to go straight home and remain indoors. The one was Zoltán Czibor, who immediately involved himself in the fighting, finding himself a gun and partaking in one of the most bitter and prolonged battles of the revolution, on Buda's Széna Square, close to his home.

The other Golden Team member who had never hidden his dislike of Soviet rule, Gyula Grosics, also played his part. From the window of his Buda apartment overlooking Gellért Hill, Grosics watched a gun battle in which rebels tried to take a heavily defended Soviet arms store. As darkness fell and a stand-off ensued, Grosics passed word down to the rebels that they could store their guns in his building's cellar, where he would look after them. That night and for the next four successive nights, a fretting Grosics, never a man with the steadiest of nerves, took responsibility for a pile of guns and hand grenades. 'That was my small part,' Grosics said years later of his actions that, if they had been discovered during the repercussions that followed, could easily have had him sentenced to death.

Czibor and Grosics were the exceptions, but this is not to say that the rest of the team did not have empathy with the revolution. Each was torn by the dilemma over whether or not to become involved. Lines had been drawn: you were either for the revolution or against it. Not getting involved was considered as an act of compliance, but at the same time the players were essentially soldiers and policemen, under orders to remain at home.

Damned if they did, and damned if they didn't.

On 28 October, five days after the revolution had begun, a ceasefire between the two sides was agreed. The Soviets requested 36 hours to retreat and did so, running the gauntlet of sniper fire, forcing them to leave their dead in the streets. Once the Soviet army had wholly departed Budapest, its citizens began celebrating the sweet taste of freedom: dancing, singing, releasing political prisoners, hunting down and lynching[137] ÁVO officers and demolishing Soviet statues ….

> **Lieutenant Kiss** – Comrade Colonel, people are pulling down the statue of Stalin in the City Park. Please send us orders immediately!
>
> **Colonel Kopácsi** – Okay Comrade Lieutenant, tell me how many people are there?
>
> **Lieutenant Kiss** – About 100,000. They are in the park and all over the square.

Colonel Kopácsi – And how many men have you got?

Lieutenant Kiss – Eh … 25..

Colonel Kopácsi – Are you really willing to sacrifice your life to save a statue of Stalin? Let them get on with it.[138]

A new democratic coalition government was formed, led by Imre Nagy and involving the Social Democrat former president Zoltán Tildy. The Budapest police chief, Sándor Kopácsi, set up a national guard; Colonel Pál Maléter took charge of the army; and the foreign minister, Zoltán Vas, halted food exports to the Soviet Union.

However, the euphoria was tainted by the nagging fear that the Soviets were sure to be planning to return with even greater manpower and an eye for revenge. The insurgents knew that their weapon stockpiles were minute compared with those of the Red Army, so hope was pinned upon an American military intervention, or at least the United States government placing pressure on Moscow.

The insurgents believed that the Americans were prepared to help because the CIA had actively encouraged the revolution by funding Radio Free Europe and distributing millions of leaflets throughout Hungary with messages such as 'The regime is weaker than you think!'

What the Hungarians did not know or even anticipate was that the American president, Dwight D. Eisenhower, had decided from the very beginning that the United States would not get involved in any way in assisting the revolution. Eisenhower was close to a general election and did not want to upset the American electorate by going to war with the Soviet Union over a former ally of Nazi Germany. Nor did Eisenhower wish to recognise the Moscow-trained communist Imre Nagy as Hungary's leader. In all, the best the Americans offered were a few words of comfort and the advice that Hungary should take its problem to the United Nations.

And indeed, as many an insurgent believed, Moscow was very much using the ceasefire to prepare its armies for revenge. Initially the Kremlin had been divided as to how to handle the revolution: the reformists wanted a political solution, whereas the hard-liners urged an instant crushing. To begin with, the reformists had held sway until similar protests began to spring up across the Soviet bloc. Fearing that their hesitancy was being seen as a weakness, the Soviets decided to damn international opinion and, for once and for all, crush the Hungarian revolution. 'It will take me three days,' the Soviet army's commander told Khrushchev.

On 1 November, the Red Army returned to Budapest with a vengeance. The full might of its military swept across Hungary from all directions, reaching Budapest within days. As the capital's citizens bunkered down in their basements and the freedom fighters again took to arms, Imre Nagy appealed to the United Nations for help, only to be informed that the Suez canal crisis[139] in Egypt took precedence. Matters worsened when Nagy's military chief, Colonel Pál Maléter, was lured by the Soviet command to the Russian embassy for supposed ceasefire talks, but was instead placed under arrest – essentially decapitating Hungary's military command in one underhand swoop.

With no leadership, and outgunned, the Hungarian defences swiftly crumbled. The isolated small pockets of resistance that remained were easily and quickly overwhelmed by the Soviet infantry. Captured freedom fighters were executed on the spot.

Imre Nagy and three of his ministers took sanctuary[140] in the Yugoslav embassy, where they remained for three weeks, only leaving after being given assurances from the politburo in Moscow that they would be unharmed. On stepping out from the embassy, the four were immediately seized by the Russian secret police and taken to Romania, where, for the next 18 months, they were held under armed house arrest, their families not knowing if they were alive or dead.

In total, 2,600 Hungarians were killed in the revolution. And in the aftermath, a further 22,000 were arrested and sentenced to prison terms ranging from a few weeks to life; 330 of the arrested were given death sentences and hanged. The revolution's failure and the bloody reprisals caused a mass exodus[141] in the weeks that followed. An estimated 180,000 Hungarians put their and their families' lives at risk to flee across the border into Austria. The majority of them were young and educated – the impact of this would be felt for decades after. Once in Austria, they were offered a safe and warm welcome. In fact, Hungarian refugees were welcomed the Western world over: Canada, the United States, Australia, New Zealand, Sweden, South Africa,

France, Spain and Great Britain all willingly took their fair share of refugees – much to their benefit, much to Hungary's loss.

On the same day that the Soviet army re-entered Budapest, Honvéd left Hungary for Vienna. Their plan was to remain in the Austrian capital for three weeks before continuing on to Spain to play a European Cup second-round match (having had a bye in the first round) against Athletic Bilbao on 22 November.

The match had initially been scheduled to take place at the Népstadion on 7 November, but could not go ahead because of the ban on public gatherings in the city; in any case, UEFA had forbidden the Spanish champions from travelling to Budapest. Sportingly, Bilbao agreed to reverse the two legs, playing the first in Spain and the second in Budapest once the situation had calmed. It was an admirable gesture from the Basque club, seeing as they were under no obligation to swap dates and could have taken a bye through to the quarter-finals. Furthermore, if Honvéd had not fulfilled their obligation to play the two ties, they would have faced a two-year ban from the competition.

In charge of the Honvéd party in Vienna, and indeed the man responsible for the club's timely departure from Hungary, was the club's general manager, Emil Östreicher. The 41-year-old Östreicher was to play a significant role in the future of Puskás and co. He was not a military man, rather a self-enterprising businessman who Honvéd had employed to look after the club's everyday running. He had held a similar position at Vasas, while at the same time owning a bar in Pest that become a favourite haunt of footballers, and it was there that he had struck up a close friendship with József Bozsik; this was also how he had become employed at Honvéd.

Once in Austria, Östreicher openly admitted that he had no intention of returning to Hungary and that in his eyes Honvéd was a commodity, from which they could all do very well. Still with three weeks to kill before the match in Bilbao, Östreicher arranged for Honvéd to undertake a lucrative five-match tour of West Germany, Belgium and France, taking along as a coaching assistant an old acquaintance – one Béla Guttmann.

Since leaving Hungary in 1949, Guttmann had coached in the first divisions of Italy and Argentina[142], and with APOEL in Cyprus, arguing with chairmen and players all the way. In 1953, he was appointed coach of the mighty AC Milan, whose technical director, one Antonio Busini, had been impressed by Guttmann's brief, fiery but altogether successful spell at Padova – Guttmann's first club in Italy and Busini's home-town club.

In typical Guttmann style, he upped the Milan players' training, disregarded their ultra-defensive tactics and persuaded the club directors to part with a world record fee to sign the Uruguayan star Juan Schiaffino. In his first season, Guttmann reached a respectable third in Serie A, but that was as good as it got. Guttmann's handing-out of fines for tardiness, and his exhaustive and inordinate training regime, soon lost him the dressing room.

Milan were top of the league in February 1955 when they sacked Guttmann. 'Misunderstandings between Guttmann and the players have been going on for weeks,' was the statement issued by the club. Guttmann famously replied, 'I have been fired even though I am neither a criminal nor a homosexual.'[143]

Contrary to these parting words Guttmann was none too concerned by the sacking. Milan paid him off handsomely, and there was no shortage of other clubs wanting his services. Nor was he in a rush to return to work, thus with money in his pocket he decided to see the football season out, relax and enjoy an Italian summer – and then in the April of 1955 a moment of madness changed everything.

Guttmann didn't have a driving licence, but this did not stop him taking the wheel of a friend's sports car for a spin around Milan's city centre. The two were zooming along merrily when suddenly Guttmann lost control, mounted the pavement and ploughed into two pedestrians, killing one instantly and placing the other in a serious condition in hospital.

The perception of Béla Guttmann as a shrewd, grandfatherly figure, strict but essentially kind, was countered by the hard cold streak that saw him walk out on clubs and turn his back on people in an instant. It was the same unpleasant side to his character that saw him heartlessly run away from the scene of the crash leaving' the two young students lying by the roadside.

Guttmann's choice of friends at times also left a lot to be desired. His passenger in the car was a fellow Hungarian Jew by the name of

Desző Solti, a dubious character probably best described as living on the margins of the law.[144] Solti was also an Auschwitz survivor, maybe the reason why he and Guttmann (who had witnessed his share of atrocities during the war) were cold-hearted enough to abandon the car at the scene and scurry away to concoct a story which placed their self-preservation paramount by placing a cloud of confusion over the whole sorry episode.

Once they'd had time to gather their thoughts, the two conspired to say that Solti was driving, a 'favour' for which Guttmann agreed to pay any fines and compensation. Not that Solti handed himself into the police. It took the Italian authorities a week to track him down (to the Austrian Alps), and once under arrest Solti stuck to his story for which he was charged with manslaughter and released on bail. However, witnesses of the crash were adamant that Guttmann had been the driver, so the police arrested and charged him, also with manslaughter, similarly releasing him on bail.

While the wheels of Italian justice slowly turned, Guttmann headed for Vienna, the one place he considered home. He and his wife were granted Austrian citizenship, but only after a process that required them to give up their Hungarian citizenship – Guttmann thought he had already done so. He spent the next year fretting about the criminal investigation, the welfare of his remaining family in the revolution-torn Budapest and the lack of money in his pocket. Guttmann was a man with a gambling habit and never took to poverty well. Therefore, on learning that the Honvéd team were staying in a Vienna hotel, Guttmann 'dropped by' to catch up on old times – like the time when Puskás forced him out of Kispest. Guttmann, though, could not afford to hold a grudge, so was pleased when Puskás, who rarely held one, greeted him warmly with a smile and a hug.

Emil Östreicher too was pleased to see Guttmann. The pair knew each other from the war, when they'd served alongside each other in a Jewish slave battalion.[145] Östreicher immediately invited Guttmann to join Honvéd on a five-match tour; Guttmann, who one suspects already had his bags packed, did not need to be asked twice.

It is not known what Honvéd coach Jenő Kalmár made of Guttmann's inclusion, though what is known is that Kalmár had made up his mind not to return to Hungary, so therefore was probably none too perturbed. Kalmár's wife was Austrian, and they had long made plans to live in the West, where Kalmár hoped that his Honvéd credentials would catch the eye of a top European club. He wasn't the only one … so did Guttmann.

It was, however, not to be a happy tour party. Despite the warm welcomes and ever-present contingent of Hungarian support, draping visiting stadiums with Hungarian flags with a hole symbolically cut in the middle, the worry about their families and the stream of bad news coming from Hungary had the players at each other's throats; fist fights were a regular occurrence as friendships that had blossomed in the good times failed miserably to endure the bad.

However, by the time Honvéd reached Spain, they were fit and rich in the pocket – though in no shape mentally to face the Spanish champions at home in front of their partisan Basque support in a full-on competitive match. Wearing black armbands seemed to sum up the Honvéd team's sombre mood, and they were fortunate to scrape two late goals to escape with a 3–2 defeat.

To many an observer, it appeared that Honvéd hadn't tried, that the match had been a mere duty to perform, and that their minds were on other matters – which, of course, they were …

The day before the match, the team had been visited at their hotel by László Kubala. The Barcelona star was a welcome sight, with his good humour and infectious optimism lifting the Honvéd players' spirits. But Kubala's visit was not to catch up with old friends – he had been despatched by Barça chiefs to sound out the Honvéd stars to see whether any of them would be interested in joining the club.

Over the years, Honvéd's star players had become used to being tapped up by foreign clubs, but because most deals were done under the table and instigated by shady strangers using translators, the players always felt at a disadvantage and unsure as to whether the offers were genuine or not. The popular 'Kuksi', though, was one of their own: a straight-talking, rough-and-ready Budapest boy who spoke directly to them in their own language – football as well as working-class Hungarian. Kubala was also living proof that Hungarian footballers could not just survive outside of Hungary but indeed thrive.

He enlightened the Honvéd players and coaching staff as to what they could expect from life abroad – a ban, homesickness, guilt, worry, money, freedom, a higher standard of living and a better future for their families. But, as the players pointed out, their families were all still in Hungary.

Honvéd's return tie against Athletic Bilbao was scheduled to be played in Budapest a month later on 20 December; but, with the United Nations still classing Budapest as a war zone, UEFA was forced to hold the match in a neutral venue – with the Belgian capital, Brussels, being the chosen city.

For Emil Östreicher, this was fantastic news. A whole month for Honvéd to continue touring! And, as they were already in Spain, Östreicher went all out to organise three matches, primarily to place the Honvéd players on display, intending to earn a hefty commission from any deal that might result from it.

The first match was against a combined Atlético and Real Madrid side, held in a packed Bernabéu Stadium (holding a minute's silence for the dead of the Hungarian revolution). Only an injury to their goalkeeper, Lajos Faragó, caused Honvéd to concede two late goals and settle for a 5–5 draw.

For Honvéd's next match, against Barcelona, Faragó's understudy, Ágoston Garamvölgyi, was thought to be too inexperienced to face the might of Barça at the Nou Camp, so Emil Östreicher contacted Gyula Grosics in Hungary and asked him to come to Spain immediately.

This, of course, was no simple matter, as pointed out by Grosics himself. Besides being forbidden from leaving Hungary, Grosics didn't want to leave his wife and two daughters behind. 'No problem – I'll sort it,' replied Östreicher. 'Bring them with you, but leave them in Vienna.' The next morning, a car arrived at Grosics's apartment and took him and his family to 5km from the Austrian border, from where they walked the rest of the way (the policeman chauffeur who drove the car also escaped).

From Vienna, Grosics caught a flight to Barcelona, making it to the Nou Camp just in time for kick-off, entering the Honvéd changing room to a round of smiles and back slaps, along with a few groans. 'It was as if I had never been away.' With Grosics back in goal, Honvéd beat the Kubala-led Barcelona 4–3, but in their next game against Sevilla FC, they imploded, bickering, to a 6–2 defeat, the heaviest loss in the club's five-year history.

From Spain, Honvéd headed to Italy for a match against AC Milan at the San Siro. Some of the team questioned the wisdom of another full-on match, but Östreicher merely replied that Honvéd had to make the most of being in demand. The good times wouldn't last forever. In truth, though, Östreicher had an ulterior motive for going to Italy: during Honvéd's match against Atlético/Real Madrid, he wangled it so that he was sitting next to the Real president, Santiago Bernabéu, using the opportunity to talk himself (both men spoke English) into a job at the club. Bernabéu, impressed by Östreicher's credentials as Honvéd's 'president', offered him a trial as a scout, with the mission to report on AC Milan.

Honvéd's arrival in Italy coincided with the much-welcomed news that some of their wives and children had arrived safely in Vienna and would be making their way down to Italy at the first opportunity.

For the wives, crossing the border into Austria had been the most hazardous of journeys. Puskás's wife, Erzsi, had had to pay people smugglers, then, with her four-year-old daughter in her arms, trudge across miles of open fields in the dark of a harsh December night in order to cross into Austria. A pregnant Alíz Kocsis and her infant daughter trudged the same path days later. Írisz Czibor was turned away twice at the border before her husband finally became resigned to what was required of him and paid a hefty bribe to the smugglers to ease her and their three children's way into the West. Not all of the wives left Hungary, though: József Bozsik's wife, for example, refused to leave her elderly parents.

The wives' arrival and a meeting with the Pope at the Vatican (neither was reported in Hungary) calmed the players considerably, and this was reflected in their play, Puskás scoring both goals in a 2–1 win over AC Milan.

Having had the opportunity to speak with their wives privately and at length for the first time in weeks, the Honvéd players now had a clearer picture of the dire situation in Hungary that faced them – begging an answer to the question: should they return?

Did they want to return to a life behind the Iron Curtain? A life that, certainly in the short term, would – in the wake of the failed revolution – be harsher than it had been in recent years. In short, the players did not know. The original plan was for them to return to Hungary straight after the Athletic Bilbao match in Brussels, but with their families safe in Milan, plus the amount of strife it had taken to get them there, it was decided to stay put in Italy and try to enjoy Christmas, and thereafter see what the future might bring ...

CHAPTER 19

I didn't leave Hungary,
I just didn't come back.

Ferenc Puskás

JUST as the Honvéd squad and families were settling into their Milan hotel preparing for Christmas (and the trip up to Belgium to play Athletic Bilbao on 20 December), two pieces of stunning news reached them on the émigré grapevine. The first was from Hungary, regarding the Hungarian Olympic squad, who had travelled to Melbourne for the summer Games a month earlier. Hungary had done well at the event, finishing fourth in the overall table – an over-achievement considering that the Hungarian authorities had decided not to send a host of the nation's best athletes, fearing that they were liable to defect (the very reason Hungary did not send a football team despite them being the defending champions). It was a fear that proved to be justified when, at the tournament's end, 48 of Hungary's 60-strong squad did indeed fail to return to Hungary.

The second – perhaps more astonishing to the players – was the news of the similar defection of the *entire* Hungarian under-21 football squad while in Switzerland.

The under-21 squad of 16 had been touring England when the revolution began. On learning of the events in Budapest, they cut short the tour and decided to head home. On the way back, they had to stop in Vienna for two days to wait for the return of the very same bus which had carried the Olympic squad to Prague airport. It was while waiting in Vienna, and talking to their fleeing countrymen, that the youngsters began to have misgivings about going home.

The team's coach, Jenő Vincze, was approached by Karl Rappan, the highly respected former manager of the Swiss national team, and the inventor of the 'Swiss Bolt', better known as the 'Sweeper System'. Rappan convinced Vincze to take the young team on a tour of Switzerland to play four matches against Swiss first-division clubs. As it was, Vincze, a member of Hungary's 1938 World Cup Final team, was a man long dissatisfied with life in communist Hungary and had made up his mind not to return. Once the tour was over (the young Hungarians won all four games), Vincze took the manager's job at the Geneva-based club Servette, taking three members of the young Hungarian team with him. He then urged the rest of the team to follow suit, as they duly did. Another four went to Belgian club FC Liege, three to Eintracht Frankfurt in West Germany, two to clubs in Vienna, and one to England and Wolverhampton Wanderers, while another joined up with Honvéd when they were in Italy.

In desperation, the Hungarian FA sent out the fathers of those boys playing in Switzerland to 'talk some sense' into their offspring. The fathers were under the promise of promotions at work if they returned with their sons, and the unspoken threat of demotions if they did not. And yet, to a man, the fathers returned home alone. Each damned the consequences, telling their sons to remain abroad. Demotion held little fear for men who already laboured 14 hours a day for a pittance. At least now they had the knowledge that their sons were safe and doing well in life.

But, of course, everything was set against them in doing well. The softly-softly approach having failed, the Hungarian FA set out to make an example of the young players, and, by using the Soviet bloc's powerful influence at FIFA, had all 16 of them banned from all football for 18 months.

Their respective clubs immediately let them go. Stuck in limbo, the young players were at a loss. Four of them returned to Hungary, where, after serving the entirety of their bans, they resumed playing football but were never again trusted with selection for the national team. The rest, far from home and away from football, drifted out of the sport altogether.

The 18-month bans dished out to the defecting under-21 players gave the Honvéd team food for thought – maybe they would be better off not antagonising the FA and going home after all? But then an offer from Brazil changed everything.

The president of the Brazilian club Flamengo contacted Emil Östreicher offering Honvéd an enormous sum of $10,000 per game plus travelling expenses to undertake a ten-match, six-week tour of Brazil in the new year.

The offer was enormously tempting. Money, or rather the lack of it, had become a severe problem for the players. While they had earned money from their recent friendly matches across Europe, they had also collectively donated a substantial amount from every match fee to the Hungarian Red Cross. Also, keeping their wives and children in hotels, which charged Western prices, wasn't cheap.

Östreicher organised a vote, the result of which was to accept the offer. The next hurdle, however, was obtaining the relevant permission from the Hungarian FA – who immediately replied with a negative, telling the players to come home first, rest, practise, then go on the tour in the spring.

The players replied with a unanimous 'No!' They had once before been promised a tour of South America after the 1954 World Cup, but, in the wake of their failure to win the tournament, the money-spinner had been cancelled at the last minute – so how could the players trust the FA to keep their word now? The Hungarian FA could feel the players slipping away. The only way the association could see to prevent the tour was to have it made illegal in the eyes of FIFA, so that any Brazilian clubs who faced Honvéd would be liable to punishment from football's world governing body.

Re-entering the picture comes Comrade Sebes. Since his sacking as Hungary's national team coach, Sebes had been a man out in the cold. The sports minister, Gyula Hegyi, had prevented him from travelling to the Melbourne Olympics, while Hegyi himself went to Australia – where according to Sebes he 'sunned himself while I dealt with the more serious problems at home'. Once the Olympics were over, Sebes handed in his resignation as vice-president of the Olympic Committee. Hegyi, refusing to give him the dignity of a personal reply, had his driver deliver the confirmation back to Sebes.

Sebes, though, was still revered in football circles (outside of Hungary), and for this reason, he retained his position as Hungarian football's representative at FIFA. Sebes was therefore quickly despatched to Zurich to personally ask FIFA general secretary Kurt Gassmann to have the Honvéd tour of Brazil made illegal. Gassmann readily agreed, and at the same time inadvertently informed Sebes that the Hungarian FA had a new president – one Marcell Nagy. 'It was the first I knew about it,' grumbled Sebes, embarrassed at his obvious isolation from the real goings-on in Hungarian football.

Seeing as he was in Switzerland, Sebes went off on his own accord to find Jenő Vincze, to try to persuade the former under-21 coach to return home and face the music, hopefully with some players.

Vincze laughed in Sebes's face. He had zero intention of ever returning to Hungary, telling Sebes he felt that he was never treated fairly because he had never been a member of the Communist Party. It was an explanation which Sebes felt deserved no reply:

> A man who defends himself with that sort of talk, and in doing so takes an entire generation of our best young footballers away, didn't deserve dealing with a moment further.[146]

Sebes was no less judgemental when he arrived, unannounced, at the Honvéd team's hotel in Brussels. He'd been permitted to travel on to Belgium by Marcell Nagy in the hope that he was the one man with whom the players would reason. The reality, however, was that none of the players, bar Puskás, were happy to see him. Reluctantly, Sebes was awarded a meeting (at a separate hotel) with Honvéd president Endre Madarász and players' representative József Bozsik. Predictably, Sebes ordered the team to return home to help build a new socialist football – they would be permitted to tour South America in the spring.

Bozsik was polite but adamant in his refusal. The players had voted to go on the tour to Brazil, and no threats or bans would stop them. Sebes was dumbstruck – flat out of weaponry. Not that he'd carried any. He'd expected that his standing among the players meant they would instantly do as he bid. He left the meeting not knowing what made him sadder: that his beloved Bozsik had turned on him or that his words no longer carried any weight.

Only Puskás sensed this, or cared, and he later visited Sebes at his hotel to ask him, 'Why don't you come with us, Uncle Guszti?'

'You know I can't go, Öcsi,' Sebes replied sadly.

Sebes remained in Brussels to watch Honvéd's match against Athletic Bilbao. The first half ended level at 1–1; then, in the opening minutes of the second half, Honvéd goalkeeper Lajos Faragó suffered a kick to the head and was unable to continue. They had no replacement goalkeeper (Grosics was not officially a Honvéd player and therefore not eligible to play), so Zoltán Czibor went in goal after convincing his sceptical team-mates that goalkeeping was yet another talent of his.

The first shot he faced, Czibor headed straight to a Bilbao forward (1–2), and minutes later he was dispossessed while needlessly dribbling out of his goal (1–3).

From the stands, Sebes was convinced that Czibor was deliberately attempting to lose the match so that Honvéd would fall out of the European Cup and therefore be able to tour South America for a longer period. He raced down to the Honvéd bench to shout at Jenő Kalmár, 'Get Faragó back on!'

A groggy Faragó was hauled out of the ambulance preparing to take him to the local hospital and returned to the field. A semi-concussed goalkeeper being better than a crazy one, Honvéd regained their composure and drew level, with Kocsis scoring a late brace to make the final score 3–3, though ultimately Honvéd lost 6–5 on aggregate.

Immediately afterwards, Sebes confronted the players to tell them of his disgust. The players vehemently denied losing on purpose and took umbrage at Sebes, who had no authority in their dressing room, daring to accuse them of such nonsense.

But Sebes, who had seen Honvéd play possibly more than anyone else present, remained eternally convinced that he was right. He left for Hungary the next morning: 'I knew then that I would never again see those great players of the Golden Squad combined in one team.'[147]

His trip, though, was not in vain. Accompanying Sebes home were five young players, each concerned that touring Brazil would ruin their chances of ever playing for the Hungarian national team. More so, one of the five was the teenage forward Lajos Tichy,[148] Hungarian football's brightest talent and the one Honvéd player whom László Kubala had insisted that Barcelona go all out to sign.

The (slightly) reduced Honvéd squad returned to Italy to spend Christmas Day with their families, and to play Inter Milan at the San Siro on Boxing Day, a match they won 2–1. But while staying in Italy was pleasant, it was too far from Hungary, so the next day the entire party upped and left to make their base in Vienna.

The Honvéd team arrived in the Austrian capital at the same time as Vörös Lobogó, who had likewise just returned from their own vagabonding around Europe. Under the club's original name, 'MTK', they'd undertaken a 15-match, six-week tour of West Germany, Luxembourg, Belgium and England. In Vienna, the MTK players were facing the same dilemma as their Honvéd counterparts – should they go home or not? – but without the added enticement of a lucrative tour of Brazil. Östreicher seized on their hesitation, inviting their three star players, Mihály Lantos, Károly Sándor and Nándor Hidegkuti, to join the tour. All but Hidegkuti accepted – he was his family's sole breadwinner and didn't want to risk a ban. A day later, Ferenc Szusza, who had been touring with Újpest in Yugoslavia, also arrived in Vienna, having accepted a similar invite from Östreicher – the bigger the names, the bigger the crowds.

After a 36-hour train ride from Budapest to London and then a 28-hour flight to Rio de Janeiro, Honvéd landed in Brazil. There was apprehension among the players that the Brazilians would seek revenge for Hungary's beating of Brazil in the filthy-tempered 1954 World Cup quarter-final – the 'Battle of Berne'. But, the moment they stepped off the plane, their fears were proved instantly unfounded. All the Brazilians wanted was to see the legendary Hungarians in action. The sunny weather and warm welcome eased the tension in the squad, and while there remained the concern for their families back home, the money earned by the tour went some way to alleviating those worries. Honvéd played all ten of their scheduled matches, the Brazilian clubs simply ignoring FIFA's ruling that the tour was illegal, calculating that the gate money generated by playing against one of Europe's very best teams would more than cover any imposed fine. It was only when FIFA upped the ante and vowed to ban from international competitions any future Brazilian clubs who played Honvéd, that the tour came to a temporary halt. Temporary, that is, until someone had the idea to play their last two games in Venezuela, a country that was not a member of FIFA.

As expected, offers abounded for the Honvéd players to remain in South America. It was rumoured that one Colombian millionaire businessman was willing to buy the entire team and have them play in the Colombian league, while Gyula Grosics even went so far as to sign a contract with Flamengo, telling the club he would return later with his wife and children (he did not). But ultimately South America was just too distant from the lives the players knew, although one of the party did remain in Brazil – the perennial wanderer Béla Guttmann.

The first member of the Honvéd team returning to Vienna to make it evident that he had no intention of returning to Hungary was the coach, Jenő Kalmár. Met by his Austrian wife at Vienna airport, Kalmár disappeared without so much as a goodbye. He would never return to Hungary.

Zoltán Czibor was equally quick to follow. His active role in the fighting had made his returning home without facing some punishment a virtual impossibility. From Vienna airport, Czibor headed straight for Italy, where, before Honvéd's tour of Brazil, he had secretly signed a one-year contract with AS Roma. Czibor would not return to Hungary for another 30 years.

> I didn't play football for myself but for the Hungarian public, the Hungarian race. That our flag should be raised higher than the next, but with respect to the second and third places. I'm like this. Not for myself, but for my family – for my homeland. I always desired that whenever we played a match abroad, they play the real Hungarian national anthem – because in communist Hungary they wouldn't play it because it goes 'God save the Hungarians'. Those barbarians and sons of whores didn't want to know it, and they did everything they could so that we didn't know our motherland, our flag, our anthem. At the time I said exactly this, and that is why I had to leave.[149]

The rest of the team made for a city-centre hotel, where they were soon caught up by Marcell Nagy. The FA president informed them that they were each banned for three months (Puskás as captain for one year) from all participation in football, and that they had a minimum of 48 hours to return to Hungary or face an extra ban of at least 18 months.

Eleven chose to return to Hungary immediately, the most prominent of whom was József Bozsik. With his wife and children still in Hungary, Bozsik had never made a secret of the fact that he would return home whatever the cost, though Puskás remembered his childhood friend returning 'without much enthusiasm'. The two would not see other again for another five years, and never again on Hungarian soil.

For his part, Puskás seriously contemplated returning with Bozsik but resisted, feeling that he had been dealt an injustice in being handed a one-year ban compared with his team-mates' three-month bans. Initially, Puskás believed that he was singled out for harsher punishment because he was the club captain – but it wasn't the case. Puskás was given an extended ban because the Sports Ministry had learned from the returning players that he had been the most instrumental in persuading players to go to Brazil. Puskás sent word to the Sports Ministry that he would consider returning to Hungary if his ban was reduced to three months.

The Ministry's reply was a resounding and swift negative, and they were equally quick in taking a dim view of being held to ransom by an overindulged and ungrateful footballer and his manager:

> We have had enough of the issues concerning Puskás and Östreicher. More than enough of their every-day changing developments. But it won't hurt for us to once and for all nail our opinion to the mast. In Hungary, lots of people have good reason to complain about the past. The leading footballers, including Puskás and Czibor, are not among them. It is well known that a blind eye was turned to their behaviour and actions for a very long time. These football kings earned more money and travelled abroad more times than anyone else in the country.
>
> It seemed at times that the world rotated around them. It will be a surprise if these ungrateful champions of ours are paying attention to the damage caused to the nation's sport by their actions, actions which have nothing to do with sport and everything to do with greed.[150]
>
> *Népszabadság, January 1957*

Quickly, the press's condemnation of Puskás mushroomed into a rumour that he and Emil Östreicher had engineered the tour so that they could fleece the Honvéd players out of the tour money.

Puskás's fellow footballers knew he never sold himself short, but he was no crook. Of Östreicher, they were not so sure. As far as the Honvéd players were concerned, their club's general manager had had his true colours exposed when he had charged some of them to arrange for their wives to be smuggled out of Hungary – and from this resentment the rumour may have stemmed. The truth was that the Brazil tour's income had been placed under the supervision of Puskás, Östreicher and the trained accountant Ferenc Szusza, and the three of them had ensured that the money was divided fairly (if not *evenly*) between the players.

But being accused of being a swindler was the final straw for Puskás, or rather his wife, Erzsi. Fearing her husband would be imprisoned should he return to Hungary, it was she who ultimately decided to remain abroad. And they had every reason to be fearful: in March 1957, Puskás's 'pal' Mihály Farkas was sentenced to 16 years in prison for crimes committed during the Rákosi regime. Many believed that 'The Wolf' got off lightly, only spared the rope because if the Soviets started hanging all those with soiled hands, they would have to hang the lot …

It would be 25 years before Puskás returned to Hungary.

A week later, just in time to beat the FA deadline, another double-figure batch of players also decided to return to Hungary, among them Szusza, Lantos and László Budai.

Kocsis had been choked to see his best friend return home and was sorely tempted to follow, but daren't defy his wife. The heavily pregnant Alíz Kocsis had no such notion of returning to a country that she had struggled for so long to leave, telling her husband, 'You can go, but me and the children are staying here.' When Budai broke the news to Kocsis's mother that her beloved Sanyi was not coming home, she collapsed.

With some of the players still not having returned, the deadline was extended for another week, time in which Károly Sándor sheepishly went back – claiming he'd turned down offers from Real Madrid to do so.

But one extension was all the authorities were willing to offer. Once the final deadline date had passed and it was apparent that the seven remaining exiles – Czibor, Grosics, Kocsis, Puskás and three reserve team players – would not be returning, the FA withdrew their playing licences: Puskás and Czibor for two years, and Grosics, Kocsis and the three reserves for one year.

Czibor was initially hit the hardest. Roma, on learning that their new winger would be unable to play for the next two years, withdrew his $1,000 monthly wage but allowed him to remain, for the duration of his ban, rent-free in the villa they had provided for him. Roma's good grace towards Czibor was down to the club's Hungarian coach, György Sárosi. The captain of Hungary's 1938 World Cup Final team, Sárosi had been coaching in Italy since 1948 and had earned a reputation as one of the best *technicos* in Italian football, having led Juventus to the Serie A title in 1952. Sárosi had enticed Czibor to Roma, and so undoubtedly felt a little sympathy for his fellow countryman's plight, especially having himself fled communist Hungary a just under a decade previously.

The other six banned players weren't affected immediately. Emil Östreicher's understanding was that the FIFA bans did not extend to 'exhibitions', so, resourceful as ever, he rustled together the six exiles and seven players from the Hungarian under-21 squad who had defected the year before, to form a team he called 'Hungária'. Their first match was in Athens against a team made up of Greek footballers, themselves without clubs. It was such a resounding success, attracting a crowd of 60,000, that Östreicher began plans to play similar 'exhibitions' right across the world. But FIFA was quick to burst his balloon. Football's governing body could not afford to have banned players so blatantly bending the rules. Puskás, Grosics and Kocsis were told that any further such 'exhibitions' would result in their bans being extended.

Unable to earn a living from *playing* football, the three had little option but to grab the first opportunities that came their way. Kocsis signed for the Swiss lower league club Young Fellows, who offered to pay him full wages while he sat out his one-year ban, on the agreement that he remained at the club for two seasons thereafter. Grosics accepted a similar offer from the Austrian first-division club

FC Austria, receiving a car, a rent-free flat and the opportunity to train regularly with the club's first team, in return for him signing for the club once his ban was over. Meanwhile, Puskás took to keeping in shape by quietly training with Vienna FC who one imagines were more than pleased to have among them the world's greatest footballer. Delighted to be back involved in football on a daily basis, Puskás's thoughts turned to coaching, but as soon as he made enquiries, he learned that 'coaching', according to FIFA, was the same as playing.

At his wits' end, Puskás took it upon himself to lodge an appeal against his, and his team-mates', bans with FIFA, travelling to Rome to seek the advice of a lawyer in the city who dealt solely with football matters. The Hungarian authorities, on learning that Puskás had left Austria, revoked his passport, classing him as a *persona non grata*, and thus preventing him from returning to his wife and daughter in Vienna.

On being turned away from the Austrian border, Puskás headed for the only person he knew in Rome – Zoltán Czibor. Considering that the pair's relationship had bordered on open hatred since their recent falling out, Czibor was shocked to see Puskás on his doorstep; and Czibor, being Czibor, offered his help in an instant.

The pair went to the Hungarian embassy in Rome, and while Puskás sat outside in the car, Czibor went in and waited for hours for a meeting with the ambassador. Once given a few minutes of the ambassador's valuable time, Czibor begged him to pull the appropriate strings to have Puskás's citizenship reinstated. It was not easy, but days later someone somewhere in the Hungarian foreign office saw sense.

Puskás was eternally grateful to Czibor for helping him in his hour of need, and never forgot the favour. From this moment on, the two former sworn enemies would become the greatest of friends, and never again ended an evening in an argument about which of them was the better player.

Yet these moments of camaraderie were few and far between for the exiled four. The reality was that there were days when they believed that they would have been better off returning home to Hungary, especially once they learned that their team-mates who had returned had fared nowhere near as badly as feared. The returnees' bans were quickly cut to three months from league football and six months from international football, and they were also allowed to retain all the money they had earned from their tour of Brazil – a very substantial amount, comparable to a year's wages.

The leniency awarded to the returnees was possible because Marcell Nagy was no longer the FA president. The man who had been so adamant that the touring players should each be banned for a minimum of 18 months had fled Hungary for Australia. Fortunately for the good of Hungarian football, Nagy's replacement was his predecessor, Sándor Barcs.

Nagy had originally replaced Barcs, who had been demoted to vice-president because his role as a witness at the László Rajk trial had tainted his name. Nagy was entirely different to Barcs: he was a hard-line communist, who took a hard-line stance on any defiance to communist rule, hence his blind refusal to offer even the slightest of compromises to the Honvéd players. Barcs was a far more moderate man, realising that Nagy's unyielding approach had been to the detriment of football in Hungary. By Barcs's own calculation, an astonishing 12,000 registered footballers left Hungary in the six months in which its football was suspended from October 1956 until March 1957.

Hungary's domestic football suffered the most: without Puskás, Kocsis and Czibor, crowds felt short-changed and attendances at matches dropped considerably. In an attempt to bring them back, the authorities allowed clubs to revert to their original names. Vörös Lobogó again became MTK, Budapest Kiniszi became Ferencváros, Budapest Vasas plain Vasas, and Budapest Dózsa became Újpest Dózsa. Notably, Budapest Honvéd remained so,[151] but they were the mighty Honvéd in name only.

Without their stars, bar the forlorn figure of Bozsik, the club finished the 1957 season second from bottom of the league, only being saved the indignity of relegation because for that one season clubs could not be relegated.[152]

In late March 1958, the trial of Imre Nagy was held in secret at Budapest's Central Prison. Alongside Hungary's former premier were the Budapest police chief Sándor Kopácsi, military commander Colonel Pál Maléter and a journalist called Miklós Gimes. Since their arrest 18 months earlier, the four had first been held for six months under armed house arrest in a villa in Romania, and then for a year in solitary confinement in the same Budapest prison where they now faced their fate.

While clearly showing the effects of their imprisonment, the four accused[153] stood defiant as they were sentenced to death for the crime of attempting to overthrow the state – one which each had readily admitted. Nagy, who failed to recognise the court, supposedly made one last statement before he was taken away:

> If me giving my life is needed to prove that communists are not the enemies of the people, then it is a sacrifice I shall make. Besides, after this [court case] it is not worth anything. I know that one day there will be a new Imre Nagy trial, one that will exonerate me, and at my reburial there will be three times more mourners than there were at László Rajk's. I only fear that my funeral oration will be given by those that betrayed me.[154]

Like the accused themselves, everyone concerned knew that the verdict had long been a foregone conclusion. The Soviet leader, Nikita Khrushchev, had initially contemplated a reprieve for the four, more worried about Russia's standing with the United Nations than he was about the health of four traitors, but then decided otherwise. Soviet rule could not be challenged., and dead martyrs were better than living rebel rousers.

Hungary's leader, János Kádár, was of a similar mind. Not a vindictive man by nature, Kádár was simply hardened by his own experience of torture, show trials and prison at the hands of his fellow comrades.[155] Kádár did, however, show some humanity, commuting Sándor Kopácsi's death sentence to life imprisonment. Nagy, Maléter and Gimes, though, were hung at dawn on 16 June 1958, and buried face down in the prison cemetery. The executions were condemned universally across the Western world. Membership levels of communist parties across the West dropped considerably. Few (former) comrades saw the good in supporting a political ideology that had to resort to closed borders and hangings to keep its people in check.

CHAPTER 20

Who is this FIFA to tell me what to do in my own country?

General Franco

THE problems of a few self-exiled 'rich' footballers somewhat paled into insignificance alongside the execution of Imre Nagy – but at the time of Nagy's trial, Puskás, Czibor, Grosics and Kocsis learned from FIFA the result of their appeal against their bans. Against all expectations, FIFA reduced Puskás's and Czibor's two-year bans to 18 months, and Kocsis's and Grosics's one-year bans to three months – meaning Kocsis and Grosics were able to return to playing football immediately.

The reductions were partly a result of FIFA's sympathy towards Hungary's plight in general, and partly of the Hungarian FA offering Kocsis and Grosics an olive branch in the hope that they would return home to help Hungary qualify for the 1958 World Cup finals.

In June 1957, Hungary returned to international football just in time to begin the qualifying matches for the 1958 finals, to be held in Sweden. Hungary's first qualifier was against Norway in Oslo, a game for which coach Márton Bukovi had little option but to select an unprepared, inexperienced team that consisted of only two players from the Golden Team period – Sándor and Hidegkuti. Hungary lost 2–1. A week later Bozsik, having served his ban, was recalled as captain for the second qualifier against Bulgaria, a 4–1 win, at a Népstadion that was only two-thirds full.

The loss against Norway left Hungary needing two wins from the return-leg qualifiers, considerably narrowing their chances of qualification for a tournament that a year earlier they were considered one of the favourites to win. Bukovi didn't react well to the pressure placed upon him and quit, citing ill health. Never the most robust of men since his nervous breakdown as coach of the ÁVO-run MTK, Bukovi had despaired at the Hungarian FA's mishandling of the Honvéd tour of Brazil, the fallout from which lost him his team's best players.

In Bukovi's place was appointed a three-man committee consisting of Bukovi's former assistant Károly Sos, the 'B' team coach Lajos Baróti and the 'C' team coach Károly Lakat; and it was they, with an eye to the future, who pressed for the return of Kocsis and Grosics. At 28 years old, Kocsis was at the absolute peak of his goalscoring powers, and Grosics remained one of the very best goalkeepers in the world. In contrast, the 'unhinged' Czibor and 'greedy' Puskás were not considered worth contacting.

Kocsis, though, wasn't going anywhere. Besides the no small matter of his wife Alíz's point-blank refusal to return to Hungary, Kocsis was also being held to his contract at Young Fellows, for although the club may have been small, its Zurich-based banker owners had no need to sell their star asset. Grosics, however, did not want to remain abroad for a moment longer. Both he and his wife, Tünde, had long wished to return home, despite having the luxury of a rent-free flat in Vienna courtesy of the president of FK Austria Wien. Grosics remembered the homesickness they suffered as being 'close to physical pain'. Indeed, they would have returned to Hungary sooner, but Grosics had been scared to do so because of a fear that his hiding weapons for the insurgents during the revolution had been discovered. Only once he was sure that there was no warrant for his arrest did Grosics, his wife and two daughters head home (in a car given to him by his Austrian club). Still unsure of what reception awaited him, Grosics crossed the border into Hungary alone to see if he would be arrested. Once it was clear that he would not, he signalled for his wife and daughters. Just as they passed through the final barrier, an officer flagged them down, sauntered over to the car window and said, 'Don't try to run away again – we are a small country and will find you within an hour.'

Despite this welcome Grosics was highly relieved to be back home, returning straight to his former club Tatabányai Banyász, and within a week of his return re-secured his spot as Hungary's number one goalkeeper – just in time to help them qualify for the 1958 World Cup.

From their bases in Austria, Italy and Switzerland, Puskás, Czibor and Kocsis learned of Hungary's qualification for the World Cup with a cheer for their nation and a heavy heart for themselves, knowing that, at the peak of their careers, they had foregone an opportunity to play in a World Cup.

Deciding not to return to Hungary had been heart-wrenching for each of them, but the vindictiveness directed towards them by the authorities had made them adamant that they were not going home in the near future. In turn, Hungary was angry at them too. Many of those who stayed behind in Hungary to face the music of the vengeful Soviets felt nothing but bitterness towards those who had upped and left. How were they ever going to defeat the communists if everyone ran away? What sort of patriot leaves their country in a time of trouble? And especially the footballers! What did they have to complain about?

Puskás, Czibor and Kocsis thus became non-persons in their homeland, written of only in the past tense. If their names were mentioned at all in football books, it was only with the most necessary and cursory of references.[156] A new reader would never have known that the F. Purczeld referred to was Hungary's greatest ever footballer. If they were spoken of, it was with an air of envy. The public notion was that the three were dripping in riches, a rumour that stemmed from the players who had returned to Hungary. Lajos Tichy, one of the very first Honvéd players to return, admitted that he'd had offers from Barcelona and Italian clubs. And Károly Sándor, possibly to place himself in the authorities' good books for having returned a week after the deadline date, told anyone who'd listen that he had been offered $140,000 to sign for Real Madrid but had turned it down for the love of his country.

The myth that the trio were living like lords had them constantly cornered by Hungarian refugees to help financially – anything from the price of a coffee to the cost of a car. Kocsis, the only wage earner, was never the most sociable of men, so had little problem in saying no. But Czibor and Puskás, both generous men by nature, were sympathetic to a fellow Magyar's suffering, and literally gave people the coats off their backs. Which, of course, only caused to spread the word of their wealth.

The truth was that both Puskás and Czibor were living on loans and charity. And while offers from clubs willing to pay up front to sign either of them weren't thin on the ground, these were generally lesser clubs that didn't meet the pair's expectations. They did not want to end up like the unhappy Kocsis in Switzerland, tied to a contract that meant playing sub-standard football for sub-standard money.

For a brief while, Manchester United showed an interest in Puskás. The English club had hoped to receive a special dispensation from FIFA to sign him to help boost their devastated squad (and morale) after the 1958 Munich air disaster. However, any notion of the move was blocked by the FA, fearing the arrival of one foreign professional would lead to an influx of others and put British footballers on the sidelines.

Inter Milan, though, did make Puskás a concrete offer, but then backed out a few days later once they learned of his ever-expanding waistline. Puskás had always been chunky and a scoffer of epic portions, but during his year of inactivity, he'd become fat, his weight ballooning by an extra 20kg. Inter, whose players existed on strict diets of pasta and fruit, took one look at Hungary's former captain, asked after his age (31), and chose to save their money for younger, slimmer players at their peak of physical well-being.

Equally hard for the exiled trio was their missing out on what was a particularly eventful summer of football. Firstly, there was the European Cup. The 1957 Hungarian league champions, Vasas, entered the tournament and proceeded to demonstrate that Hungarian clubs were still forces to be reckoned with by reaching the semi-finals, losing only to the eventual winners, Real Madrid, 4–2. In Budapest, a crowd of 40,000 turned up just to watch the Real players train.

The World Cup was probably harder to bear. Had the three been present, Hungary would have easily been among the tournament's favourites – but as it was, their new coach, Lajos Baróti, was forced to construct a team around Grosics, Bozsik and Hidegkuti, fading veterans in comparison to the fast and colourful teams sent by West Germany, France and Brazil.

Baróti was formerly the coach of Vasas, rewarded with the national team role after the club's European Cup achievement. If he was looking, however, for guidance and wisdom from his wizened predecessor, Sebes, he caught short shrift. 'I have never seen a Hungarian team in such a deplorable physical condition and nervous state,' was all Sebes offered, perhaps with more than a tad of jealousy.

In the group stage, Hungary drew against Wales, lost to the host nation, Sweden, and beat Mexico, to finish level with the Welsh. Because goal difference was not accounted for, the two nations then had to contest a play-off to see who went through to the quarter-finals. The match took place in the small town of Sulna, in front of a paltry crowd of just under 3,000. Hungary took the lead in the first half through Lajos Tichy, but that was as good as they got. The Wales centre-half Mel Charles was not impressed:

> It soon became clear very early on in the game that these eleven guys we were facing were nothing out of the ordinary. They were known as the Magyars but I think they were clinging to past glories a little. Without Puskás and co their magic had ebbed away.[157]

In the second half, Wales scored twice, clinging on to their lead until the end to win 2–1. In the next round, they went on to lose to the eventual winners, Brazil: a team coached by Vicente Feola, until recently an assistant to Béla Guttmann at Brazilian club FC São Paulo. 'The victory is 50% down to Mr Guttmann because I copied his method,'[158] was Feola's explanation for Brazil's triumph.

Back in Hungary, the national team's early exit was met apathetically, which was somehow worse for the players than four years previously when there had been riots. At least in 1954 they had expected to win it.

Puskás and Czibor were, though, for a change, happy. The end of the 1958 World Cup coincided with their bans coming to an end, and immediately the pair's situation turned full circle, and they once again became the ones calling the shots – or in Puskás's case, Emil Östreicher called them.

Östreicher, having landed himself a job as a scout for Real Madrid, had made it his mission to bring Puskás to the European Cup holders. But the Real president, Santiago Bernabéu, was reluctant. He acknowledged Puskás's skills, but also believed him to be too old and too fat. Undeterred, Östreicher urged his boss: 'At least size Puskás up in person before you make a final decision.' Bernabéu did, and still thought Puskás too old and too fat. But he liked him, liked his enthusiasm, his warmth. Bernabéu himself was an ex-footballer who was forced into exile during the Spanish Civil War, so he empathised with Puskás's predicament. The two men hit it off from the start in a meeting that Puskás remembered as being very surreal. No translator was present, so they got by with hand signals, and in the ensuing laughter Puskás pointed at his stomach to say, 'Have you seen the size of this?'

'How is that my problem?' was Bernabéu's reply. Or at least that's what Puskás thought he said.

Puskás signed for the European Cup holders there and then, on a four-year contract worth a very tidy four million pesetas (worth almost £1m in 2019).

At the same time that Puskás was in Madrid, Czibor was in Barcelona via an invitation from László Kubala. A week earlier, Kubala had arrived out of the blue at Czibor's apartment in Rome, offering a three-year contract at Barça worth two million pesetas. The offer gave Czibor an unexpected dilemma. He'd given his word as a Hungarian to Roma that he would sign for them once his ban was over, plus the club had been kind to him, supplying him with a rent-free flat. But Czibor was beyond broke. Of the exiled trio, it was he who had the biggest outgoings, as the sole breadwinner for his wife, two children and an adopted daughter (who they had got from a Hungarian orphanage), plus his sister-in-law.

On sitting down with the Barça president to discuss the offer, Czibor claimed that he suddenly remembered some advice that an old Italian had once given him: 'When you are selling yourself, you name your price.' With this in the forefront of his mind, Czibor proceeded to ask Barça to double their offer, saying he'd then think about it. 'It was there and then I realised that I, Zoltán Czibor, son of an honest railway worker, had become a prostitute.'

Stunned by Czibor's front, Barça sent him packing. But three days later, at Kubala's pressing, the Barça board relented and gave in to Czibor's demand – four million pesetas. Czibor turned his back on Roma, to surpass Kubala as Barcelona's highest-paid player.

The Spain that Czibor and Puskás arrived in during the summer of 1958 was a fascist dictatorship under the rule of one General

Francisco Franco. In 1936, Franco led a military coup against the then socialist-leaning government, and the ensuing war, the Spanish Civil War, lasted for three long years, causing the death of over a million people.

Once in power, the victorious Franco implemented an ultra right-wing nationalist regime upon Spain, of which Madrid became the all-powerful centre. He took control of the city's biggest football club, Real Madrid, a club that had already always been a focal point for Spanish nationalists (Royal Madrid),[159] appointing as club president one of his most loyal officers: Santiago Bernabéu, himself a former Real Madrid player during the 1920s. The pair's ambition was to make Real the biggest club in the world, thus a reflection of the superiority of Spain and the Spanish people. But the men knew that for Real to succeed they had to regularly face top-class opposition, so he let the leading Basque and Catalan clubs – Athletic Bilbao and FC Barcelona – remain powerful, while at the same time stripping the regions of their independence. Hereafter Real versus Barça matches, *El Clásico*, became even more poisonous affairs than they were already, described by one Spanish football historian as 'virtual reenactments of the Civil War itself'.

Puskás and Czibor had little care for the politics, although it was not lost on their foes in Hungary that in going to Spain they had merely swapped life in a communist regime for life in a fascist one with, fittingly, Puskás, the darling of the communist regime, joining the club of the dictatorship, and Czibor the freedom fighter joining Barça.

In joining Barcelona, Czibor was adding to the club's long, proud tradition of signing foreigners, dating right back to their inaugural match in 1899, when they had fielded only foreign nationals, the majority of whom were Englishmen – the British having introduced the sport to Spain around a decade earlier. Hungarians had also had a role in the club's history.

The first was a goalkeeper called Ferenc Plattkó, who joined Barça in 1923 after touring Spain with MTK. Plattkó, or Franz Platko as he became known in Spain, remained at the club for the next seven seasons winning a host of titles and cups, his bravery in goal enshrining him in Catalan legend, inspiring the Catalan poet Raphael Alberti to pen 'An Ode to Platko': 'no one will forget that golden bear from

Hungary!' In 1924, Plattkó was joined by coach Imre Pozsonyi, Barça's first non-British coach, who, as Jesza Pozsony, coached for one semi-successful season, 1924/25. And in the 1930s a former Ferencváros wing-half, Elemér Berkessy,[160] landed at the club for one indifferent season. He would become more famous in the city in his later years as a permanent fixture at Czibor's city-centre bar.

But of all the Barça Magyars, none came close to László Kubala. From the very moment 'Kubi' had stepped on to a pitch in the Barcelona strip, he'd taken the club by storm. He was everything the Catalans loved in a footballer – lion-hearted, aggressive, strong, quick, and with a complete Danubian mastery of the ball. The Catalan newspaper *Destino* gushed:

> Kubala has arrived with a new style of football. Having watched him play spectators come out of matches with a sense of amazement.

The Catalans weren't the only admirers: General Franco was also impressed by Kubala's skills, as well as seeing the immense propaganda value of a player risking his life to escape the repression of communism for a better life in fascist Spain.

Franco first watched Kubala playing in 1951, when the player was still halfway through his one-year ban imposed by FIFA for fleeing Hungary the year before, and so was only able to play friendly matches. When told the reason why this great footballer was not gracing La Liga, Franco famously replied, 'Who is this FIFA to tell me what to do in my own country?' The general cut short Kubala's ban, threatening to withdraw Spain from international football if FIFA dared impose any further punishment on the player. FIFA did not, and in March 1952 Kubala officially became a Barcelona player.

His immediate presence in the Barcelona first team transformed the club's fortunes. In his first full season, they won La Liga, the Spanish Cup and the Latin Cup;[161] he also scored seven goals in one match,[162] a still-standing La Liga record. Almost single-handedly, Kubala lifted post-Civil-War Barça up and out of the doldrums, hastening the club's plans to build a new stadium to cope with public demand to see their star player in action. And duly the Nou Camp (New Field) was completed in 1954, a stadium fit to rival Real Madrid's.

The reverence with which the Barça fans treated Kubala was contrasted by the harsh treatment dished out to him by opponents and opposition fans to try to thwart him. On the pitch, Kubala was the target of endless fouls, and whenever he played away from the Nou Camp, he was met with howls of anti-foreign and anti-communist abuse. None of this duly concerned Kubala. He was no shrinking violet. Having grown up in the toughest of Budapest districts, he'd long learned to look after himself and was not above seeking revenge when the referee's attentions were elsewhere.

Czibor's arrival at Barcelona coincided with the club appointing a new coach in Helenio Herrera. It was an appointment that was seen as a very daring move by the usually conservative Barcelona directors. Herrera was an arrogant eccentric who demanded full control of the team – perhaps not best suited to a club like FC Barcelona, where the reputation of Catalonia was first and foremost, and directors and fans alike believed they had a right to interfere in team selection.

According to Czibor, he immediately approached the new boss to ask him to bring Sándor Kocsis to the Nou Camp:

> Now, you see, Herrera was half Red Indian, so he was very superstitious. So I said to him, 'Bring Kocsis here, and he will bring you luck. Wherever and whenever he and I have played together, we have won the league title. At both Ferencváros and Honvéd. Also, our national team went four-and-a-half years unbeaten with us playing side by side.
>
> Herrera laughed: 'Hee-hee-hee.' He liked my style. He was daft. He knew as much about football as a pig knows about interest rates. A footballing imposter. His trick was to always go to a team that had four or five world-class players. As simple as that.'[163]

History proves Czibor's 'football imposter' description of Herrera at best disingenuous: in his two seasons at Barça, the Argentinian would win La Liga twice, and he would later lead Inter Milan to two European Cup victories, as well as in time becoming coach of the French, Italian and Spanish national teams. Herrera's strength lay in motivating his teams. He dabbled in black magic, was not beneath nobbling a referee and encouraged the use of performance-enhancing drugs. He prided himself on being a psychologist, going to great lengths to get close to his players, becoming their friends so that he could find out what made them tick – but Herrera was stumped in trying to find out what made Zoltán Czibor tick, especially with Kubala translating. But surprisingly the two had very few problems, probably because of Czibor's lack of Spanish – Herrera even described Czibor as 'reserved' a word which no Hungarian-speaking coach ever used when speaking of him. They only crossed swords once, after Czibor refused to drink any more of Herrera's own pre-match amphetamine-laced tea. Czibor was a staunch alcohol and cigarettes man: he had no time for damaging drugs. Only once, against his better judgement, did he try Herrera's potion, only to find it made no difference to his performance but had made him feel 'madder than usual'. Meanwhile, Kubala, a whisky man to whom hangovers were mere inconveniences, had no aversion to Herrera's concoctions, though he would quickly develop an aversion to the man himself.

Kocsis duly arrived at Barça, although he wasn't signed by Herrera, and nor on Czibor's recommendation. In Spanish football at the time, the manager and coach performed two different roles. At Barça, the manager, Pepe Samitier, signed players, negotiated contracts and was the link between the directors and the coach. The coach, Herrera, was responsible solely for team selection and coaching the players. The club directors were impressed by the technical skills of Czibor and Kubala, not to mention Kocsis's formidable goal record, so they decided to take a chance on one more *Hungáro*.

Kocsis's time in Switzerland had been largely unhappy. His wife, Alíz, had been pregnant when she fled Hungary, and by the time they were in Switzerland, the stress of it all and the uncertainty over her family's future caused her to miscarry. Adding to Kocsis's problems was his debilitating homesickness. He felt guilty for abandoning his elderly parents, and his malaise was reflected in his lacklustre performances for his club, Young Fellows, who possibly were none too concerned to see him leave, convinced that Barcelona wouldn't be getting their money's worth either.

Other clubs, mainly Italian, had also wanted to sign Kocsis, but Alíz reasoned that Barça, with Czibor and Kubala, would give her husband some Hungarian-speaking company. Also, Alíz Kocsis had recently given birth again, to a son named Sándor junior, and the money offered by Barça would provide a very secure future for their burgeoning family. One month after the arrival of Czibor and his family, Kocsis and his arrived in Barcelona.

Such was the Barça fans' interest in their new Hungarian signings that when the pair made their debuts in a pre-season friendly, a crowd of 60,000 came out to watch. 'Those 60,000 paid for my contract,' remembered Czibor.

Two hundred kilometres to the west, Ferenc Puskás was receiving a somewhat more lukewarm reception at Real Madrid. At 31 years old, with a bulging belly and two years without playing top-flight football, Puskás did not appear to many of the Real fans as the shrewdest of signings.

The Real coach, Luis Carniglia, was unimpressed with the latest acquisition brought to him by Santiago Bernabéu. In Puskás's first game for Real, during a pre-season tour of Argentina, he struggled severely to keep pace with the game, and so was dropped by Carniglia for the following match; it was only after Bernabéu insisted that Puskás be reinstated that he returned to the first team.

On returning to Spain and La Liga, Puskás continued to struggle: the tempo of the football in Spain was far faster than in Hungary, where the players were taught to let the ball do the work. His total lack of Spanish also isolated Puskás; he'd always been a player to talk continuously throughout matches: cajoling, scolding and directing his team-mates, and mocking or goading the opposition. In Spain, in his early days at least, he played in total silence.

Nonetheless, Puskás was determined to succeed. The Spanish climate and pace of life suited him and his wife very much. They had bought a villa in one of Madrid's more salubrious suburbs, and in a resolve to immerse themselves in Spanish life had begun to learn the language, taking inspiration from their infant daughter Anikó, who had become fluent in no time.

Through sheer willpower, a strict training regime and his wife's support in feeding him 'healthy Spanish food' (i.e. not bowls of goulash), Puskás slowly and surely got back into shape. When Hungarian FA president Sándor Barcs was in Spain, he visited Puskás and was astonished to see football's most notorious glutton grazing a salad. 'I'm a professional now, Uncle Sanyi,' Puskás explained.

A leaner Puskás (although he would never lose his paunch) with a smattering of Spanish began to resemble the player of old, and slowly he began to win over the Bernabéu crowd, who nicknamed him 'Pancho', an affectionate term for the forename Francisco – Francis in English, Ferenc in Hungarian.

He also began to win over the notoriously grouchy Real captain, Alfredo Di Stéfano, a man who held high expectations for himself and others. The Argentinian-born centre-forward was to Real what Kubala was to Barça: an all-action leader, the fans' favourite, and very much with a say in who his team-mates were. Ironically, considering how much he was revered at Real, Di Stéfano had so nearly been a Barça player. He had initially come to Spain in 1953 on tour with the Colombian club Millonarios, who, as their name suggests, were a rich club, able to lure the very best South and Central American stars. On seeing Di Stéfano, the Real president, Bernabéu, quickly agreed on a deal with Millonarios; but the Barcelona manager, Pepe Samitier, was cannier and agreed on a deal with Di Stéfano's Argentinian club, River Plate, who, under FIFA's rules, held the player's registration.

The ensuing bitter dispute between the two giants was to last nine months. Eventually, it was Real who triumphed. It is not known exactly why, but it is believed that either the club directors resorted to blackmailing dishonest Catalan politicians, or a fed-up Di Stéfano chose for himself and preferred Real because he did not want to share the limelight with Kubala. Whatever the reason, it was Barça's loss. In his first season, Di Stéfano led Real to their first La Liga title in over two decades, and over the next 11 seasons he would captain the club to a further seven league titles along with five European Cups.

Di Stéfano ran his critical eye over the rotund Puskás fruitlessly huffing and puffing away through matches and was impressed – Puskás showed the one characteristic Di Stéfano admired above all else: an all-encompassing desire to win even the most insignificant of matches.

Puskás, for his part, was clever in his dealings with his captain. It had been a worry that the two would clash, for in every team Puskás had played in, from the Kispest grounds to the World Cup Final, the team had revolved around him. But, at Real, for the first time in his life, this was not the case. Puskás, though, was smart enough to grasp that the onus was on him to defer to Di Stéfano, and not vice versa, and in doing so became an even better player:

> I studied Di Stéfano intensely. He could be a little unpredictable. But what dominated his life was the huge desire to win, to be the best, at any cost. Threaten that and he could be as pig headed and ruthless as a little child.[164]

Towards the end of their first season together, Puskás showed just how much he had changed and how far he was willing to go to defer to Di Stéfano. By the penultimate match of the season, both headed the league's goalscoring table on 21 goals apiece. With the score at 0–0 and just minutes remaining, Puskás had the goal at his mercy, but instead he turned and laid the ball off for Di Stéfano to score. He was only that generous the once, mind. For the next four seasons thereafter, Puskás made sure that *he* was La Liga's leading scorer.

CHAPTER 21

You must shoot immediately shoot, shoot and shoot again! It's just like when you are with your wife or your girlfriend and you keep on kissing, kissing and making small talk. You have to score a goal for them too in the end. It's only then that the satisfaction will show on everybody's face.

Béla Guttmann[165]

THE presence of Czibor, Kocsis and Kubala at Barcelona helped the club begin to match the prowess of Puskás's Real Madrid. As the two rivals battled for La Liga and European domination, the four Magyars stood at the forefront. To begin with, Real led the way, winning the 1958/59 European Cup, beating French champions Stade de Reims 2–0 in the final – but without Puskás.

A year earlier, he'd given an interview with the respected French football magazine *France Football* in which he said that West Germany's players had been doped during the 1954 World Cup Final. The West German FA professed outrage at Puskás's claim and explained that while they had injected their players, it was only ever with glucose and vitamins. Puskás refused to apologise, for which the West German FA banned him indefinitely from playing football in their country.

This wasn't a problem until Real reached the 1959 European Cup Final, staged in Stuttgart, and the West Germans stuck to their word. Puskás was therefore forced to watch from the stands as his team-mates lifted Real's fourth successive European Cup, more convinced than ever of West German foul play.

Real Madrid may have been champions of Europe, but it was Barcelona who were kings of Spain, having pipped their rivals to the 1958/59 La Liga title. The two had actually finished level on points, but Barça, having conceded fewer goals, were awarded the title on goal difference. The result was both teams entering the 1959/60 European Cup, meeting in a semi-final clash that was the first-ever *El Clásico* outside of the Spanish domestic league. Over two bruising legs, Real, with their experience of the big occasion, came out on top, winning 6–2 on aggregate, placing them in the final against West German champions Eintracht Frankfurt in Glasgow.

Maybe Puskás had a point to prove against a West German side, or perhaps he just wanted to please the mainly Scottish 135,000 crowd (he was always a firm favourite in Scotland), or maybe he was just on flying form that day. But, for whatever reason, he produced what is regarded as his, and indeed the European Cup's, greatest ever display of football – a 7-3 win in which Di Stéfano scored a hat-trick and Puskás (a record still for a final) four goals. As the game neared its end, Puskás made sure he was close to the ball, so as to prevent Di Stéfano from claiming it. The ball tucked safely under his arm, Puskás felt a tap on his shoulder. 'Would you mind giving me the ball?' asked Frankfurt forward Erwin Stein, scorer of his team's second-half goals.

'What could I do?' said Puskás later, explaining he willingly handed the ball over. 'The poor sod had scored twice in a European Cup Final and still lost.'

Barcelona's semi-final loss to Real prompted the dismissal of coach Helenio Herrera, the cost of falling on the wrong side of Kubala. Herrera had initially liked his captain, but this quickly cooled as he became jealous of Kubala's standing at the club. Herrera began to select Kubala for home games only, which baffled more than pacified the Barça faithful, and had Kubala handing the club bosses an 'Either he goes, or I go' ultimatum.

Once Herrera was sacked, Kubala quickly reverted to his old self and helped win Barça their second successive La Liga title in 1959/60, pipping Real by one point. It was a triumph that led to another *El Clásico* in the European Cup, this time in the first round of the 1960/61 tournament. The first leg at the (now named) Bernabéu Stadium ended in a 2–2 draw. Real dominated until the very last minute, only for the scores to be levelled with a disputed penalty won by a foul on Kocsis. Or 'one of Kocsis's famous forward rolls' as Puskás acidly described it.

'You must be very proud of yourself, Sanyi,' Puskás called to Kocsis as the two teams left the pitch. Kocsis refused to meet his former captain's eye.

At the return leg at the Nou Camp, the Real players shrank in the heat of the abuse that was thundered upon them by the 100,000 crowd. The English referee Reg Leafe, quivering in every decision that went against the home team, disallowed three Real goals, leading Real to accuse Barça of buying him. Of course, Barça hadn't – they didn't need to: they were good enough to reach the final of their own accord. In the quarter-final they beat the Czechoslovak champions Spartak Hradec Králové, and in the semi-finals SV Hamburg to go through to their very first European Cup Final, the opposition being the Portuguese champions, Benfica – coached by one Béla Guttmann …

Guttmann's route to Benfica had begun in Brazil, where he'd departed from the touring Honvéd team in the spring of 1957. He had attached himself to Honvéd so as to utilise his association with the club (he'd called himself the team coach) with the idea of landing a 'real' job at another top club. And Guttmann did so in Brazil, taking charge of one of the country's biggest clubs, São Paulo. As it was, Brazil already appealed to Guttmann: his younger brother Ernő had emigrated there after the war, and it was Ernő's son Imre who became his Uncle Béla's translator.

Guttmann's effect was immediate, one Brazilian journalist noting the sudden improvement in the São Paulo players: 'Under Guttmann, the players are learning to shoot, run with the ball, head the ball, and many more things which the players thought that, being Brazilian, they were born already knowing.'

But Guttmann only remained in Brazil for just over a year. His wife, Mariann, unable to tolerate the South American climate, returned to Europe, and Guttmann followed: 'I am leaving to take care of what I cherish most,' was his parting statement.

'You leave with a champion title at the end of your extraordinary work,' was the club's reply. As Feola and the São Paulo players waved him off from the airport, Guttmann must have wished that all his departures were on such pleasant terms.

Capitalising on the small amount of Portuguese he'd learned, Guttman headed for Portugal to try his luck, landing the manager's job at FC Porto. Adhering to his reputation for being able to turn a team's fortunes around instantly, Guttmann won the Lisbon club the league title in his first season. He then adhered to his notoriety as a money grabber, by dumping Porto for their rivals Benfica, who offered to double his wage. Guttmann had no qualms about leaving Porto in the lurch: 'I sell my expertise to a club for a limited time. I left Porto with a clear conscience.'[166]

At around the same time Guttmann was settling in at Benfica, a court in Milan was hearing the case of manslaughter brought against him after his arrest for reckless driving (with no driving licence) which resulted in the death of a pedestrian.

The case had actually been brought to court first some two years earlier when Guttmann was in Brazil. That time his friend and the car's owner and passenger Dezső Solti had stood in the dock alone, having conspired with Guttmann to lie and say he was the driver of the car. In turn, Guttmann agreed to pay the victims' families any compensation. Yet on the first day of the trial, Solti sensationally retracted his confession, saying that he'd taken the blame to prevent Guttmann from committing suicide. It was another tall tale designed to place the case in limbo, and it worked for it took another three years before the case came to court for a second time, time enough for Solti to utilise his dubious connections and grease palms and have witnesses forget what they saw.

The second time around neither man was in court. Solti did not have to attend and Guttmann was in Portugal, from where he learned the news that in his absence while he had been found guilty of manslaughter, his sentence was a paltry six months – pardoned if he agreed to pay the victims' families substantial damages. Unsurprisingly, Guttman paid up immediately.

With the court case off his back, Guttmann set his mind to concentrate fully on football, and within just one season led[167] Benfica to the 1961 European Cup Final, where they faced Barcelona. It took place in the Wankdorf Stadium in Berne, Switzerland, the same venue where Hungary had narrowly lost the 1954 World Cup Final. There was little between the two sides except for luck: Benfica had it and Barça didn't, Czibor, Kocsis and Kubala all hitting the woodwork as Barça crashed to a 3–2 defeat. It wasn't lost on the three Hungarians that the final score was the same as in Hungary's World Cup Final defeat. Béla Guttmann was overjoyed; Kubala remembered it as the saddest day of his football career, Czibor and Kocsis had been there before …

That same year, 1961, another Magical Magyar was also involved in a European final. Nándor Hidegkuti, as coach of the Italian club Fiorentina, won the inaugural European Cup Winners' Cup. The 'Old Man' of the Golden Team had been the first to retire from playing, quitting in 1958 to become coach of MTK. After just one indifferent season, Hidegkuti was approached by Fiorentina, eager to have the Golden Team's playmaker as their coach.

The Hungarian authorities grudgingly permitted Hidegkuti to work in Italy, but only on the condition that one of his three children remain behind as security against his not returning. Hidegkuti, feeling that the opportunity to coach a leading Serie A club was too good to refuse, accepted the condition, choosing to leave behind his eldest son.

It was a decision that would be much to his eternal regret. Hidegkuti's teenage son wasn't as enamoured with the idea, resenting being left behind. That Hidegkuti had chosen football over his son's welfare was an issue never resolved between them, and when the son died prematurely from cancer in his early forties, the devastated Hidegkuti never recovered.

The Hungarian authorities' treatment of Hidegkuti, an easy-going, apolitical man who had never purposely given the regime the slightest cause for trouble, was a reminder to the exiled Hungarians in Spain of exactly why they had chosen not to return home in the first place.

And nor were they in any hurry do so. Granted, life in Hungary as a member of the Golden Team had been comfortable, but life in Spain as a professional footballer was even better.

In Spain, the exiles' lives were simpler: they weren't expected to join the army, didn't have to attend endless mind-numbing political meetings, nor kowtow to and butter up puffed-up politicians, and could make ends meet without having to resort to demeaning black-market dealings. Puskás opened a factory that made Hungarian sausages and a restaurant in Madrid's city centre – both businesses carrying the Puskás name – while Czibor opened up a bar in central Barcelona, naming it 'Kék Duna' (Blue Danube).

Both establishments quickly became focal points for Spain's population of Hungarian émigrés. But whereas Czibor's hospitality was a result of the quiet desperation of someone not wanting to drink alone, Puskás's welcome was genuine. Combining his love of food and company, he was a born restaurateur, and business boomed.

With money in the bank, food in his belly, his family safe, and playing for the world's greatest club, Puskás was happy, and it was a joy that he was willing to share – especially with his fellow Hungarians. Much to the annoyance of his Real team-mates, who often had to wait while he insisted on introducing them one by one to yet another gawping Hungarian refugee. 'If you were Hungarian, you'd understand and do the same,' Puskás would say in response to their moans.

When in the summer of 1960 Puskás was paid a surprise visit by Gusztáv Sebes, his former coach was amazed at just how worshipped Öcsi was in Madrid:

> Puskás was as popular in the Spanish capital as he ever was at his height in Budapest. In the mornings there were taxis queuing up in front of his house for the privilege of driving him to training. If the traffic lights were red on his way, the police would stop the traffic to wave him through. It was great to see him. He had tears in his eyes when we parted at the airport.[168]

Sebes had been at the Olympic Games in Rome in an official capacity when a Spanish official had asked him if he wanted to watch Puskás play in Madrid. Sebes replied that he would love to go but did not have permission from the Hungarian government to travel to Spain. The next day, the Spanish official returned with a visa, aeroplane tickets and two tickets for the match, which Real won 5–1; Sebes recalled the twice-scoring Puskás being 'as brilliant as ever'.

Afterwards (at Puskás's daughter's eighth birthday party), the two men sat down and spoke for the first time in three years. For the first time, Sebes realised just how easy the exiled trio *hadn't* had it, but also that, despite their obvious high standard of living, they lived in goldfish bowls – in Hungary they'd never had the general public hanging around outside their front doors, not in the good times at least.

Sebes was not alone in his ignorance of the trio in Spain. Back in Hungary, news of them was purposely suppressed by the government, who didn't want the populace to learn of the success they were having abroad. And although it was impossible for the news of their European Cup results not to become known, the match reports barely, if ever, mentioned the players by name.

In their early years in Spain, the exiled trio only ever contacted their families in Hungary when necessary, and then only with the briefest of messages, either by postcard or phone call – in the knowledge that their every correspondence was eavesdropped on.

But, as time went by, the János Kádár regime softened, especially in comparison to the dark, paranoid years under Rákosi, and the trio's parents and siblings were permitted to travel to Spain for holidays. Similarly, the trio's wives were also allowed to return home to Hungary for holidays – although none of the three players themselves dared venture home.

When Real Madrid were drawn with Vasas in the first round of the 1960/61 European Cup, Puskás did not travel for the first leg in Budapest (won 2–0 by Real), much to the disappointment of the thousands who had bought tickets on the black market at vastly inflated prices just to see Öcsi in action at the Népstadion one more time. Puskás did, however, play in the return leg in Madrid, which Real won 3–1, throughout which he was referred to by the Hungarian radio commentary not by name but as 'the Madrid number ten'.

After defeating Vasas, Real proceeded through to the final to face the reigning champions, Béla Guttmann's Benfica, at Amsterdam's Olympic Stadium. Guttmann lined up with nine of the team who had won the previous year's final against Barcelona, plus a teenage forward by the name of Eusébio da Silva Ferreira – Eusébio for short[169].

Benfica (coached by a Hungarian) had a self-imposed policy of recruiting only players from Portugal or its colonies, Mozambique and Angola. This initially frustrated Guttmann, but he soon found a liking for the African players. Raw but strong, they were enthusiastic in a way that the well-fed and wealthy Europeans were no longer. Guttmann built his Benfica side around two Mozambican powerhouses, Mário Coluna and Eusébio. In Amsterdam, the 36-year-old veterans Puskás and Di Stéfano had the match of the two young Africans skill-wise, but their ageing legs were beaten for energy. Benfica won 5–3.

With a second successive European Cup to his name, Guttmann felt he could name his price: and he did, a year later, to the Uruguayan club Peñarol. The Uruguayan and South American champions had faced Guttmann's Benfica in the Intercontinental Cup Final, the match between the European and South American cup winners. Although their team beat Benfica, the Peñarol directors were still willing to lure Guttmann by offering him a substantial wage increase to replace the previous manager, who had gone on to coach the Uruguayan national team. But, after the customary good start, things quickly turned pear-shaped when he fell out with the entire team after they collectively said 'no' to an instruction. 'Players can never say "no" to a coach,' Guttmann told the Peñarol president as he handed in his notice. 'If they dare do it then the coach must say goodbye.'[170]

Benfica made diplomatic overtures to lure him back, but Guttmann was having none of it; besides, he had been offered the chance to coach the Austrian national team. Guttmann let his imagination run wild – he was convinced that he had found his calling. From now on he could stay at home with his wife in Vienna, have time in between matches to again open up a dance school, build another 'Wunderteam' to lift a World Cup … He quit after just five games amidst slurs of greed from the Austrian FA and anti-Semitism from Guttmann. 'Wonder Rabbi' was one insult slung at him. He wasn't even religious.

So he returned to Benfica. The club hadn't performed poorly without him, but neither had they won two successive European Cups. In Guttmann's absence, Benfica had seemingly tried to replace him with fellow Hungarian Jew coaches, possibly in the hope that there was some magic power in their make-up. The first was Lajos Czeizler, a wizened old veteran Danubian, coach of Italy at the 1954 World Cup, and close friend of Guttmann's – until, that is, an evening out together with their wives ended up in a fight between the two men. Czeizler led Benfica to the league title but was too long in the tooth to want to continue, so he was replaced by a Transylvanian Jew, Elek

Schwartz, who likewise won the league and further led the club to the 1965 European Cup Final, only to lose to (Helenio Herrera's) Inter Milan by a single goal.

Inter's European Cup success was Herrera's second in a row – matching Guttmann's achievement, and Guttmann wasn't having that! *He* was the world's greatest coach, not Herrera with his dull and stifling tactics! Guttmann raced to reclaim his rightful crown, hitting Benfica with an offer to work for them that made the club president wince while agreeing at the same time. At Lisbon airport, a huge crowd greeted the return of the 'old fox': Guttmann was back, therefore European domination was surely back. Only, of course, it wasn't: Benfica reached as far as the 1965/66 European Cup quarter-finals, only to run into Manchester United and a mop-haired teenage Northern Irish winger by the name of George Best.

The defeat had Guttmann turn on his players. He accused them of going soft. When he'd left in 1962, they were poor and hard, and walked everywhere; now they were rich and lazy, with cars. His protégé Eusébio, quite unfairly, took the brunt of Guttmann's tongue-lashing, being accused of letting himself go: 'It is sad to watch the end of a great footballer.'[171] Eusébio was only 24, and would be the top scorer at the World Cup two months later.

Guttmann immediately regretted and retreated from what he said, saying that a journalist had twisted his words. But the damage was done, and the tables turned. Maybe the 'old fox' was the one who was out of shape, and past it as well? 'If you ever had a great love, do not ever go back,' was Guttmann's pearl-of-wisdom parting shot.[172]

CHAPTER 22

I was where I had to be.
I did what I had to do.

János Kádár

THE emergence of Eusébio and George Best was a sign to the elder statesmen of European football that the time had come to move aside for the new generation.

The first to call it quits was 34-year-old László Kubala, playing his last game for Barcelona in late 1961. The club retained his services, appointing him as youth team coach, with one eye on his becoming manager one day. His testimonial match, against the French club Stade de Reims at the Nou Camp, was a packed and tearful affair: even Puskás and Di Stéfano donned Barça kits to pay their respects to one of Barcelona's greatest ever players. One wonders what would have been had Kubala remained in Hungary 12 years earlier. Just how good would the Golden Team have been with Kubala on the right wing – the team's one spot that Sebes never satisfactorily filled? Budai, Sándor and József Tóth all held the claim, but none would have surpassed Kubala.

Alas, Zoltán Czibor's departure from Barça soon afterwards was far less emotional – for the club at least. Czibor had always been protected somewhat by his friendship with Kubala, in that with Kubala around he had someone to bounce off, to play with. But with Kubala gone, Czibor's foibles became more noticeable, and when he began turning up for training hungover, belligerent and resentful at being told what to do, Barça were quick to decide enough was enough. The Barça historian as Casals was a lawyer at the club at the time of Czibor's departure:

> Czibor was a very, very good footballer, and he did a lot in making Barcelona a big club, but he was too problematic: there was always something. The club wanted his skills as a footballer, and only his skills, the rest they did not need. Professional clubs don't like players around whom a storm is always blowing.[173]

When Czibor's contract came to an end in 1961, it was not renewed. In fairness to him, in his latter days at Barça he was deeply unhappy in his personal life. His wife, Írisz, was born to the Hungarian educated classes and probably expected more than her train driver's son husband could ultimately provide, not financially but socially. Always a tempestuous marriage, it was placed under further strain when their four-year-old son Zoltán junior had to have his leg amputated after getting it caught between a lift door and shaft at their Barcelona apartment block. Czibor sought haven in his bar, the Blue Danube; Írisz sought the advice of a divorce lawyer.

While Czibor had to make do with a 12-month contract at Barça's cross-city rivals Españyol, Sándor Kocsis had his contract at Barcelona extended by another five years: a rarity for any player at the ripe old age of 32, let alone one at Barcelona.

Kocsis had slowly found his feet in Spain; his homesickness had abated substantially once his parents had been permitted to visit him. But, as always with Kocsis, there was a dark cloud of his own making lingering nearby. He was terrified at the prospect of one day soon having to retire from playing – perhaps the reason why he continued to push himself so hard. His fellow Hungarian exiles had their business interests to fall back on, but Kocsis was too reserved a person ever to become a successful restaurateur or bar owner. And, not so pressing, but essential to Kocsis, there was the matter of his legacy: no matter how successful he had been throughout his career, he was always overshadowed by the feats of Puskás.

Puskás's being selected to represent Spain at the 1962 World Cup had once again stirred all of Kocsis's insecurities – neither he nor Czibor was *ever* selected for the Spanish national team, despite both possessing Spanish citizenship.

Czibor always said that he never wanted to represent another national team other than Hungary, but in truth he was never asked –

being kept out of the Spanish team by the native-born Real Madrid winger Francisco Gento. Kocsis's non-selection, on the other hand, was a mystery, the only reasonable explanation being that the ultra-nationalistic Spanish government did not want too many 'foreigners' in the national team. It was a view also held by Spain's most widely read newspaper: the state-controlled *Marca*. The paper argued that Spain's failures to qualify for the 1954 and 1958 World Cups were because the foreigners in the team didn't possess 'the vitality, aggression and fury of the Spanish'. It also argued that foreign players were preventing the development of home-grown Spanish players. These sentiments were echoed by the more vocal elements at matches, but in general, the majority of the Spanish football-following public were appreciative of the skill and colour the foreigners, and particularly the Hungarians, had brought to the nation's leagues. If any player did receive an inordinate amount of abuse, it was Kubala, but that was more to do with his abrasive style of play than with his being an *extranjero*.

Puskás would recall that it was not emotionally straightforward for any of the foreigners who represented the Spanish national team, and especially for him. He felt it was somewhat easier for Kubala and Di Stéfano for two reasons: firstly because they both spoke fluent Spanish, and secondly because they were what could be best described as more 'international' people. The Budapest-born Kubala's parents were Slovaks, and he had represented both Hungary and Czechoslovakia, while Di Stéfano was born in Buenos Aires to Italian immigrant parents and had played for both Argentina and Colombia. But Puskás – Hungary's record goalscorer and undisputedly their greatest ever player – was Hungarian, pure and simple. Being Hungarian defined him. His representing another nation, even one as good to him as Spain, felt slightly treacherous, and he was aware that, perhaps, many of his fellow countrymen were of the same mind.

Ironically, considering all the fuss in Spain over foreigners in Spanish football, for the 1962 World Cup in Chile the Spanish FA's appointed coach was Helenio Herrera – born in Argentina (albeit to a Spanish father) and raised in Morocco.

Herrera came to Spain via Inter Milan, from whom he had recently parted company. At Inter, Herrera had combined his coaching role with assisting the Italian national team, but when he publicly celebrated

Juventus getting knocked out of the European Cup, the Italian FA demanded an apology. Herrera refused, so the Italians withdrew his licence for coaching in the country, allowing the Spanish to snatch him up just in time to coach their team for the World Cup.

His was not a popular appointment: many in Spanish football believed Herrera to be far too defensive-minded to be in charge of a nation of bullfighters. One of the most vocal in questioning the decision was Di Stéfano. Surprisingly, Herrera took his compatriot's criticism in his stride, mooting that Di Stéfano had a point and duly selecting him for the tournament. The Real captain had never played in a World Cup, and nor would he: once in Chile, Herrera refused to play him.

Herrera, though, held no such grudge with Puskás (who agreed with Di Stéfano but had had the sense to hold his tongue, a first for Öcsi). Herrera made Puskás his first-choice forward, indeed his only forward and Spain lost all three of their group games. Not that Herrera was unduly fussed: on his return to Europe he headed straight for Italy, apologised to the Italian FA and was immediately reinstated as coach of Inter.

Spain's crashing out in the first round did, however, relieve Puskás of the dread of maybe having to face Hungary in a later round. The Hungary team of 1962 contained the veterans Grosics and Károly Sándor, and a forward line of captain Lajos Tichy and a strapping young Ferencváros centre-forward called Florián Albert, tipped in Hungary to be the 'new Kocsis' (and who, like Kocsis had done in Switzerland in 1954, would finish the tournament as top scorer). Low expectations produced a high yield, and Hungary topped their group – beating England and Bulgaria, and holding Argentina to a draw – only going out in the quarter-final 1–0 to a strong Czechoslovak team, who themselves would go on to reach the final, to lose to Brazil.

Puskás remained in Chile, partly to watch Hungary's quarter-final but primarily to catch up with Bozsik, who was working as an adviser to the team. The two old friends had remained in loose contact by telephone and letter, but Chile was the first time that the two had seen each other in the flesh in six years, and the difference was startling. Puskás was a vision of health: muscled, tanned and relaxed. Bozsik was pale, strained and rarely without a cigarette – a prelude, perhaps, to the heart problems that would soon beset him and ultimately cause his premature death. It was evident that while Puskás had been gracing European Cup finals, Bozsik had been plugging away in the anonymity of the Hungarian domestic league. Puskás also had his outside business interests, which, combined with the wages he earned at Real, meant his retirement was assured to be one of comfort. For Bozsik there was no such satisfaction. Compared with the average Hungarian, he was far from hard up, but neither did he live in a villa – and, on a Hungarian state pension, nor would he in the future. He'd also recently, and reluctantly, quit playing, having been coerced into stopping once he'd made a record 100 appearances for Hungary. Bozsik was at both a loose end and a crossroads. He was only in Chile because the Hungarian FA felt that they should be seen to reward him for his loyalty, hence his role tagging along as an 'adviser' – though not to the team coach, Lajos Baróti, who one imagines wasn't best pleased at having a potential replacement sniffing around.

Therefore Bozsik was overjoyed to see his old friend Öcsi. Not for a moment did he hold any animosity towards Puskás – in fact, quite the reverse – but Bozsik must have pondered what would have been had he joined his friend in Spain.

Spain's below-par World Cup mirrored the beginning of the end of Real Madrid's decade-long domination of European football. In the 1962/63 European Cup, they failed to pass the first round, crashing out in a surprise defeat to the Belgian club Anderlecht. And in 1963/64, while they did make it to the final (Puskás was the competition's joint top scorer), they were beaten by Inter Milan.

The final proved to be Di Stéfano's last game for Real, but what should have been a celebratory farewell turned into a bitter feud between player and club. Real offered Di Stéfano a place on the club's technical coaching staff, with the aim of him one day taking over as coach. Di Stéfano read the offer as an insult – why couldn't he take over as coach straight away? – and signed a one-year contract at the Catalan club Españyol, where László Kubala was the player-manager.

Now it was Real's time to be insulted – how dare a Real legend join a Catalan club, and furthermore team up with a Barcelona legend! The club president, Santiago Bernabéu, vowed that all the time he himself was still alive, Di Stéfano would not be permitted to enter the Bernabéu Stadium, and so it would be.

Kubala had landed at Espanyol after being sacked as coach of Barcelona. He had been promoted to the role from youth team coach by the new Barça president, hoping to win the fans' favour. But it quickly became apparent that Kubala the coach was the same as Kubala the player. The hard-living exploits that had made him a legend were exploits not conducive to running a team of the magnitude of FC Barcelona. Like Czibor before him, Kubala moved across the city to Espanyol, the second biggest team in Catalonia and a club with a reputation for signing fading stars, hence the arrival of Di Stéfano.

Puskás, though, carried on for one more season at Real. Throughout the 1965/66 season he mostly showed his age, but also the occasional flash of brilliance, bowing out just shy of his 40th birthday – not bad for a fat guy who a decade earlier had been over the hill.

Kocsis, at Barcelona, was the last to hang up his boots, a year after Puskás, and also just short of 40. The Magical Magyars had had their day.

As well as being the last to retire, Kocsis was the first to return to Hungary. In the summer of 1976, after nearly 20 years away, he made a quiet and fleeting visit to Budapest. The Hungary Kocsis returned to was much changed from how it had been in the dark, repressive days when he had fled. Under the rule of János Kádár, Hungary, of all the Soviet satellites, was the most Westernised and possessed the highest standard of living. Kádár was no dictator, despite his siding with the Soviets in 1956: he was essentially a patriot, a communist who genuinely believed that communism was the best system for his country. He worked hard to loosen the Soviets' iron grip on Hungary, and through this, 'Goulash Communism' emerged: communism with a distinct Hungarian flavour. Hair was long, trousers were flared, and Western music blared from bars. But this is not to say the Hungarians were content with their lot. Food in their cupboards or not, still all of Hungary's major policies were decided in and by Moscow, and still Russian troops were based throughout the country.

In 1981, Puskás too plucked up the courage and decided to visit Hungary. It was a decision prompted by the makers of a documentary film about the Golden Team who wanted him to partake in a reunion match at the Népstadion before a Hungary versus England World Cup qualifier. The documentary makers despatched Gusztáv Sebes and the then Hungarian FA president, György Szepesi, to Madrid to accompany Puskás home and give assurances that he would not be arrested. But any fears that Puskás held dissipated the moment he stepped off the plane at Ferihegy airport, to an awaiting crowd of tens of thousands, and a sea of handshakes, backslaps and hugs. Even for a man as famous as Puskás, long used to being gawped at and feted, you can see, in the footage of his walking out into the arrivals terminal, his incomprehension and overwhelming emotion at such a welcome.

His first port of call was his parents' grave (he hadn't attended his mother's funeral), and then it was on to preparations for the Golden Team's old boys' reunion – a match made up of two teams of former internationals: 'Budapest', captained by Puskás, versus 'The Countryside', captained by Jenő Buzánszky. In the dressing room beforehand, the 'old boys', now in their mid-fifties, greyer, fatter and mellower, roared with laughter as they poked fun at each other's balding pates and bulging bellies, especially Puskás, for whom a big-enough shirt could not be found.

> Puskás – Fucking hell, Szusza, look at the size of your gut – have you swallowed a football?
>
> Szusza – You can talk! Yours looks like you're carrying twins.

There was sadness too for the absence of the deceased Zakariás, Bozsik, Kocsis and Lóránt (who had died only a month earlier), as well as for Czibor, still stubbornly refusing to return home all the while Hungary was under communist rule, although he himself would also relent two years later.

At a time when average attendances at football matches in Hungary were well below their 1950s heyday (they would get lower), a crowd of 65,000 turned up two hours before the World Cup qualifier to watch the reunion. The very nature of the participants meant that they took the game seriously. Puskás (his gut straining over his shirt, and thighs pushing the seams of his shorts to bursting point) offered the occasional trick, flick and dribble, much to the crowd's roared approval, and at the match's end (a 3–3 draw) he made a point of publicly thanking the watching president, János Kádár. And the World Cup qualifier, Hungary versus England? England won 3–1 – their first ever victory at the Népstadion. Well, we had to get our own back sooner or later.

Appendix 1: Unbeaten

June 1950 to June 1954

1 v Poland – Warsaw, 4 Jun 1950
5–2: Szilágyi (3), Puskás (2)
Grosics, Rákóczi, Börzsei, Lantos, Bozsik, Józsa, Sándor, Kocsis, Szilágyi, Puskás, Babolcsay

2 v Albania – Budapest, 24 Sep 1950
12–0: Budai (4), Puskás (4), Kocsis (2), Palotás (2)
Grosics, J Kovács, Börzsei, F Tóth, I Kovács, Bozsik, Budai, Kocsis, Palotás, Puskás, Babolcsay

3 v Austria – Budapest, 29 Oct 1950
4–3: Puskás (3), Szilágyi
Grosics, J Kovács, Börzsei, Lantos, Bozsik, Lakat, Sándor, Kocsis (Hidegkuti), Palotás (Szilágyi), Puskás, Czibor

4 v Bulgaria – Sofia, 12 Dec 1950
1–1: Szilágyi
Grosics, Buzánszky, Börzsei, Lantos, Bozsik, Lakat (Zakariás), Sándor, Hidegkuti (Kocsis), Szilágyi, Puskás, Czibor

5 v Poland – Budapest, 27 May 1951
6–0: Kocsis (2), Puskás (2), Sándor, Czibor
Grosics (Henni), J Kovács, Börzsei, Lantos, Bozsik, I Kovács, Sándor, Kocsis, Szusza, Puskás (Hidegkuti), Czibor

6 v Czechoslovakia – Vitkovice, 14 Oct 1951
2–1: Kocsis (2)

Henni, J Kovács, Börzsei, Lantos, Bozsik, I Kovács, Sándor, Kocsis, Palotás, Puskás, Czibor (Hidegkuti)

7 v Finland – Budapest, 18 Nov 1951
8–0: Hidegkuti (3), Kocsis (2), Puskás (2), Czibor
Gellér, Buzánszky, Börzsei, Lantos, Bozsik, Zakariás, Sándor, Hidegkuti, Kocsis, Puskás, Czibor

8 v East Germany – Budapest, 18 May 1952
5–0: Hidegkuti (2), Kocsis, Sándor, Szusza
Grosics, Buzánszky, Börzsei, Lantos, Bozsik, Zakariás, Sándor, Hidegkuti, Szusza, Puskás, Czibor (Kocsis)

9 v Poland – Warsaw, 15 June 1952
5–1 Kocsis (2), Puskás (2), Hidegkuti
Grosics, Buzánszky, Lóránt, Dalnoki, Bozsik, I Kovács, Budai, Kocsis, Hidegkuti, Puskás, Czibor

10 v Finland – Helsinki, 22 June 1952
6–1: Kocsis (3), Bozsik, Palotás, Puskás
Grosics (Gellér), Buzánszky, Lóránt, Lantos, Bozsik, I Kovács, Budai, Kocsis, Hidegkuti, Puskás, Czibor (Palotás)

11 v Romania – Turku, Finland, 15 July 1952
2–1: Czibor, Kocsis
Grosics, Dalnoki, Lóránt, Lantos, Bozsik, I Kovács, Budai, Kocsis, Hidegkuti, Puskás, Czibor

12 v Italy – Helsinki, 21 July 1952
3–0: Palotás (2), Kocsis
Grosics, Buzánszky, Lóránt, Lantos, Bozsik, Zakariás, Csordás, Kocsis, Palotás, Puskás, Hidegkuti

13 v Turkey – Kotka, Finland, 24 July 1952
7–1: Kocsis (2), Puskás (2), Bozsik, Lantos, Palotás
Grosics, Buzánszky, Lóránt, Lantos, Bozsik, Zakariás, Csordás, Kocsis, Palotás, Puskás, Czibor

14 v Sweden – Helsinki, 28 July 1952
6–0: Kocsis (2), Hidegkuti, Palotás, Puskás, Lindh (own goal)

Grosics, Buzánszky, Lóránt, Lantos, Bozsik, Zakariás, Hidegkuti, Kocsis, Palotás, Puskás, Czibor

15 v Yugoslavia – Helsinki, 2 Aug 1952
2–0 Puskás, Czibor
Grosics, Buzánszky, Lóránt, Lantos, Bozsik, Zakariás, Hidegkuti, Kocsis, Palotás, Puskás, Czibor

16 v Switzerland – Berne, 20 Sep 1952
4–2: Puskás (2), Hidegkuti, Kocsis
Grosics, Buzánszky, Lóránt, Lantos, Bozsik, Zakariás, Budai, Kocsis, Palotás (Hidegkuti), Puskás, Czibor

17 v Czechoslovakia – Budapest, 19 Oct 1952
5–0: Kocsis (3), Egresi, Hidegkuti
Horváth, Buzánszky, Lóránt, Lantos, Bozsik, Zakariás, Egresi, Kocsis, Hidegkuti, Puskás, Czibor

18 v Austria – Budapest, 26 Apr 1953
1–1: Czibor
Grosics, Buzánszky, Börzsei, Lantos, Bozsik, Zakariás, Budai, Kocsis, Hidegkuti (Palotás), Puskás, Czibor

19 v Italy – Rome, 14 May 1953
3–0: Hidegkuti, Puskás (2)
Grosics, Buzánszky, Lóránt, Lantos, Bozsik, Zakariás, Budai, Kocsis, Hidegkuti (Palotás), Puskás, Czibor

20 v Sweden – Stockholm, 5 July 1953
4–2: Budai, Hidegkuti, Kocsis, Puskás
Grosics, Buzánszky, Lóránt, Lantos, Bozsik, Zakariás, Sándor (Budai), Kocsis, Hidegkuti, Puskás, Czibor

21 v Czechoslovakia – Prague, 4 Oct 1953
5–1: Csordás (2), Hidegkuti, Puskás, M Tóth
Grosics, Buzánszky, Lóránt, Lantos, Bozsik, Zakariás, Egresi, Csordás, Hidegkuti, Puskás, M Tóth

22 v Austria – Vienna, 11 Oct 1953
3–2: Hidegkuti (2), Csordás

Grosics, Buzánszky, Lóránt (Kárpáti), Lantos, Bozsik, Zakariás, Budai, Csordás, Hidegkuti, Puskás, M Tóth

23 v Sweden – Budapest, 15 Nov 1953
2–2: Czibor, Palotás
Grosics, Buzánszky, Lóránt, Lantos, Bozsik, Zakariás, Budai, Kocsis (Palotás), Hidegkuti, Puskás, Czibor

25 v England – London, 25 Nov 1953
6–3: Hidegkuti (3), Puskás (2), Bozsik
Grosics (Gellér), Buzánszky, Lóránt, Lantos, Bozsik, Zakariás, Budai, Kocsis, Hidegkuti, Puskás, Czibor

26 v Egypt – Cairo, 12 Feb 1954
3–0: Puskás (2), Hidegkuti
Grosics, Buzánszky, Teleki, Lantos, Bozsik, Zakariás, Budai (Sándor), Kocsis (Csordás), Hidegkuti, Puskás, Czibor (Palotás)

27 v Austria – Vienna, 11 Apr 1954
1–0: Happl (own goal)
Grosics, Buzánszky, Lóránt, Lantos, Bozsik, Zakariás, Budai, Kocsis (Palotás), Hidegkuti, Puskás, Czibor

28 v England – Budapest, 23 May 1954
7–1: Kocsis (2), Puskás (2), Hidegkuti, Lantos, J Tóth
Grosics, Buzánszky, Lóránt, Lantos, Bozsik, Zakariás, J Tóth, Kocsis, Hidegkuti, Puskás, Czibor

29 v South Korea – Zurich, 17 June 1954
9–0: Kocsis (3), Puskás (2), Palotás (2), Czibor, Lantos
Grosics, Buzánszky, Lóránt, Lantos, Bozsik, Szokja, Budai, Kocsis, Palotás, Puskás, Czibor

30 v West Germany – Basel, 20 June 1954
8–3: Kocsis (4), Hidegkuti (2), Puskás, J Tóth
Grosics, Buzánszky, Lóránt, Lantos, Bozsik, Zakariás, J Tóth, Kocsis, Hidegkuti, Puskás, Czibor

31 v Brazil – Berne, 27 June 1954
4–2: Kocsis (2), Hidegkuti, Lantos

Grosics, Buzánszky, Lóránt, Lantos, Bozsik, Zakariás, J Tóth, Kocsis, Hidegkuti, Czibor, M Tóth

32 v Uruguay – Lausanne, 30 June 1954
4–2: Kocsis (2), Czibor, Hidegkuti
Grosics, Buzánszky, Lóránt, Lantos, Bozsik, Zakariás, Budai, Kocsis, Palotás, Hidegkuti, Czibor

Appendix 2: Epilogue

Coaching staff

GUSZTÁV SEBES (1906–1986)

In 1960, in the midst of reforms distancing a new communist Hungary from the old Stalinist one with which he was associated, Sebes was removed from his post as Hungary's UEFA representative, and therefore also from his position as UEFA's vice-president. In 1962, he was appointed 'technical adviser' at Honvéd, but it wasn't to be, and he lasted just one underwhelming season. His last coaching job was at lowly Diósgyör VC in 1968. Credited internationally as the mastermind behind the Magical Magyars, Sebes spent the last years of his life in constant demand as a speaker on football tactics – particularly in Britain.

> Football was his sole passion, for which he sacrificed his life and at times his family. I felt that he looked up to the outstanding players with a combination of wonder and sadness that as a player himself he was never that good. He would have loved to have been as good as Puskás – that's why Öcsi was his 'child', because Sebes was enthralled by what he could do. Sebes did, however, understand what made footballers tick. He knew exactly how much he could let players get away with. He treated each differently and accordingly. That was his strength.
>
> *György Szepesi*[174]

He was well-meaning and decent, but you couldn't envy him. He was isolated.

Zoltán Czibor[175]

We were never on the same wavelength. There was always conflict between us, and I always pulled the short straw. For him, this was purely a matter of course. He was strong, he was the Communist Party, he was everything. He was a real narrow-minded, iron-fisted communist. He did not believe in God or man, he believed in communism. But during the 1950s, if Sebes hadn't been that type of person, he would never have been made head coach. The Communist Party put him there to direct the team. From a personal, political and professional viewpoint, we did not understand each other. Yet even without these three factors, it is still possible that two people can respect one another.

Gyula Grosics[176]

Sebes was a very intelligent and fundamentally decent man. He was fair-minded and never hurt anyone. He was always ready to help those who asked for his help. He was respected enormously by us players. The truth is that he loved us. He was one of the most genuine and honest persons I have ever known and looking back, there is nothing I can find bad to say about him.

Ferenc Puskás[177]

MÁRTON BUKOVI (1903–1985)

After resigning as Hungary's national team coach in August 1958, the feted inventor of the 4–2–4 formation returned to MTK for a season. He then moved to the Greek club Olympiakos, and along with Mihály Lantos led the club to two successive league titles. Bukovi saw out his retirement in France, a country he knew well from his time there as a player in the 1930s.

GYULA MÁNDI
(1899–1969)

After being released from his position as national team assistant coach in the wake of Gusztáv Sebes's sacking in 1956, Mándi was inundated with coaching offers. He decided upon the most lucrative – in Brazil, coaching first-division club FC America. But he only remained in Brazil for a year until illness forced him to return to Hungary, and it was another two years before he was well enough to return to work, this time as national team coach of Israel, having been personally requested by Israel's president, Ben Gurion. Mándi spent four successful years in Israel before returning to Budapest in his long-held hope that one of his home town's big clubs would employ him as their first-team coach. It was a position that Mándi had always felt deserving of, but alas by the late 1960s he was looked upon as a coach from a bygone era.

Players

GYULA GROSICS
(1926–2014)

Grosics retired from playing in 1962 to take up the coaching role at his club, Tatabányai Bányász, remaining for two seasons until leaving on a sour note. After another brief spell as coach of a second-division league club, he went to work for two years in Kuwait as an adviser to the country's football association. He returned to Hungary in 1970, and for the next 20 years ran a clothes shop in central Pest with his second wife. In 1990, he became involved in politics, standing for parliament with the centre-right Magyar Demokrata Forum. Grosics and his second wife would also divorce, and thereafter he lived alone with his six dogs, travelling by public transport, carrying the names of the ÁVO men responsible for his arrest decades earlier in his wallet. He was a popular figure in Hungary, regularly appearing at football functions and on television programmes.

> Not long ago my partner and I were out in Croatia, where we met with Vladimir Beara, the world-famous Yugoslav goalkeeper of the 1950s. In conversation, he asked me how much financial help I got from the government. I told him, 'Nothing'. By that, I meant no extra money other than my pension. He was shocked. 'I don't

believe it,' he said. I told him I was telling the truth. I can't explain to you just how much Beara praised the 'Golden Team'. Like we were gods! It is a humiliating experience when a footballer from another country acknowledges the lack of respect that you receive from your own.

Gyula Grosics[178]

Gyula was a great goalkeeper. Better than Lev Yashin. He was the greatest! He was a pioneer of world football. He was the game's first-ever fourth defender, wonderfully running out from his goal. It gave me the shivers watching him from the bench. It was possible to copy him but impossible to do it perfectly. If someone can measure every single time to the exact 100th of a second when to leave their goal or when not to, that is truly wondrous. No one could handle him, though. Except for me. He was personable, a soul of gold, a dear fool! How peculiar he was! Every goalkeeper is peculiar. I am not normal either. There isn't a goalkeeper who is normal. You stand in the goal all by yourself for ages and nothing happens, then all of a sudden everything depends on you. Before every match, Gyula believed himself to be ill; before every match he would find himself an alibi which he could use later if something went wrong.

Sándor Gellér[179]

MIHÁLY LANTOS (1928–1989)

Lantos remained MTK's first-choice left-back up until 1962. Three years after retiring, he joined, as assistant, his former MTK boss Márton Bukovi at the Greek club Olympiakos, where the pair would win the league twice in succession. In 1968, Lantos returned to Hungary, coaching four lower-league clubs until his retirement in 1981.

JENŐ BUZÁNSZKY (1925–2015)

Buzánszky retired from playing in 1960 aged 35, having spent 13 years at Dorogi Banyász. A year later, he was appointed as the club's coach, and he remained in the role until illness forced him to quit in 1969. In 1972, he returned as the club's technical director, a position he would keep until his retirement in 1985. During all this time, Buzánszky continued to work as the head of recruitment for the Dorogi Coal Board. He was always a cheerful presence, willing to reminisce and represent Hungarian football in all respects. From 1994 until 1998, Buzánszky was the vice-president of the Hungarian FA.

GYULA LÓRÁNT (1923–1981)

Lóránt quit playing in 1957, aged 34, to make use of his economics degree, taking charge of a Pest plastics company, but the business venture turned sour. After a brief spell running a pub he returned to football taking charge of Váci Vasas, and thereafter Honvéd in 1962. But Lóránt's ultra-authoritarian approach endeared him to no one, and the threat of a players' revolt saw him sacked after just one season. It was the final straw for Lóránt. He spent Christmas Day 1963 with his wife and daughters, and the next day fled to Austria. He would never return to Hungary, nor see his family again. He made for West Germany, where his fluent German (he'd grown up in a town in on the Austrian border) and legacy as a member of the Hungarian Golden Team stood him in good stead.

Throughout the next 15 years he was in constant employment at no fewer than eight clubs, peaking at Bayern Munich from 1978 to 1979. German football remembers Lóránt more for his short fuse than his few successes. However, as hard a taskmaster as he was, Lóránt was also a very competent football coach, and he is credited with bringing zonal defending to the Bundesliga. And nor did all of his players dislike him: Jürgen Grabowski, a member of West Germany's 1974 World Cup-winning team, saw Lóránt's rages merely as 'his Hungarian way of sorting the men out from the boys'. On a personal level, Lóránt was forever guilt-ridden for abandoning his wife and daughters, and for their part they had to make do with following his career in the foreign press. His wife Ibolya divorced him in 1973. In the spring of 1981, Lóránt sent a message to his daughters – if he came home like Puskás, would they be prepared to see him? Lóránt never found out the answer: on 31 May 1981, while sitting on the trainer's bench, watching his team, the Greek side PAOK Thessaloniki, Lóránt suffered a heart attack. He died in hospital later the same day. Lóránt was first laid to rest in Thessaloniki, Greece, and then in 2011 his coffin was exhumed and reburied in his home town of Kőszeg.

JÓZSEF BOZSIK
(1925–1978)

In April 1962, the 36-year-old Bozsik played his last game for Kispest Honvéd, after a record-breaking 447 appearances. Three days later, he established another record in playing his 100th and last international match for Hungary, an achievement that made him just the third player in the world to reach a century of appearances for his country.

From 1962 to 1966, Bozsik remained at Honvéd as the club's 'football supervisor', and in 1966, he became the club's head coach, but only lasted a season before he quit, unable to tolerate/understand the new generation of footballers.

In 1974, Bozsik resurfaced to be appointed as coach of Hungary's national team, but the stress of the job and the fact that Bozsik was a lifelong heavy smoker saw him suffer a heart attack after only a year in charge. Advised by doctors not to return to management, Bozsik remained employed at the Hungarian FA as a 'technical supervisor', but again had to retire after suffering a second heart attack in 1977. In May the following year, Bozsik suffered his third and final heart attack. Kispest Honvéd's stadium is named in his honour – Bozsik József Stadion.

His son Péter would himself go on to have a successful career as a footballer, and for a spell in 2006 was the head coach of Hungary's national team.

JÓZSEF ZAKARIÁS
(1924–1971)

'Zaki' never played for Hungary after the 1954 World Cup Final defeat to West Germany, the only Golden Team member not to do so. He retired from playing four years later, opening a pub with his wife in central Budapest. In contrast to Zakariás's reputation as a dull footballer, he was an excellent and lively host and cashed in on customers wanting to meet a Golden Team member. He only gave up the business to return to football, taking a coaching role at the small Pest club Szigetszentmiklósi SE. A year later, the national team of Guinea toured Hungary (the first African nation to do so), combining their trip with a search for a Hungarian coach, and Zakariás was the perfect candidate: fluent in French (Guinea was a French colony) and ever eager to broaden his horizons. In total he spent seven years coaching in Guinea, at the cost of his marriage. In 1968, he returned to Hungary hoping to find a coaching role at a first-division club, but the best offered was at a lowly third-division club, where he remained for the next three seasons. Then, one morning in November 1971, Zakariás collapsed at his Budapest home, to die in hospital two days later. He was 47 years old.

Interestingly, the press was forbidden to investigate precisely how Zakariás died; the authorities told them it was cancer. Even to this day, the file on Zakariás's death remains a government secret. Why should this be? According to many, Zakariás was resentful at what he considered his shoddy treatment by Hungarian football, and was preparing to spill the beans and let it be known that he had been ordered to underperform in Hungary's 1954 World Cup Final against West Germany.

> In the 1970s, it was very easy to die. There was the case of one Hungarian sportswriter who went for a stroll from his Berlin hotel and his body was discovered the next day, nine kilometres away. Another, more modern one, concerns the family of a well-known sports administrator. The father disappeared, and his body was found drowned in only a few centimetres of water in Lake Balaton, and when his son began to investigate he was killed in a strange accident. How did they die and why? They knew something that they shouldn't have. Simple as that.
>
> *Gyula Grosics*[180]

LÁSZLÓ BUDAI
(1928–1983)

Budai played his last game for Hungary in 1959 and for Honvéd in 1961. Afterwards, he remained in the army as a physical training instructor, and in 1967 was appointed coach of an army team, Szentendri Honvéd, where he would stay for the next 15 years.

In 1983, Budai gave an interview, alongside Zoltán Czibor, to a room full of sports reporters and inadvertently said that the Golden Team had been ordered to lose the World Cup Final. When pressed further, Budai, an upstanding, honest man with no reputation as a teller of tall stories, refused to elaborate, indeed refused to speak further. It was only the intervention of Czibor that finally got the pressmen to leave Budai alone. Czibor did not disagree with what Budai had said. The pressmen present were forbidden from reporting Budai's comment all the time Hungary remained a communist country.

To believe, though, that Hungary purposely threw the World Cup Final is unfathomable (though many think this to be the case). For a start, there is no proof, and there is the question of what could have motivated the Hungarian government in wanting their national team to lose the World Cup Final. Yet neither is the whole scenario unfeasible, in a world where betrayal had come to be considered a natural action.

Weeks after the interview, the hitherto perfectly healthy Budai died from a stroke. He was 54. He is buried in the Pest suburb of Rákospalota, where he lived his entire life. The local football club's ground is named in his honour – Budai László Stadion.

SÁNDOR KOCSIS (1929–1979)

Of all the Golden Team members, quitting football hit Kocsis the hardest – he literally knew nothing else. His lack of confidence in dealing with people, combined with his faltering Spanish, prevented him from becoming a coach, so instead he followed Zoltán Czibor's example and opened a café in central Barcelona. Then in 1974 a freak accident changed everything. Kocsis was in his bathroom having a shave when a cabinet fell from the wall and landed on his right foot, causing a serious gash. Kocsis's aversion to doctors had him refusing to seek medical help, but when the wound became infected he was forced to – but it was too late: gangrene had set in and the foot had to be amputated. The loss devastated the already fragile Kocsis. Self-conscious and ashamed of his orthopaedic shoe, he became depressed and began to drink heavily.

When, in 1976, he returned home for a visit to Hungary for the first time in 20 years, the bloated, limping Kocsis was hardly recognisable to those that had known him as a lithe young man. In 1979, he was diagnosed with stomach cancer. While undergoing treatment at a Barcelona hospital, he jumped to his death out of a second-floor window. Kocsis was 49 years old.

In 2012, Sándor Kocsis's ashes were moved from Barcelona to Budapest and placed in the crypt of the city's St Stephen's Cathedral.

PÉTER PALOTÁS (1930–1967)

Palotás was forced to retire from football in 1960 when it was discovered that he had a weak heart. For the next few years, he worked as a clerk in the textiles industry, dying from a heart attack in 1967, aged just 37.

KÁROLY SÁNDOR
(1928–2014)

'Csikar' remained at MTK for the rest of his playing days until 1964, and the same year also played his last international match after 75 appearances and three World Cup tournaments. Ever cheerful, he remained involved in football up his death in 2014 aged 86. MTK's training academy is named the Károly Sándor Academy.

FERENC PUSKÁS
(1927–2006)

Straight after retiring from playing for Real Madrid in 1966, Puskás became coach of second-division Vitoria. But the dual workload of coaching and running his two businesses in Madrid (a restaurant and a sausage-making factory) soon had Puskás quitting the club. Before long, though, he began to miss football, so he accepted a lucrative coaching job in Canada with Vancouver Royals, giving up his businesses to do so. The North American Soccer League was founded that year, 1968, and needed big star names to attract crowds, and Puskás was one such. Alas, for numerous reasons, mostly issues concerning money or the lack of it, Puskás's time in the States did not work out. He stayed for nine months before returning to Madrid empty-handed, forever regretful of closing his beloved restaurant.

For a brief while he coached second-division Spanish club CD Alavés, until one day he was contacted out of the blue by the president of Greek club Panathinaikos, offering him the manager's job at the club, which Puskás readily accepted. Puskás warmed to Greece, and Greece to him. He led Panathinaikos to two league titles and the 1971 European Cup Final, where they lost 2–0 to the 'Total Football' of Johan Cruyff's Ajax. One king watching the other.

After four happy years at Panathinaikos, Puskás returned to Spain, coaching second-division Real Murcia for a brief period, then, as a favour for a friend, undertaking a coaching job in Chile for a season. From Chile, Puskás went to Saudi Arabia to coach the country's newly formed national team; but the country was not to his wife's liking, so he returned to Greek football, taking AEK Athens to the second round of the 1978/79 European Cup – where they lost to eventual winners Nottingham Forest. His time in Greece, though, only lasted that one season. At his home in Athens, Puskás was visited by the president of the Egyptian club Al-Masry with a job offer. Puskás's wife, Erzsi, was keen on going to Egypt, so they went, although she would soon change her mind and return intermittently to Madrid. Puskás would stay in Egypt for another five well-paid years (it was while working as coach of Al-Masry that, in 1981, Puskás returned to Hungary for the Golden Team's reunion match).

In 1985 Puskás (again as a favour to a friend) moved to Panama to coach Club Sol de America, remaining for a season before moving on to Cerro Porteño where he stayed for three more. From Panama Puskás then headed to Australia, coaching South Melbourne Hellas for three successful seasons.

Immediately on his return to Hungary, Puskás was offered the job as coach of Honvéd, but he refused, feeling that he was too old for the stresses of managing a league club. But he did, against his better judgement, allow himself in 1993 to be convinced into accepting the post of head coach of the Hungarian national team. The team was in dire need of a miracle, and Puskás was hoped to be it. He wasn't. He and the players immediately clashed: they felt he lived in the past, while Puskás told them they were not a patch on the players of his day. In his short reign, Hungary lost to the Soviet Union, Sweden and most notably lowly Iceland in a World Cup qualifier.

He spent his last years living in comfort with his wife in Buda and working as an ambassador for Hungarian football: 'handshaking duties' as he called the role. In 2000, he was named by FIFA as the sixth greatest footballer of the 20th century behind Pelé, Cruyff, Beckenbauer, Di Stéfano and Maradona. In 2002, the Népstadion was renamed the Puskás Ferenc Stadion in his honour.

In 2004, Puskás was diagnosed with Alzheimer's, and he died from complications stemming from the disease in 2006, aged 79. Hungary awarded its most famous son a state funeral. His ashes were placed in the crypt of Budapest's St Stephen's Basilica.

NÁNDOR HIDEGKUTI
(1922–2002)

For a player who relied on intelligence more than stealth, it is not surprising that Hidegkuti would prove to be the most successful of the Golden Team players when it came to coaching. After retiring from playing in 1958, he was immediately appointed coach of MTK, but only remained for a season before leaving to coach in Italy with Fiorentina. In his first season, 1960/61, Hidegkuti led the club to victory in the newly established European Cup Winners' Cup. In 1965, he returned to Hungary, taking charge of Vasas Győr, leading them to the Hungarian league title and the remarkable achievement of reaching the semi-finals of the 1964/65 European Cup. In the 1970s, he coached in Egypt at Al Ahly, winning the league title five times. In 1985 he was tempted back to coach for a season in Dubai, and again in 1996 for a season as technical adviser at the Egyptian club Alexandria. It was Hidegkuti's last appointment in football. MTK's stadium is named in his honour.

ZOLTÁN CZIBOR
(1929–1997)

After leaving Barcelona in 1961, Czibor joined their cross-city rivals Españyol, making just ten sporadic and indifferent appearances before moving down two divisions to join CE Europa. He ended his career a year later after an equally underwhelming and brief spell in Canada. Back in Barcelona, he continued running his bar, the Blue Danube – a great success, popular with Barça fans and Hungarian émigrés. But Czibor and alcohol were never a great combination, leading his wife, Írisz, to divorce him in the early 1970s; the expense of the divorce would eventually cost him his business.

In 1983, Czibor finally returned to Hungary, essentially for a family wedding but primarily because a biography of him and Kocsis had been published and he needed the money from the book. The book signing alone attracted a crowd of 15,000 and brought central Budapest's main thoroughfare to a standstill. While in Hungary, Czibor found the time to marry a woman some 29 years his junior. He also did the rounds, visiting his old friends, who included László Budai. Rather than knock on Budai's door, Czibor clambered through an open front-room window to confront Budai sitting on his sofa.

'You've come back, Crazy,' said Budai, not getting up.

'I couldn't live any longer without you, Hunchback.'

Hungary was still, however, under a communist regime, something Czibor refused to tolerate, so he and his bride returned to Barcelona. As good as his word, Czibor only returned to Hungary for good in 1990 once the communist regime was no longer. He spent his last years poor but happy in his home town of Komárom. A heavy smoker all of his life, Zoltán Czibor died of cancer in 1997 aged 68. His funeral in Komárom was attended by thousands and his passing marked with a minute's silence at Barcelona's Nou Camp.

FERENC SZUSZA
(1923–2006)

Szusza finished his playing career at his sole club Újpest in 1960 after 19 years, 463 appearances and 383 goals, a world record for a player at a single club (until recently surpassed by Lionel Messi). He became a successful coach, first in Hungary with Vasas Győr and Újpest, then in Poland with Górnik Zabrze, and later in Spain, with Real Betis from 1971 to 1976 and Atlético Madrid for a season. His last coaching job was at Újpest in 1981. Újpest's stadium is named the Szusza Ferenc Stadion in his honour.

JÓZSEF TÓTH
(1929–2017)

Winger Tóth retired from playing in 1961 having spent his entire 13-year career at the one club, Csepel SC. He remained in Csepel (a district of Budapest) for the rest of his days, working in a local factory. In 1982, 28 years after his knee was kicked out of joint in the brutal World Cup quarter-final against Brazil, Tóth had an operation to rectify the damage. He was the very last of the Golden Team to pass away, aged 88 in 2017.

MIHÁLY TÓTH
(1926–1990)

The 1954 World Cup finalist Tóth retired from playing for his one club, Újpest, in 1963. He remained at the club as reserve team coach until 1970 and thereafter worked as a physical education teacher at a Budapest secondary school.

ISTVÁN NYERS
(1924–2005)

In 1956, a 32-year-old Nyers left Inter Milan to spend two seasons at Roma before joining Barcelona, at the behest of an invitation by László Kubal. Unfortunately Nyers was a tad past his best for the Catalan club to want to sign him permanently, but he remained in Spain for a couple of seasons at lower-league clubs before returning to Italy. In 1961, he retired from playing to become coach of Serie A club Bologna, but heart problems soon forced his resignation. Unable to continue in football and out of money, the France-born Nyers returned to his parents' home town of Szabadka, formerly in Hungary but since 1921 in Yugoslavia. He took Yugoslavian citizenship and lived quietly in Szabadka until his death in 2005. Practically unheard of in communist Hungary for his goalscoring feats in Italian football, Nyers's funeral was attended by only a handful of mourners. Later, Inter Milan would pay for a headstone fit for one of their all-time greats.

LÁSZLÓ KUBALA (1927–2002)

From leaving the Spanish club Españyol in 1964, it was another two years before Kubala returned to football, as player-manager of the Swiss club FC Zurich, where at the age of 41 he played in the opening round of the 1966/67 European Cup against the eventual winners Celtic. From Switzerland, Kubala took one final payday in Canada, again as player-manager, at Toronto Falcons – but Spain was home, and he returned to coach lower-league Córdoba for a season before readily accepting the job as coach of the Spanish national team. Kubala would remain in charge of Spain for 11 years, remarkable in itself but even more so considering how miserably they underachieved during his time as coach, failing to qualify for the 1970 and 1974 World Cups. And although they qualified for the 1978 tournament, they failed to get beyond the group stage. In 1980, he took over as a coach of his beloved FC Barcelona, but his second spell was even briefer than his first six-month stint in charge some 17 years earlier. What followed were spells as a coach in Saudi Arabia and at lower-league clubs across Spain. He did eventually find success as coach of the gold-winning Spanish team at the 1992 Olympics, fittingly in Barcelona. His last coaching position was in 1995, aged 68, with the Paraguay national team, but Kubala only lasted a few months: he missed his home – Barcelona.

In his ripe old age, Kubala continued to turn out for Barça veteran teams, and was a regular face at the Nou Camp, remaining as popular as ever with the supporters. His last years were spent in financial hardship – not that anyone besides his family knew. This toughest of Budapest boys was never one to complain. László Kubala died in Barcelona in 2002 from complications stemming from Alzheimer's. In his honour, Barcelona's city council named a street after him, and FC Barcelona erected a bronze statue of him in front of the Nou Camp. In 2000, FIFA rated Kubala as the 32nd greatest player of the 20th century, while at the same time Barça fans voted him the club's greatest ever player.

Others

BÉLA GUTTMANN
(1899–1981)

After being sacked in 1966 by Benfica, Guttmann, by then in his mid-sixties, spent the next decade living off his reputation, coaching undramatically in Switzerland with Servette, in Greece with Panathinaikos, and in Austria with Austria Vienna, finally returning to Portugal for a two-season spell at Porto, before quitting when he was 75 years old. A lifetime of high living saw him and his wife live their last days practically penniless. He died in Vienna in 1981 and is buried in the city's Jewish cemetery.

In 2013, in a poll of the greatest managers of all time, compiled by *World Soccer,* Guttmann finished ninth. In a similar poll of Hungarian journalists choosing the greatest Hungarian manager of all time, Guttmann came first, Sebes second.

JENŐ KALMÁR
(1908–1990)

In 1957, after Honvéd's tour of Brazil, Kalmár remained in Austria to manage league club Wacker and thereafter Wiener SC. In 1960 he moved to Spain, where, using his credentials as a former coach of the mighty Honvéd, he was never out of work for nearly two decades at numerous first- and second-division clubs. After a brief spell in Portugal at FC Porto, Kalmár returned to Spain, where he spent the rest of his days.

GYÖRGY SZEPESI
(1922–2018)

The Golden Team's 'Twelfth Man' continued commentating well into the 1990s. In total Szepesi commentated on 14 World Cup tournaments, earning himself a place in the Guinness Book of Records. From 1978 until 1986, Szepesi was president of the Hungarian FA, and from 1982 until 1994 he was a member of FIFA's inner committee.

SÁNDOR BARCS
(1912–2010)

Barcs remained the president of the Hungarian FA up until 1963. He was vice-president of UEFA from 1964 to 1972, and president from 1972 to 1973.

GYULA HEGYI
(1897–1978)

Hegyi remained influential in Hungarian sport for the rest of his life. Between 1964 and 1969 he was president of the Hungarian FA.

MIHÁLY FARKAS
(1904–1965)

In 1957, Farkas was sentenced to 16 years in prison for his role during the Rákosi regime, but he ultimately served only four years before being released in 1961. Thereafter he worked as a proofreader for a renowned Budapest publisher, but longed to return to politics. In 1965, when his application to rejoin the Communist Party was *again* refused, Farkas committed suicide.

> Of all the top leaders of the time, Mihály Farkas embodied the Golden Team. It was a comfort for us that we need only deal with Farkas. He adored football – a minister who hated the sport would have never been such a helping hand. I am also sure that he loved basking in our popularity.
>
> For us, he was our boss, and when we needed help we could always count on him.
>
> *Ferenc Puskás*[181]

GÁBOR PÉTER
(1906–1993)

The once feared chief of the ÁVO was released from prison in 1959 after serving six years of a life sentence. He was never again permitted to join the Communist Party. He spent the rest of his working days as a librarian in Budapest.

ERNŐ GERŐ
(1898–1980)

After his failure in the eyes of the Soviets to prevent the 1956 revolution, Gerő was sent to live in the Soviet Union. Four years later in 1960, he returned to Hungary, but he was never again entrusted with any role in any governmental office; indeed in 1962 he was dismissed from the Communist Party outright. He spent the rest of his days working as a translator.

IMRE NAGY
(1896–1958)

After his execution in June 1958 the former prime minster's body, and those of Pál Maléter and Miklós Gimes, were buried face down in the cemetery of the prison in which they were executed. Four years later, their bodies were moved secretly to a Pest cemetery, and it was only towards the end of the communist regime in the 1980s that their families were told of the graves' locations. In 1989, the then still leader János Kádár oversaw that the three were given state reburials fit for national heroes.

JÁNOS KÁDÁR
(1912–1989)

From the end of the '56 revolution, Kádár remained in power for over 30 years. In the late 1980s, when well into his seventies, and going senile, he was ousted by younger members of the Communist Party. Although Hungarians never truly forgave him for his role in siding with the Soviets in 1956, they did grow to respect Kádár, surmising that it could be worse – while neighbouring Romania was enduring the terror that was the Nicolae Ceauşescu regime, Hungarians had the highest standard of living in any of the Soviet satellites. In comparison to the Romanian dictator, Kádár was a saint. When he died aged 77 in July 1989, thousands attended his funeral and the day was classed as a national day of mourning.

Communism in Hungary did not survive long after Kádár. On 23 October 1989, 33 years to the day since the revolution began, communism in Hungary was replaced with a multi-party democracy. The last Russian troops left Hungarian soil on 19 June 1991.

MÁTYÁS RÁKOSI (1892–1971)

In 1967, Rákosi was offered the opportunity to return to Hungary, but only if he promised not to get involved in politics. Despite being desperate to return home, Rákosi refused to promise. He never returned to Hungary. 'The Bald Butcher' (or 'Stalin's Best Pupil' depending on who you asked) died in Nizhny, central Russia in February 1971 aged 78. His body was cremated in Moscow, but his relatives were permitted to have his ashes interned in Budapest's Farkasréti Cemetery, in a ceremony that was held in secret and attended by only a scattering of relatives.

> It was almost impossible to get close to Rákosi. He was unbelievably inflexible. Of course, we met a few times. I was in awe. He had a massive authority and the power to decide life or death. Once at a reception we ran into each other; he looked me up and down, put his hand on my shoulder and asked, 'What's up, Puskás? Will you win on Sunday? You know it would make a lot of people happy.' All I replied was, 'We will win, Comrade Rákosi – we will win.'
>
> *Ferenc Puskás*[182]

Endnotes

1 At the time of writing, Hungary are ranked 54th.

2 Initially Hungarians simply called the sport 'futball', but, thanks to the government's insistence that national sporting associations use Hungarian terms, a new word was coined: 'labdarugás', translating to 'ball-kick' – hence 'Magyar Labdarúgás Szövetség' (Hungarian Football Association).

3 The very first visit by a British club to Hungary was earlier in 1901, when the leading amateur side Richmond AFC played six matches in seven days, winning all with ease. The visitors' first match was against a Hungarian league representative side.

4 Jacobs, N., *Vivian Woodward: Football's Gentleman*. Tempus, Stroud, 2005.

5 Ibid.

6 In Hungary, the club is commonly known as *Fradi*, derived from *Franzstadt*, the German name for Ferencváros.

7 'MTK' stands for *Magyar Testgyakorlók Kőre*, translating to the 'Hungarian Gymnastics Circle Committee'.

8 The MTK stadium was the location for the football match scenes in the 1981 movie *Escape to Victory*, starring Michael Caine, Sylvester Stallone, Pelé, Bobby Moore and a host of Ipswich Town footballers. The movie was based on a wonderful 1962 Hungarian film, *Két Felidő a Pokolban* – 'Two Half Times in Hell'.

9 Also known as John Tait Robertson.

10 Hogan was once selected for the Irish national team, only for them to back out once they learned that, although of Irish parentage, he had been born in England.

11 Meisl was himself a former referee, and in 1908 had refereed the first international match between Hungary and England.

12 Fox, N., *Prophet or Traitor? The Jimmy Hogan Story*. The Parrs Wood Press, Manchester, 2003.

13 Ibid.

14 Ibid.

15 Ibid.

16 A royal role that cannot bestow titles of nobility nor commute death sentences.

17 Bukovi, M. & Csaknády, J. *Learn to Play the Hungarian Way*. Hungarian Sport Publishing House, Budapest, 1954.

18 Hungarians now call the Puskás team of the 1950s the 'Golden Team', whereas the record-breaking MTK team of the 1920s are referred to as the 'First Golden Team'. The terms 'Magical Magyars' and 'Magnificent Magyars' were coined by the British press in the 1950s.

19 The very first coach of Juventus was a former MTK forward called Jenő Károly who as a player was legendary for his goal scoring prowess and notorious for diving, though whether he is the man responsible for introducing the latter to Italian football is unknown. Károly died in 1926, aged 40, while coach of Juventus – the club going on to win that season's Serie A in his absence.

20 Fox, N., *Prophet or Traitor?*

21 Named after the Palace of Versailles' summer house, Trianon Petit.

22 Five of the Hungarian team that played in the historic 6–3 win over England at Wembley in 1953 had 'Hungarianised' surnames: Mihály (Ledenmeyer) Lantos, Gyula (Lipovics) Lóránt, László (Bednarik) Budai, Ferenc (Purczeld) Puskás and Nándor (Krautenbrunner) Hidegkuti. 'Lantos' means 'flute player', 'Lóránt' is the Hungarian spelling of 'Roland', Budai means 'of Buda', Puskás 'gunner' and Hidegkuti 'of the village Hidegkut'.

23 Fox, *Prophet or Traitor?*

24 A former Ferencváros and Hungary international, Eisenhoffer was born a gentile (József Aczel) but converted to Judaism so that he could marry his Jewish fiancée.

25 Hakoah's pinnacle was a 5–1 victory over West Ham United in London, the first time an English club lost to continental opposition on home soil.

26 In fairness, the Dutch East Indies (Indonesia) were no real competition. The last-minute replacements for Japan were woefully inexperienced, fielding a team containing nine debutants and a captain so myopic that he had to wear glasses even when playing.

27 Today, 60 Andrássy Boulevard is a tourist attraction: The House of Terror.

28 Today a floodlight pylon stands where the tenement block once stood.

29 Docherty, Tommy, *The Doc: Hallowed Be Thy Game.* Headline, London, 2006, pp 103–104.

30 Puskás's sister Éva would live in the house for life.

31 One US dollar would have bought you 400,000,000,000,000,000,000,000,000,000 Hungarian pengő.

32 Malonyai, P., *Aranykór*. Novotrade, Hungary, 1989, p 53.†

33 L. Réti, A., *Miért Vesztettünk?* Sport, Budapest, 1982, p 76.†

34 Burgess, a former Manchester United full-back, had replied to an advert placed in a London newspaper by Alfréd Brüll seeking a British coach.

35 Surányi, A., *Aranycsapat*. MAFILM, Budapest, 1982.†

36 Kő, A., *A Grosics*. Apriori International, Hungary, 2008, p 51.†

37 Malonyai, P., *Aranykór*. Novotrade, Budapest, 1989, p 115.†

38 Bocsák, M., *Kocsis és Czibor*. Sport, Hungary, 1983, pp 34–35.†

39 Malonyai, P., *Aranykór*. Novotrade, Budapest, 1989, p 87.†

40 Ibid., p 83.†

41 While interviewing Gyula Grosics for this book, I asked him who was the better player: Puskás or Kubala? 'Puskás', he replied without hesitation, looking slightly incredulous that I had to ask such a question.

42 Bocsák, *Kocsis és Czibor*, p 149.†

43 Kő, A., *A Grosics*. Apriori International, 2008, p 47.†

44 Peterdi, P. & Somos, I., *Lóri: Lóránt Gyula Életregénye*. Lapkiadó Vállalat, Budapest, 1986, p 33.†

45 Hungarians never took up learning Russian with any enthusiasm – indeed, there was a certain patriotic pride in not being able to speak the language.

46 Török, F., *Mandula: Mándi Gyula, Fradi-MTK-Aranycsapat*. Nyik-ki Bt, Budapest, 1999, p 119.†

47 The MAC was abolished under nationalisation, but its stadium and training facilities remained.

48 Football league seasons in the Soviet Union ran from March through to October, whereas the Hungarian seasons had run from August through to October – followed by a three-month winter break – then continuing from March through to May. In Hungary, therefore, the season that should have been 1950/51 instead became just 1950.

49 Named after György Dózsa, a 16th-century Transylvanian peasant executed for leading a revolt against the aristocratic gentry.

50 Deák was arrested for drunkenly punching to the ground two ÁVO officers who had ordered him to stop singing the Fradi anthem, an overtly nationalistic song, in a hotel

bar. But instead of being taken to Andrássy Avenue, Deák was taken to a police station in Újpest, where the Dózsa president, Sándor Csáki, visited him. 'Decide what you want, Deák,' said Csáki. 'Prison or play football for us?' Ferenc Deák may have saved his career by joining Dózsa, but the incident had Sebes excluding him from any further involvement in Hungary's national team. At just 27 years old, Deák – the world record holder for scoring the most goals in a season (66 goals in the 1945/46 season) – never represented his country again.

51 Szöllősi, G., *Czibor: Dribli az Égig.* Self-published, Hungary, 1997, p 111.†

52 Bocsák, M., *Kocsis és Czibor*. Sport, Hungary, 1983, p 39.†

53 MATEOSZ was a Buda-based club (formely Gamma FC) formed at the end of the war by members of the Hungarian National Haulage As-sociation (Magyar Teherfuvarozók Országos Szövetkezete). To generate funds to form a sports club, the association signed a deal with its members that 5 per cent from every profit made on a hauled cargo would be directed to the club, and thus within a year MATEOSZ's sports club was flush with enough funds to purchase outright the team and stadium of a Buda club, Gamma FC, who were then languishing in the second division. A year later, under the name MATEOSZ, the club were promoted to the first division.

54 Kő, A., *A Grosics*. Apriori International, Hungary, 2008, p 70.†

55 The International Federation of Football History & Statistics rates Szusza's 392 league goals for Újpest between 1941 and 1960 as a world record for a player at one club.

56 The exact same injury had ended the playing career of Rudas's professional footballer father some 20 years earlier, when he also was aged 29.

57 Szöllősi, G., *Czibor*, p 128.†

58 Ibid., p 87.†

59 The actual origins of the 4–2–4 are impossible to distinguish. Some football historians credit Bukovi, but in Hungary it is also written that he learned the formation during his playing days at Ferencváros. Only in 1958 at the World Cup did the formation become recognised as a 4–2–4, when the tournament's winners, Brazil, lined up with a four-man defence, two midfielders and a four-man forward line. And who was the man said to be responsible for taking the formation to Brazil? Izodor Kürschner, a former MTK player in the 1920s.

60 Surányi, A., *Aranycsapat*. MAFILM. Budapest, 1982, p 46.†

61 Bolgár, I., *Suttyó a Császár*. Sportpropaganda, Budapest, p 82.†

62 Olympic rules meant that Sebes could not coach the football team at the tournament as well as hold the position of Hungary's Olympic Committee president. Therefore the Honvéd coach, Jenő Kalmár, was named as Hungary's coach for the tournament.

63 Joy, B., *Soccer Tactics*. Phoenix House, London, 1962.

64 Sebes, G., *A Magyar Labdarúgás*. Sport Lap és Könyvkiadó, Budapest, 1955.†

65 Borsi-Kálmán, B., *Az Aranycsapat és a Kapitánya*. Kortárs Kiadó, Hungary, 2008, p 86–87.†

66 Puskás, F., *Captain of Hungary: An Autobiography*. Stadia, Stroud, UK, 2007, p 131.

67 Rejtő, L., *Az Aranycsapat és Árnyai*. Sport, Budapest, 1966, p 62.†

68 The site of a huge bronze statue of Stalin.

69 Péter's birth name was Benjámin Eisenberger.

70 Sebestyen, V., *Twelve Days: Revolution 1956*. Phoenix, London, 2007.

71 First round: Switzerland 4–0; quarter-final: Eire 4–0; semi-final: Turkey 2–0; final: Yugoslavia 2–0.

72 Sebes, G., *Örömök és Csalódások*. Gondolat, Budapest, 1981, pp 227–228.†

73 In 1961, Sztalinváros was renamed Dunaújváros (Danube-New-Town).

74 Both Hogan's biography, *Prophet or Traitor? The Jimmy Hogan Story*, and Raynor's, *George Raynor: The Greatest Coach England Never Had* are great reads.

75 Hyne, A., *George Raynor: The Greatest Coach England Never Had*. History Press, Stroud, 2014.

76 Joy, B., *Soccer Tactics*. Phoenix House, London, 1962.

77 Feleki first asked a recently retired Arsenal player, Jack Lambert, but the newly married Lambert didn't want to leave his young wife. Lambert in turn recommended Arthur Rowe. This explains why the Arsenal fan Feleki turned to a Tottenham player for assistance.

78 Fox, N., *Prophet or Traitor?* The Parrs Wood Press, Manchester,, p 184.

79 Kő, A., *Szemétből Mentett Dicsőégünk*. Magyar Könyklub, Budapest, 1997, pp 89–90.†

80 Ibid., p 90.†

81 Ibid., p 91.†

82 Tossell, D., *Big Mal: Biography of Malcolm Allison*. Mainstream Publishing, Edinburgh, 2009.

83 Wright would be magnanimous enough to admit later, 'It was not the cleverest thing I've ever said.'

84 When Wright and Puskás shook hands on meeting for the first time in 40 years at a dinner function in England, one wag yelled, 'That's the closest you've ever got to him, Bill!'

85 The Tottenham winger Robb was selected because he had seen the Hungarians play at the 1952 Olympics.

86 Gellér and Grosics had a rather bizarre form of friendship. Gellér was quite clearly Grosics's downtrodden understudy, and content to be so. As Gellér explained in an interview in his later life, 'Grosics would say to me, "I am cleverer than you, I am more handsome than you and I am better than you, because I am Grosics, whereas you, Gellér, are a dick." But tell me the truth – is it that difficult to accept that a genius who played 80 times for his country is better than you?' (Bocsák, M., *A Grosics – Villa Titka*. Sport,Budapest, 1986, pp 49–50.†)

87 *Daily Telegraph*, 24 November 1953.

88 Matthews, S., *The Way It Was: My Autobiography*. Headline, London, 2000.

89 Agnew, P., *Football Legend: The Authorised Biography of Tom Finney*. Milo Books, Bury, 2002, p 110.

90 Puskás, F., *Captain of Hungary: An Autobiography*. Stadia, Stroud, 2007, p 134.

91 Fox, *Prophet or Traitor?*, p 11.

92 Ibid., p 11.

93 Surányi, A., *Aranycsapat*. MAFILM. Budapest, 1982, p 78.†

94 Bocsák, M., *Kocsis és Czibor*. Sport, Hungary, 1983, p 108.†

95 Wright, B., *Football Is My Passport*. Stanley Paul, London, 1957.

96 Bocsák, *Kocsis és Czibor*, pp 54–55.†

97 The house on Colombus Street in the Pest suburb of Zugló (where Puskás was born) would have ordinarily been the residence of a high-ranking party official. Set back from the road behind trees and surrounded by an iron fence, it awarded Puskás, his wife and their infant daughter the much-needed privacy that had been absent from their previous home in downtown Pest.

98 Kő, A., *A Grosics*. Apriori International, Hungary, 2008, p 127.†

99 Ibid., p 127.†

100 Ibid., p 127.†

101 Bocsák, *Kocsis és Czibor*, p 56.†

102 Ferencváros took advantage of Imre Nagy's 'softer' government to change their club's name from the over-complicated 'ÉDOSZ' to the patriotic-sounding 'Budapest Kiniszi', 'Kiniszi' being the surname of Pál Kiniszi, a legendary 15th-century Hungarian general.

103 Also accompanying the squad was one Ignac Pióker, a Pest factory hand who, for his production rate at work, had won 'worker of the year', the prize being a trip to the World Cup.

104 Kasza, P., *A Berni Csoda: Amikor Foci Történelmet Ír*. Alexandra Kiadója, Pécs, 2004, p 101.†

105 Ellis refereed the Uruguay versus Brazil 1950 World Cup Final, along with Hungary's win over Yugoslavia in the final of the 1952 Olympics.

106 Szöllősi, G., *Czibor: Dribli az Égig*. Self-published, Hungary, 1997, p 106.†

107 *Munka Vörös Zászló Érdemrend*. Perhaps best thought of as the socialist equivalent of the British MBE.

108 Bocsák, M., *Kocsis és Czibor*. Sport, Hungary, 1983, p 69.†

109 Adolf 'Adi' and Rudolf Dassler were brothers born at the turn of the 20th century in the small German town of Herzogenaurach. They continued and expanded their father's shoemaking business, finding a profitable niche market in sports shoes, inventing the Dassler spiked running shoe, a pair of which the American sprinter Jesse Owens bought and wore when he won four gold medals at the 1936 Berlin Olympics.

But in 1948 the brothers fell out (according to rumour, over a woman) and split the business, agreeing that neither would use the name 'Dassler' in their new, separate, shoe businesses. Rudolf moved to the opposite side of town, opening up a sports shoemaking business called 'Ruda', later renamed when an advertising expert told him 'Puma' sounded better. Adi also opened up a sports shoe factory in Herzogenaurach and, wanting to incorporate his new name into his business, settled on 'adidas', written with a small letter 'a'. As it still is today.

110 For his blasphemous remark, the commentator, Herbert Zimmermann, was forced to apologise to the German Church authorities. However, this was countered by his legendary (in West Germany) commentary of the match becoming a hit record.

111 Kasza, P., *A Berni Csoda: Amikor Foci Történelmet Ír*. Alexandra Kiadója, Pécs, 2004, p 93.†

112 There were a small number of brand-new Mercedes Benzes cruising the streets of Budapest at this time, all belonging to high-ranking politicians.

113 At the same time, the ÁVO were destroying millions of celebratory stamps, commissioned by Mihály Farkas to commemorate Hungary's World Cup win.

114 Hungary's quarter-final win over Brazil saw them surpass Vittorio Pozzo's Italy's world record of 30 games unbeaten between 1935 and 1939. Hungary's 32-match unbeaten record lasted up until 1996, when it was broken by Brazil.

115 The statues were, supposedly, to have been placed on the entrance to the Népstadion, but this has now been proven as an empty promise of Mihály Farkas.

116 Bocsák, M., *Kocsis és Czibor*. Sport, Hungary, 1983, p 87.†

117 Wright, B., *Football Is My Passport*. Stanley Paul, London, 1957.

118 The Mitropa Cup would be resumed in 1955 and last up until 1992. Six-time winners Vasas are the club to have won it the most.

119 Buckingham would go on to manage Ajax and is said to be responsible for 'discovering' Johan Cruyff.

120 Wolves won the 1954 FA Cup as well as the league title, so in the annual Charity Shield match they played second-placed West Brom, in a 4–4 draw that led to both clubs keeping the trophy for six months apiece.

121 Chelsea 2 v Vörös Lobogó 2.

122 FA Cup finals and the annual England versus Scotland matches had been broadcast live in Britain since the late 1940s.

123 Holden, J., *Stan Cullis: The Iron Manager*. Breedon Books, UK, 2005.

124 Ibid.

125 Ibid.

126 Ironically, neither Honvéd nor Wolves entered the tournament. Vörös Lobogó lost 8–6 on aggregate in the quarter-finals to the eventual losing finalists, Stade de Reims.

127 Csernai would play for the next decade in the West German first and second divisions, but it was as a coach that he would become most renowned, most notably with a successful

five-year stint at Bayern Munich, building a team around a young Karl-Heinz Rummenigge. After Bayern, Csernai managed numerous clubs across the world, including Panathinaikos, Benfica and Fenerbahçe, and ended his coaching days in the 1990s as manager of the North Korean national team – a bizarre choice for a man who had once risked everything to escape communism.

128 One did not have to be a footballer in 1950s Hungary to be successful with the ladies. Sexual intercourse became less taboo under the communist regime as, with the vigour of the oppressed, people partook in the only pleasurable activity that was not state-owned. A lack of privacy in the cramped living conditions meant that people fornicated in alleyways, parks, cars or wherever possible, with, as one historian wrote, 'the speed of sparrows and the discretion of dogs'.

129 Szöllősi, G., *Czibor: Dribli az Égig*. Self-published, Hungary, 1997, p128.†

130 In Hungary, it was common practice for a woman to take her husband's entire name. So, for example, Alíz Kocsis, while still using her forename, was officially known as Mrs Sándor Kocsis.

131 Bocsák, M., *Kocsis és Czibor*. Sport, Hungary, 1983, pp 19–20.†

132 Sebestyen, V., *Twelve Days: Revolution 1956*. Phoenix, London, 2007.

133 Wright, B., *Football Is My Passport*. Stanley Paul, London, 1957.

134 Sebestyen, V., *Twelve Days: Revolution 1956*. Phoenix, London, 2007, p 118.

135 For 30 years after, the Hungarian government never made any mention of the atrocity.

136 So exasperated did Puskás become at having to explain he was fine that he eventually phoned the national press to ask them to print the news that he was alive and well.

137 The most infamous incident was the lynching of 23 suspected ÁVO officers outside the Communist Party headquarters.

138 Sebestyen, *Twelve Days*, p 118.

139 British and French forces were preparing to invade Egypt to regain control of the Suez canal.

140 One of the released political prisoners was the head of the Catholic Church, Cardinal József Mindszenty. He would take refuge in the American embassy, where he would remain for the next 15 years, despite being given many assurances that no harm would come to him should he leave. The Cardinal only left when ordered to do so by the Pope.

141 An excellent account of this mass exodus is in James Michener's book *The Bridge at Andau*.

142 Guttmann was invited to Argentina by a fellow Hungarian Jewish coach called Imre Hirschl, coach of first division club San Lorenzo. Hirschl is perhaps the finest example of the esteem in which Hungarian coaches were held, and of the fact that just being Hungarian was enough to land a man a coaching job. Hirschl claimed to have been a Ferencváros player, a claim that was not backed up by any evidence (Guttmann reckoned that he'd been a butcher in Budapest); but he used it in South America to land a job as coach of the mighty Argentinian club River Plate. Whether he was telling the truth or not became irrelevant for Hirschl, as he – under the name Emérico Hirschl – proved to be an outstanding coach, earning the nickname 'El Mago' ('The Wizard') and leading River Plate to two Argentine league titles, later doing the same with the Uruguayan giants Peñarol after the war.

143 Bolchover, D., *The Greatest Comeback: The Story of Béla Guttmann*. Biteback Publishing, London, 2017.

144 In the 1970s Dezső Solti was revealed as a 'fixer' hired by Inter Milan and Juventus, and who for a fee bribed referees in major European Cup ties with money, lavish presents and ladies of the night.

145 Östreicher, like Guttmann, evaded certain death in the battalion by escaping – clad only in his underwear – and hiding in a church.

146 Surányi, A., *Aranycsapat*. MAFILM. Budapest, 1982, p 151.

147 Bolchover, D., *The Greatest Comeback*

148 Tichy would go on to become one of Hungarian football's all-time greats. In a career lasting up until 1971, he scored 247 goals in 320 games for Honvéd and 51 goals from 72 games for the national team.

149 Szöllősi, G., *Czibor: Dribli az Égig*. Self-published, Hungary, 1997, p 135.†

150 Malonyai, P., *Aranykór*. Novotrade, Budapest, 1989, p 277.†

151 In 1991 the club changed its name to Kispest Honvéd, but in 2004 it went into voluntary liquidation after a tax scandal. In its place, a new club was formed, Budapest Honvéd FC, which remains the name of the club to this day.

152 The 1957 league season was purposely cut short to accommodate the six months during which football was suspended due to the revolution.

153 Alongside the accused was the former president Zoltán Tildy, sentenced to six years for the same crime. It is believed that his life was spared because even the Soviets were unwilling to hang a former president, who had been democratically elected and recognised internationally.

154 This version of Imre Nagy's 'final statement' was the first to be published – in 1968 by a French newspaper and in an article written by its Budapest correspondent. For many years it was a version taken as a given, but in 1989, after the fall of communism, doubt was thrown upon this. In fact, now no one knows for sure what the exact wording of Nagy's final statement was – although it is proved that he did give one and it was along the lines of the one in the text.

155 It was said that Kádár was sterile due to his testicles being crushed during his interrogation after his arrest in 1951, as well as having Mihály Farkas piss into his mouth while he lay bloodied and beaten on the floor.

156 Probably the best example of the authorities' attempts to eliminate Puskás from Hungarian history was his cameo walk-on part in the 1956 comedy football film *Csodacsatar* (Wonder Striker) being deleted and re-shot a year later using Nándor Hidegkuti.

157 Charles, M., *In the Shadow of a Giant*. John Blake Publishing, London, 2009.

158 Bolchover, D., *The Greatest Comeback: The Story of Béla Guttmann*. Biteback Publishing, London, 2017.

159 Formed in 1902 as Madrid FC, the club received royal patronage in 1920 changing its name to Royal Madrid – Real Madrid.

160 In the wake of Hungary's 6–3 and 7–1 trouncings of England, Berkessy decided to make the most of his credentials as a Hungarian and travelled to England in search of coaching work, and thus spent a season as caretaker manager of Grimsby Town, taking over from the previous manager – a young man by the name of Bill Shankly.

161 La Copa Latina, a competition between the league champions of Spain, Portugal, Italy and France. It lasted from 1949 to 1957.

162 In a 9–0 win over Sporting Gijon in 1952.

163 Szöllősi, G., *Czibor: Dribli az Égig*. Self-published, Hungary, 1997, pp 146–147.†

164 Hawkey, I., *Di Stéfano*. Penguin, London, 2016.

165 Bolchover, D., *The Greatest Comeback*

166 Ibid., p 229.

167 En route, Benfica beat Újpest 2–1 in Budapest, but Guttmann did not go to the match. He listened to it on the radio from his home in Vienna.

168 Dénes, T. & Jamrich, K., *Egy Legenda Életre Kel: Puskás Ferenc Életregénye*. Puskás Marketing és Tanácsaadó Kft, Hungary, 1998, p 236.†

169 Guttmann had learned of Eusébio from Carlos Bauer, a player he knew from his time in Brazil. The pair accidentally met in a Lisbon barber's shop, and while they were both receiving a trim, Bauer told Guttmann of a teenage footballer he had seen in Mozambique playing for Sporting Lisbon's nursery club. By offering him more money, Guttmann immediately had Eusébio sign for Benfica, much to the anger of their bitter cross-city rivals Sporting Lisbon. Sporting launched legal proceedings that delayed

Eusébio's arrival in Portuguese football by months but still ended with him remaining a Benfica player. Sporting had a right to feel hard done by: Eusébio would become the highest scorer in Portuguese league history, with 727 goals from 715 games.

170 Bolchover, *The Greatest Comeback*, p 229.

171 Ibid., p 229.

172 Ibid., p 229.

173 Bocsák, M., *Kocsis és Czibor*. Sport, Hungary, 1983, p 142.

174 Kő, A., *Szemétből Mentett Dicsőégünk*. Magyar Könyklub, Budapest, 1997, p 295.†

175 Ibid., p 260.†

176 Ibid., p 270.†

177 Jamrich, K. and Taylor, R., *Puskas on Puskas: The Life and Times of a Footballing Legend*. Robson Books, London, 1997.

178 Kő, A., *A Grosics*. Apriori International, Hungary, 2008, p 266.†

179 Bocsák, M. & Mátyás, I., *Örökség: Puskásék és a Történelem*. Self-published, Hungary, 2002, p 115.†

180 Bocsák, M., *Aranykönyv: Hogyan Éltek? És Akik Elmentek – Hogyan Haltak?* M.Sport, Hungary, p 105.†

181 Bocsák & Mátyás, Örökség, pp 54–55.†

182 Ibid., pp 54–55.†

Bibliography

Aczel, T. & Meray, T., *The Revolt of the Mind*. Thames & Hudson, London, 1960.

Agnew, P., *Football Legend: The Authorised Biography of Tom Finney*. Milo Books, Bury, 2002.

Alberti, J. & Grosics, G., *Kapusiskola*. Sport, Budapest, 1965.

Antal, Z. & Hoffer, J., *Alberttől Zsákig*. Sport, Budapest, 1968.

Applebaum, A., *Iron Curtain: The Crushing of Eastern Europe*. Penguin, London, 2013.

Balázs, G., *The Story of Hungarian: A Guide to the Language*. Corvina, Budapest, 2000.

Ball, P., *Morbo: The Story of Spanish Football*. WSC Books, London, 2003.

Barber, N., *Seven Days of Freedom: The Hungarian Uprising 1956*. Stein & Day, New York, 1974.

Bart, I., *Hungary and the Hungarians – The Keywords: A Concise Dictionary of Facts, Beliefs, Customs, Usage & Myths*. Corvina Books, Budapest, 1999.

Bellos, A., *Futebol: The Brazilian Way of Life*. Bloomsbury, London, UK, 2002.

Bliss, D., *Erbstein, Ernő: Az Elfeledett Futballhős*. Kanári, Hungary, 2017.

Bocsák, M., *A Grosics – Villa Titka*. Sport, Budapest, 1986.

Bocsák, M., *Aranykönyv: Hogyan Éltek? És Akik Elmentek – Hogyan Haltak?* M.Sport, Hungary.

Bocsák, M., *Hogyan Élnek Olimpiai Bajnokaink?* Miksport Bt, Hungary, 1998.

Bocsák, M., *Kocsis* és *Czibor*. Sport, Hungary, 1983.

Bocsák, M. & Mátyás, I., Örökség*: Puskásék* és a *Történelem*. Self-published, Hungary, 2002.

Bodnár, Z. & Szöllősi, G, *Az Aranycsapat Kincskönyve*. Twisther Media Kft, Budapest, 2015.

Bodonyi, L. & Walter, B., Gól Volt, Gól Nem Volt. Media Knox, Budapest, 2002.

Bolchover, D., *The Greatest Comeback: The Story of Béla Guttmann*. Biteback Publishing, London, 2017.

Bolgár, I., *Suttyó a Császár.* Sportpropaganda, Budapest, 1987.

Borhi, L., *Hungary in the Cold War 1945–56.* CEU Press, New York, 2004.

Borsi-Kálmán, B., *Az Aranycsapat és a Kapitánya.* Kortárs Kiadó, Hungary, 2008.

Bowler, D., *Danny Blanchflower: A Biography of a Visionary.* Vista, London, 1998.

Bowler, D. & Reynolds, D., *Ron Reynolds: The Life of a 1950's Footballer.* Orion, London, 2003.

Briggs, S., *Don't Mention the Score.* Quercus, London, 2008.

Budai, M., Sinkovics, G. & Tóth, P., *Rudi Bácsi: Az Rudolf Illovszky Életregény.* Vasas Média és Reklám Kft, Hungary, 2009.

Bukovi, M. & Csaknády, J., *Learn to Play the Hungarian Way.* Hungarian Sport Publishing House, Budapest, 1954.

Burns, J., *Barça: A People's Passion.* Bloomsbury, London, 1999.

Burns, J., *La Roja: A Journey Through Spanish Football.* Simon & Schuster, London, 2012.

Burns, J., *When Beckham Went to Spain: Power, Stardom and Real Madrid.* Penguin, London, 2005.

Campomar, A., *Golazo! A History of Latin American Football.* Quercus, London, 2014.

Castro, R., *Garrincha: The Triumph and Tragedy of Brazil's Forgotten Footballing Hero.* Yellow Jersey Press, London, 2005.

Chapman, H., *Herbert Chapman on Football.* GCR Books, UK, 2011.

Charles, J., *King John: John Charles – The Autobiography.* Headline Publishing, London, 2003.

Charles, M., *In the Shadow of a Giant.* John Blake Publishing, London, 2009.

Charlton, B., *My England Years.* Headline Publishing, London, 2008.

Claussen, D., *Béla Guttmann: A Világfutball Edzőlegendája.* Akadémmiai Kiadó, Budapest, 2015.

Connolly, K. & MacWilliam, R., *Fields of Glory, Paths of Gold: The History of European Football.* Mainstream Publishing, Edinburgh, 2005.

Cresswell, P. & Evans, S., *The Rough Guide to European Football.* Rough Guides, London, 1997.

Crouch, T., *The World Cup: The Complete History.* Aurum Press, London, 2002.

Csanádi, Á., *Labdarúgás I&II.* Tankönykiadó, Budapest, 1955.

Demjén, Dr L., *A Nagyváradi AC: A Magyar Nemzeti Bajnokságban 1941–44.* Self-published.

Dénes, T. & Jamrich, K.: *Egy Legenda Életre Kel: Puskás Ferenc Életregénye.* Puskás Marketing és Tanácsaadó Kft, Hungary, 1998.

Dénes, T. & Sándor, M., *Baj-Nok-Csa-Pat! A Magyar Labdarúgás 14 Bajnok Klubjának Története.* Campus Kiadó, Debrecen, Hungary, 2011.

Dent, B., *Budapest 1956: Locations of Drama.* Europa Könyvkiadó, Budapest, 2006.

Dlusztus, I., *Barcs Sándor.* Délmagyarország Kft, Szeged, 1997.

Docherty, T., *The Doc: Hallowed Be Thy Game.* Headline, London, 2006.

Downing, D., *The Best of Enemies: England v Germany.* Bloomsbury, London, 2000.

Downing, D., *Passovotchka: Moscow Dynamo in Britain 1945.* Bloomsbury, London, 2000.

Faludy, G., *My Happy Days in Hell.* William Morrow & Company, New York, 1963.

Fekete, P., *Csikar.* Sport, Budapest, 1965.

Fekete, P., *Orth és Társai ...* Sport, Budapest, 1963.

Finney, T., *Finney on Football.* The Sportsmans Book Club, London, 1960.

Finney, T., *My Autobiography.* Headline, UK, 2003.

Fischer, T., *Under the Frog.* Vintage Books, London, 2002.

Foot, J., *Calcio: A History of Italian Football.* Fourth Estate, London, 2006.

Fox, N., *Prophet or Traitor? The Jimmy Hogan Story.* The Parrs Wood Press, Manchester, 2003.

Földessy, J., *A Magyar Labdarúgás és a 60 Éves MLSZ.* Sport Könyvkiadó, Budapest, 1960.

Fűrész, A. & Privacsek, A., *Ria, Ria! Hajrá, Magyarok, Avagy Egy Évszázad Válogatott Törtenetei.* Inverz Media Kft, Hungary, 2016.

Gál, L., *Az Aranycsapat Elfeledett Legendái:* Tóth II József és Vár*hidi Pál Élete.* Aposztróf Kiadó, Budapest, 2015.

Gál, L., *Hittel, Sporttal és Kultúrával: Az Aranycsapat Alapitvány Első Évtizede.* Aposztróf Kiadó, Budapest, 2013.

Giller, N., *Billy Wright: A Hero for All Seasons.* Robson Books, London, 2003.

Giller, N., *Football and All That: An Irreverent History.* Stodder & Hodder, London, 2004.

Glanville, B., *England Managers: The Toughest Job in Football.* Headline, London, 2007.

Glanville, B., *Football Memories.* Virgin Publishing, London, 1999.

Glanville, B., *The Joy of Football.* Hodder & Stoughton, London, 1986.

Glanville, B., *The Story of the World Cup.* Faber & Faber, London, 2005.

Godsell, A., *Europe Utd: A History of the European Cup / Champions League.* SportsBooks, Cheltenham, UK, 2005.

Goldblatt, D., *The Ball Is Round: A Global History of Football.* Penguin, London, 2007.

Gough, R., *A Good Comrade: János Kádár, Communism and Hungary.* I.B. Tauris, London, 2006.

Greaves, J., *Greavsie: The Autobiography.* Time Warner Books, London, 2003.

Greaves, J., *The Heart of the Game.* Time Warner Books, London, 2005.

Green, G., *Soccer: The World Game.* The Sportsmans Book Club, London, 1954.

Greenwood, R., *Yours Sincerely*. Willow Books, London, 1984.
Grosics, G., Így Láttam a Kapuból. Sport, Budapest, 1963.
Gunther, J., *Behind the Curtain*. Harper & Brother Publishers, New York, 1949.
Gyarmati, G., *A Rákosi-Korszak. Rendszerváltó Fordulatok Évtized Magyarországon, 1945–56*. Ábtl-Rubicon, Budapest, 2011.
Gyenes, A., *Fradi Gyászinduló: Jenő Dalnoki Élete*. Self-published, Budapest.
Hanák, P., *The Corvina History of Hungary: From the Earliest Times until the Present Day*. Corvina Books, Budapest, 1991.
Handler, A., *From Goals to Guns*. East European Monographs, USA, 1994.
Hapgood, E., *Football Ambassador*. Sporting Handbooks, London, 1945.
Harris, N., *England, Their England: The Definitive Guide to Foreign Footballers in the English Game since 1888*. Pitch Publishing, Worthing, 2003.
Hawkey, I., *Di Stéfano*. Penguin, London, 2016.
Hámori, T., *Puskás: Legenda és Valóság*. Sportpropaganda, Budapest, 1982.
Hámori, T., *Régi Gólok, Edzősorsok*.....Lapkiadó Vállalat, Budapest, 1984.
Hegyi, I., *Magyarok Nagy Pályán*. Sprint Kft, Budapest, 2010.
Henderson, J., *The Wizard: The Life of Stanley Matthews*. Yellow Jersey Press, London, 2013.
Hesse-Lichtenberger, U., *Tor! The Story of German Football*. WSC Books, London, 2003.
Hidegkuti, N., *Óbudatól Firenzéig*. Sport, Budapest, 1965.
Holden, J., *Stan Cullis: The Iron Manager*. Breedon Books, Derby, 2005.
Holland, J., *Spurs: A History of Tottenham Hotspur Football Club*. The Sportsmans Book Club, London, 1957.
Hoppe, L., *Labdarúgó Bajnokságaink 1901–1969*. Self-published, Hungary, 1970.
Hoppe, L., *Vasas: Ne Hagyd Magad!* Sport Lap és Könyvkiadó, Budapest, 1958.
Hoppe, P. & Szabó, F., *Labdarúgó Bajnokságaink 1945–1986*. Sport, Budapest, 1987.
Horváth, A., *Informális Tanulás az Aranycsapat Korában*. Gondolat Kiadó, Budapest, 2011.
Hyne, A., *George Raynor: The Greatest Coach England Never Had*. History Press, Stroud, 2014.
Irving, D., *Uprising! One Nation's Nightmare: Hungary 1956*. Hodder & Stoughton, 1981.
Jacobs, N., *Vivian Woodward: Football's Gentleman*. Tempus, Stroud, 2005.
Jamrich, K. & Taylor, R., *Puskas on Puskas: The Life and Times of a Footballing Legend*. Robson Books, London, 1997.
Jeffrey, G., *European International Football*. Nicholas Kaye, London, 1963.
Joy, B., *Soccer Tactics*. Phoenix House, London, 1962.

Kasza, P., *A Berni Csoda: Amikor Foci Történelmet Ír.* Alexandra Kiadója, Pécs, 2004.

Kenez, P., *Hungary from the Nazis to the Soviets.* Cambridge University Press, New York, 2006.

Kincses, G. & Pongrácz, G., *Ferde Fák: Tichy Lajos Életregénye.* Zrinyi Katonai Kiadó, Budapest, 1971.

Kő, A., *A Grosics.* Apriori International, Hungary, 2008.

Kő, A., *Bozsik.* Sport, Budapest, 1979.

Kő, A., *Papp Laci.* Budapest-Print Kft, Hungary.

Kő, A., *Szemétből Mentett Dicsőégünk.* Magyar Könyklub, Budapest, 1997.

Kő, A. & Török, P., *A Magyar Futball Anekdotakincse.* Self-published, Hungary, 1988.

Koltay, G., *Szep Volt Fiúk ….* Self-published, 1987.

Koltay, G., *Verebes, a Magus.* Self-published, Budapest, 1987.

Kopacsi, S., *In the Name of the Working Class.* Fontana Paperbacks, London, 1989.

Korda, M., *Journey to a Revolution.* HarperCollins, New York, 2006.

Kuper, S., *Ajax, the Dutch, the War.* Orion, London, 2003.

Lázár, I., *Hungary: A Brief History.* Corvina, Budapest, 2001.

Lázár, L. & Lévay, G., *A Golkirály: Szusza Ferenc Életútja.* Alakart Dtp Stúdió, Szombathely, 2004.

Lázár, S.. *A Vereség Forradalma.* Válasz Könyvkiadó, Budapest, 2003.

Lendvai, P., *The Hungarians: 1000 Years of Victory in Defeat.* Hurst & Company, London, 2006.

Lepies, Dr G., *Baróti Lajos, Kapitányságom Története ….* Népszarva Lap, Budapest, 1984.

Lessing, E., *Revolution in Hungary: The 1956 Budapest Uprising.* Thames & Hudson, London, 2006.

Lévai, G., *Csanádi Emlékkönyv.* Trio Produkció Kiadó, Budapest, 1983.

Lewis, B., *Hammer & Tickle: A History of Communism Told through Communist Jokes.* Phoenix, London, 2009.

L. Réti, A., *Miért Vesztettünk?* Sport, Budapest, 1982.

Lukács, L. & Szepesi, G., *100+1: A Magyar Olimpiai Aranyérmek Története 1896–1972.* Sport, Budapest, 1976.

Lukács, László, Rejtő, László, & Szepesi, György, *Felejthetetlen 90 Percek.* Sport, Budapest, 1964.

Major, J., Nagy, B. & Szűcs, L., *Fradi Labdarugó-Szakosztály Története.* Sportpropaganda, Budapest, 1972.

Malonyai, P., *Aranykór.* Novotrade, Budapest, 1989.

Márai, S., *Memoir of Hungary, 1944–48.* Corvina, Budapest, 1996.

Margitay, R. & Margitay, Z., *Az Idegenlégió: Magyar Játékosok és Edzők a Futballvilágban.* ABA Könyvkiadó, Budapest, 2012.

Margitay, R. & Margitay, Z., *Kubala*. Aposztróf Kiadó, Budapest, 2014.
Marquis, M., *Sir Alf Ramsey: Anatomy of a Football Manager*. The Sportsmans Book Club, Newton Abbot, 1972.
Matthews, S., *The Way It Was: My Autobiography*. Headline, London, 2000.
Matthews, T., *Football Oddities*. Tempus Publishing, Stroud, 2005.
McKinstry, L., *Sir Alf*. HarperSport, London, 2006.
Meray, T., *Thirteen Days That Shook the Kremlin: Imre Nagy and the Hungarian Revolution*. Thames & Hudson, London, 1958.
Mező, Dr F., *A Helsinki Olimpia*. Sport Lap és Kiadó, Budapest, 1952.
Mező, L., *Futball Adattár*. Sportpropaganda, Hungary, 1986.
Michener, J. A., *The Bridge at Andau*. Random House, London, 1957.
Mikes, G., *The Hungarian Revolution*. Comet Books, London, 1958.
Miller, D., *England's Last Glory: The Boys of '66*. Pavilion Books, London, 2006.
Moldova, G, *A Szent Labda*. Urbis Kiadó, Budapest, 2012.
Montefiore, S. S., *Stalin: The Court of the Red Tsar*. Phoenix, London, 2004.
Morris, P., *West Bromwich Albion*. The Sportsmans Club, London, 1966.
Morse, G., *Sir Walter Winterbottom: The Father of Modern Football*. John Blake Publishing, London, 2013.
Motson, J., *Motson's World Cup Extravaganza*. Robson Books, London, 2006.
Motson, J., *Second to None: Great Teams of Post-War Soccer*. Pelham Books, London, 1972.
Mourant, A. & Rollin, J., *The Essential History of England: The Complete Story 1872–2002*. Headline, London, 2002.
Moynihan, J., *Football Fever*. Quadrant Books, London, 1974.
Muha, J., *Bajnokokkal Szemtöl Szembe*. Sportpropaganda, Budapest, 1986.
Müller, R., *Politikai Rendőrség: A Rákosi-Korszakban*. Jaffa Kiadó, Budapest, 2012.
Mullery, A., *The Autobiography*. Headline, London, 2006.
Nagy, B., *Fradi Meccskönyv. Az Első Negyszázad FTC Mérkőzései*. Fradi futballmúzeum, Budapest, 1993.
Nagy, B., *Futball Évtizedek: 125 Magyar–Osztrák Válogatott Története*. Self-published, Budapest, 1984.
Nagy, B., *Hajrá Magyarok: Valogátott Mérkőzesek és Tórténetek 1931–1949*. Hárót János, Hungary, 1980.
Nagy, B., *Toldi Géza: A Fradi Szív* és *Szellem Megtestesítője*. Self-published, Budapest, 1984.
Nagy, Dr L., *Száz Éves az MTK-VM Sportklub*. Self-published, Budapest, 1988.
Nemere, I., *Rákosi Mátyás Maganélete*. Anno Kiadó, Hungary.
Norridge, J., *Can We Have Our Balls Back, Please? How the British Invented Sport*. Penguin, London, 2008.

Ocsovai, G., *Micsoda Gólok!* Sport, Budapest, 1969.

Okwonga, M., *Will You Manage?* Serpent's Tail, London, 2010.

Page, S., *Herbert Chapman: The First Great Manager.* Heroes Publishing, Birmingham, 2006.

Pelé, *The Autobiography.* Pocket Books, London, 2007.

Peterdi, P. & Somos, I., *Lóri:* Lóránt Gyula Életregénye. Lapkiadó Vállalat, Budapest, 1986.

Pickering, D., *Cassell's Sports Quotations.* Cassell & Co, London, 2000.

Pintér, I., *Pokol és Mennyország.* Sportpropaganda, Hungary, 1985.

Pluhár, I. & Szepesi, G., *Szerelmünk a Mikrofon.* Sport, Budapest, 1967.

Pongrácz, G., *A Bamba: Deák Ferenc Élete.* Szac Kiadó, Budapest, 1992.

Pongrácz, G., *Puha Vagy Jenő!* Népszava Lap, Budapest, 1984.

Pongrácz, G., *Szikrázó Cipők: Tichy Lajos Elet Regenye.* Lapkiadó Vállalat, Budapest, 1983.

Puskás, F., *Captain of Hungary: An Autobiography.* Stadia, Stroud, 2007.

Rees, P., *The Three Degrees: The Men Who Changed British Football Forever.* Constable, London, 2015.

Rejtő, L., *Az Aranycsapat és Árnyai.* Sport, Budapest, 1966.

Riordan, J., *Comrade Jim: The Spy Who Played for Spartak.* Fourth Estate, London, 2008.

Romsics, I., *Hungary in the Twentieth Century.* Corvina Books, Budapest, 1999.

Ronay, B., *The Manager: The Absurd Ascent of the Most Important Man in Football.* Sphere, London, 2009.

Rónay, T., *A Magyar Foci Legendája.* Múzsák Kiadó, Budapest, 1993.

Rous, S., *Football Worlds: A Lifetime in Sport.* Faber and Faber, Newton Abbot, 1978.

Rózsa, A., *Fociológia.* Sport, Budapest, 1981.

Rózsaligeti, L., *A Futball Aranykora,* Alma Mater Zala Bt, Hungary, 2014.

Rózsaligeti, L., *A Nagy Honvéd: Az Elfogott Piros Ulti.* Alma Mater Zala Bt, Hungary, 2013.

Rudas, F., *Nyolc Évtized a Magyar Futballban.* Építészet Műveszet Sport Kiadó, Hungary, 2011.

Sándor, M., *Vasutasból Aranybányász: Beszélgetések Buzánszky Jenővel.* Campus Kiadó, Debrecen, Hungary, 2007.

Sárközi, M. & Vámos, M., *A Xenophobe's Guide to the Hungarians.* Oval Books, London, 1999.

Schlosser, I., *Fél Évszázad a Futballpályán.* Sport Lap és Könyvkiadó, Budapest, 1958.

Sebes, G., *A Magyar Labdarúgás.* Sport Lap és Könyvkiadó, Budapest, 1955.

Sebes, G., *Örömök és Csalódások.* Gondolat, Budapest, 1981.

Sebestyen, V., *Twelve Days: Revolution 1956*. Phoenix, London, 2007.

Service, R., *Comrades: Communism, a World History*. Pan Books, London, 2007.

Shiel, P., *Olympic Babylon: The True Story of the Olympic Games*. Macmillan, Sydney, 1998.

Smith, R., *Mister: The Men Who Taught the World to Beat England at Their Own Game*. Simon & Schuster, London, 2016.

Stone, N., *The Atlantic and Its Enemies: A History of the Cold War*. Penguin Books, London, 2011.

Surányi, A., *Aranycsapat*. MAFILM, Budapest, 1982.

Swatridge, C., *A Country Full of Aliens*. Corvina, Budapest, 2010.

Syposs, Z., *Ez a Szép Játek*. Sport, Budapest, 1976.

Szász, B., *Volunteers for the Gallows: Anatomy of a Show Trial*. Chatto & Windus, London, 1971.

Szegedi, P., *Az Elsö Aranykor: A Magyar Foci 1945-ig*. Kanári Kiadó, Budapest, 2016.

Szeidl, I., *Az Aranycsapat Szürke Eminenciása: Zakariás József élete*. B-Humanitas Stúdió, Budapest, 2002.

Szekeres, J., *7:1*. Sport Lap és Könyvkiadó, Budapest, 1954.

Szepesi, G., *Búcsu a Mikrofontól*. Paginarum Kiadó, Budapest, 1998.

Szepesi, G., *Gól! Góóóól! 2000 Gól!* Sport Kiadó, Budapest, 1962.

Szepesi, G., *Sport-Mikrofon*. A tömegkommunikácios kutatóközpönt kiadása, Budapest, 1982.

Szöllősi, G., *Czibor: Dribli az Égig*. Self-published, Hungary, 1997.

Szöllősi, G., *Puskás Ferenc: A Legismertebb Magyar*. Rézbong Kiadó, Hungary, 2015.

Szücs, L., *A 70 Éves Magyar Labdarúgás*. Self-published, Hungary, 1970.

Takács, T., *Szoros Emberfogás: Futball és Állambiztonság a Kádár-Korszakban*. Jaffa Kiadó, Budapest, 2014.

Taylor, R. & Ward, A., *Kicking and Screaming: An Oral History of Football in England*. Robson Books, London, 1995.

Tibballs, G., *Great Sporting Eccentrics*. Robson Books, London, 1998.

Tongue, S., *Turf Wars: A History of London Football*. Pitch Publishing, Worthing, 2016.

Tossell, D., *Big Mal: Biography of Malcolm Allison*. Mainstream Publishing, Edinburgh, 2009.

Toth, K.; *Puskás* és az *Aranycsapat Diadalai: The Zenith & Decline of the Hungarian Golden Team*. Self-published, 2014.

Tóth-Szenesi, A., *Baróti*. Alexandra, Pécs, 2004.

Török, F., *Mandula:* Mándi Gyula, Fradi-M*TK-Aranycsapat*. Nyik-Ki Bt, Budapest, 1999.

Ungváry, K., *Battle for Budapest: 100 Days in World War II*. I.B. Tauris, Chicago, 2010.

Vándor, K., Üllői Úti Kapufák: Sárosi György Dr, Futballtörténeti *Visszaemlékezései*. Kossuth Könyvkiadó, Budapest, 1988.

Végh, A., *Gyögyít6atlan?* Lapkiadó Vállalat, Budapest, 1986.

Végh, A., *Miért Beteg a Magyar Futball?* Magvető Könyvkiadó, Budapest, 1974.

Végh, A., *Miért Vesztettek Puskásék? (Világbajnokság '54 Svájv)*. Self-published, Hungary, 2000.

Vitray, T., *Hivatásos Sportajongó*. Sport Zsebkönyvek, Budapest, 1981.

Walvin, J., *The People's Game: The History of Football Revisited*. Mainstream Sport, Edinburgh, 1994.

Williams, R., *The Perfect 10: Football's Dreamers, Schemers, Playmakers and Playboys*. Faber & Faber, London, 2007.

Wilson, J., *Behind the Curtain: Travels in Eastern European Football*. Orion, London, 2006.

Wilson, J., *Inverting the Pyramid: The History of Football Tactics*. Orion, London, 2008.

Wilson, J., *The Anatomy of England: A History in Ten Matches*. Orion, London, 2010.

Wilson, J., *The Outsider: A History of the Goalkeeper*. Orion, London, 2013.

Winner, D., *Brilliant Orange: The Neurotic Genius of Dutch Football*. Bloomsbury, London, 2001.

Winner, D., *Those Feet: A Sensual History of English Football*. Bloomsbury, London, 2005.

Wright, B., *Football Is My Passport*. Stanley Paul, London, 1957.

Wright, B., *One Hundred Caps and All That*. Robert Hale, London, 1962.

Zeidler, M., *A Labdaháztól a Népstadionig: Sportélet Pesten és Budán a 18–20. Században*. Kalligram, Pozsony, 2012.

Zeidler, M., 'English Influences on Modern Sport in Hungary'. *Hungarian Quarterly*, issue 182, 2006.

Zeidler, M., *Sporting Spaces*. Municipality of Budapest, Budapest, 2000.

Zsolt, I., *A Pálya Közepén*. Magvető Kiadó, Budapest, 1974.

Zsolt, R., *Labdarúgók Sportolók: Magyarország Felfedezése*. Szépirodalmi Könyvkiadó, Budapest, 1978.

Zsolt, R., *Puskás Öcsi*. Szabad Tér Kiadó, Budapest, 1989.

Zsolt, R., *Sportolók, Sporterkölcsök*. Sport, Budapest, 1983.

Zweig, R., *The Gold Train: The Destruction of the Jews and the Second World War's Most Terrible Robbery*. Penguin, London, 2002.

Acknowledgements

My sincere thanks and gratitude to Paul Camillin and the team at Pitch Publishing, and to Graham Hughes at GH Editorial. To Miklós Nagy, Zsolt Szász, Judit Schultz, Róbert Iles, Márton Turi and András Pál at Helikon Publishing in Budapest. For their time, input and encouragement, and in no particular order: Donald MacRae, Mihály Sándor, Gyula Grosics, Phil Saltmarsh, Andy Clark, Nigel Greer, Spencer Vignes, Dean Rockett, Norbert Tadanaj, Nándor Horváth, György Orodán, Attila Márton, Billy Szentpeteri and Steve Redai. Not forgetting the hidden gems that are the Hungarian Museum of Sport and Budapest's Foreign Language Library. And simply for being them: my wife, Kriszta, and our daughter, Emma.

Index

AC Milan 186, 208, 212
AEK Athens 269
Albania national team 90, 256
Albert, Florián 252
Alexandria FC 271
Államvédelmi Osztály – ÁVO 41
Allison, George 100
Allison, Malcolm 133, 293
Anderlecht 253
Andrade, Victor 160
Andrews, Jimmy 133
Argentina national team 28, 207, 237, 251–252
Arkadiev, Boris 80–81
Arrow Cross Party 31, 39
Arsenal FC 82, 100, 105, 127–128
AS Roma 220
Aston Villa FC 138
Athletic Bilbao 207, 211, 212–214, 218, 233
Atlético Madrid 272
Atkinson, Ron 184–185
Attila the Hun 13
Auschwitz 31, 54, 209
Austrian Football Association 18, 19, 27, 247
Austria national team 15, 18, 27–28, 40, 46, 71–72, 75–76, 89, 90, 115, 120, 143, 151, 162, 177, 192, 198, 247, 256, 258–9, 265
    Wunderteam 27–28, 180, 247

Barcelona FC 68, 119, 210, 211, 218, 229, 232–238, 240–1, 243, 245–246, 249, 250, 253–254, 271–273
Baróti, Lajos 228, 230, 253, 290, 293
Bayern Munich 265
Bem, General Josef 200–201
Benfica FC 10, 242–244, 246–248, 274
Beria, Lavrenty 80, 82, 117
Berkessy, Elemér 234
Bernabéu, Santiago 211–212, 231–233, 237–238, 241, 253
Best, George 249
Blackburn Rovers FC 80, 133
Bozsik, István 45
Bozsik, József 45–46, 55, 81, 83–84, 88, 90, 92–94, 96–97, 103–105, 107, 119, 123–124, 132–136, 138, 145–148, 152, 157–160, 162–163, 166–167, 175, 199, 207, 212, 217, 221, 225, 227, 230, 252–253, 255–260, 266, 290
Bozsik, Péter 45
Brandaozinho 157
Brazil national team 25, 129, 151, 155–157, 160, 167, 172, 216–222, 225, 228, 230–231, 242–243, 252, 259, 263, 272, 274
Broadis, Ivor 148–149
Brundage, Avery 122
Brüll, Alfréd 16, 18–21, 24–25
Buckingham, Vic 181
Budai, László 87–90, 95–96, 104–105, 133–134, 145–146, 148, 152, 160, 163–164, 222, 249, 256–260, 267–268, 271
Budapest Torna Club 14
Bukovi, Márton 78–79, 94, 100–102, 152, 162, 197–199, 203, 227–228, 262, 264
Bulgaria national team 46, 56, 74, 90, 227, 252, 256
Burgess, Herbert 52

Busini, Antonio 208
Buzánszky, Jenő 93–95, 104–105, 123, 132–133, 136–137, 147, 152–153, 157, 160, 166, 198, 255–260, 264–265, 292

Cardiff City FC 82
Carniglia, Luis 237
CD Alavés 269
Challenge Cup 180
Chapman, Herbert 100
Charles, Mel 183, 231
Charnock, Clement & Harry 80
Chelsea FC 17, 82, 130, 182
Chinezul Timişoara 53
Coluna, Mário 247
Costa, Flávio 156
Cruyff, Johan 43, 269–270
Csáki, Sándor 91
Csepel AC 39, 69, 97, 148, 157, 188, 272
Csernai, Pál 188, 190
Cullis, Stan 183–185
Czeizler, Lajos 247
Czibor, Zoltán 10, 81, 87, 94–97, 101, 104–107, 109–111, 124, 132–134, 136–137, 145–149, 152, 155–160, 164, 166, 168, 171, 173, 176–177, 179, 190–191, 198–199, 203–204, 212, 218, 220–221, 223–225, 227–237, 240, 244–245, 249–250, 254–260, 262, 267–268, 271

Dassler, Adi 167
Daučík, Ferdinand 67–68
Deák, Ferenc 71–72, 74, 87, 101, 292
Debrecen Lokomotív 85
Denmark national team 188
Dietz, Károly 29–30
Dinamo Zagreb 78
Distay, Baron 19
Di Stéfano, Alfredo 238–239, 241, 247, 249, 251–254, 270
Docherty, Tommy 44
Dorogi FC 77, 94
Duckworth, Teddy 24–25
Dynamo Moscow 80, 99, 122

East Germany national team 151, 257
Eckl, Horst 166
Egresi, Béla 71, 73, 258
Egypt national team 142, 259, 270–271
Eintracht Frankfurt FC 215, 241
Eisenhoffer, József 27–29
Eisenhower, Dwight D. 205
Elektromos 39
Ellis, Arthur 106, 157–159
England national team 9–10,15, 28, 117–121, 123, 125, 127–131, 133–139, 141–144, 146–149, 151, 161, 166, 181–185, 197, 252, 254–255, 259
Erbstein, Ernő (Ernesto Erbstein) 52–54, 65, 67
Espanyol 254
European Cup Final
  1959 Real Madrid v Stade de Reims 186, 240
  1960 Real Madrid v Eintracht Frankfurt 241
  1961 Benfica v Barcelona 244
  1962 Benfica v Real Madrid 253
  1964 Inter Milan v Real Madrid 235, 248
Eusébio 43, 246–249

Faragó, Lajos 185, 211, 218
Farkas, Mihály 82–84, 87, 90, 92, 94, 97, 108–112, 116–118, 137, 147, 161–162, 172, 174–175, 200, 222, 275
FC Austria 224
Feleki, László 100, 128–129, 131, 174
Fenyvesi, Máte 177
Feola, Vicente 231, 242
Ferencváros Torna Club 16, 37, 40, 46, 53, 55, 71–72, 78, 83, 85–88, 93, 96, 100, 146, 192, 225, 234–235, 252
  Élelmezési Dolgozók Szakszervezete – ÉDOSZ 85
  Budapest Kiniszi 85, 225

FIFA 11, 67, 118, 151, 165, 169, 186, 197, 215–217, 219, 223–224, 227, 229–231, 233–235, 237–239, 270, 274
FIFA World Youth Cup Tournament 1953 118
Finland national team 99, 101, 103, 188, 257
Finney, Tom 130, 138, 148
Fiorentina 244, 270
Flamengo 155–156, 216, 220
Franco, Francisco General 233–234
Franz Ferdinand, Archduke 17
Franz Ferdinand, Emperor 17
Fulham FC 127, 148

Gallowich, Tibor 36–37, 39–40, 48–50, 53–54, 66
Garamvölgyi, Ágoston 211
Gassmann, Kurt 217
Gellér, Sándor 137, 152, 177–178, 189, 257, 259, 264
Gento, Francisco 251
Gerő, Ernő 49–50, 116, 196, 200–203, 276
Gimes, Miklós 225–226, 276
Glasgow Rangers FC 82
Gramlick, John 180
Green, Geoffrey 130, 135, 185
Griffiths, Mervyn 160, 168, 173
Grosics, Gyula 70–71, 77, 81, 89–90, 93–95, 104–105, 112, 124, 133, 135–137, 146–149, 152, 158, 160, 164, 166–167, 169, 171, 177–179, 189, 198–199, 203–204, 211, 218, 220, 223, 227–228, 230, 252, 256–260, 262–264, 267
Guinea national team 266
Guttmann, Béla 10, 27, 50–57, 65, 207–210, 220, 231, 242–244, 246–248, 274

Hamrin, Kurt 124
Hanot, Gabriel 186
Harris, Peter 148
Hegyi, Gyula 48–49, 53–54, 64, 118, 137, 145–146, 158, 162, 178, 192, 196–198, 216, 275
Herberger, Sepp 153–154, 162, 165–167
Herrera, Helenio 235–236, 241, 248, 251–252
Hidegkuti, Nándor 10, 101–102, 104–105, 112, 123, 128, 131, 133–137, 147–149, 152, 154, 156, 158, 160, 166, 168, 219, 227, 230, 244, 256–260, 270–271
Hirschl, Imre 283
Hitler, Adolf 30–31
Hohberg, Juan 160
Hogan, Jimmy 18–21, 23–26, 55, 80, 100, 123, 138–139, 145, 155
Horn, Leo 134, 136–137, 197
Horthy, Miklós Regent 22, 25, 29–31, 35, 37, 41, 69, 102, 195
Howcroft, James 18
Humberto 158
Hungarian Communist Party – Kommunistak Magyarországi Partja 34–35, 37, 39, 47–48, 50, 64, 68, 75–76, 80, 83, 97, 99, 114, 117, 164, 191, 195, 217, 262, 275–276
Hungarian Football Association – Magyar Labdarúgó Szövetség 27, 29, 36–37, 39, 67–68, 75–76, 100, 108, 118–119, 131, 143, 145, 181, 215–217, 227–228, 237, 253–254, 265–266, 274–275
Hungarian National League – Magyar Nemzeti Liga 50
Hungarian Secret Police – Államvédelmi Osztály 41
Hungarian Socialist Workers Party – Magyar Szocialista Munkás Party 47

Italy national team 28–29, 54, 72, 105, 115, 118–119, 151, 192, 219, 247, 257–258, 270, 272

Járay, József 68–69

Jezzard, Bedford 148
Joy, Bernard 105, 127
Julinho 158

Kalmár, Jenő 60, 77, 87, 176, 178, 209–210, 218, 220, 274
Karl IV, Emperor 17
Kádár, János 39, 48, 73, 90, 202, 226, 246, 254–255, 276
Károlyi, Count Mihály 17, 21
Kéri, Károly 71
Khrushchev, Nikita 117, 187, 193–194, 196, 202, 206, 226
Kispest AC
  Budapesti Honvéd 83–84
Kocsis, Alíz 191, 212, 222, 236
Kocsis, Sándor 10, 72, 74, 87–90, 101, 103–106, 111, 119, 123, 133, 136, 142, 145–149, 152, 154, 157–158, 160, 163–164, 166, 168, 171, 184–185, 191–192, 218, 222–223, 225, 227–230, 235–237, 240, 242, 244, 250–252, 254–260, 268, 271
Kohut, Vilmos 29
Kopácsi, Sándor 200, 202, 204–205, 225–226
Korányi, Lajos 29
Kosztolányi, Andre 140
Kovács, Béla 41–42
Kovács, Erzsebet 197
Kovács, Imre 91–92, 103–104, 152, 256–257
Kléber, Gábor 50, 54, 59–60
Kubala, László 10, 65–68, 119, 210–211, 218, 232, 234–236, 238, 240–241, 244, 249, 251, 253–254, 273–274, 291
Kun, Béla 21–22, 25, 35
Kürschner, Dori 19, 24–26, 28, 155–156

Lakat, Károly 228, 256
Lantos, Mihály 104–105, 132–135, 147–148, 152, 157–158, 166–167, 198, 219, 222, 256–260, 262, 264
Lausanne FC 260
Leafe, Reg 242
Liebrich, Werner 154, 166
Ling, Bill 154, 168, 173–174
Lóránt, Gyula 10, 69, 71, 73–74, 89–90, 94, 104–105, 111, 133–136, 147, 152, 157–158, 166–167, 179, 255, 257–260, 265, 292

Machos, Ferenc 152, 185
Madarász, Endre 217
Malenkov, Georgy 117, 187
Maléter, Pál Colonel 202, 205–206, 225–226, 276
Manchester United FC 44, 129, 148, 184, 230, 248
Marik, György 66–67
MATEOSZ – Magyar Teherfuvarozók Országos Szövetkezet 70, 89
Matthews, Stanley 10, 130–133, 135–136, 138
Maurinho 159
Mándi, Gyula 76–78, 80, 198, 263, 293
Mears, Joe 130
Meazza, Giuseppe 115
Meisl, Hugo 18–19, 27, 180
Meisl, Willy 186
Merrick, Gil 133–135, 144, 148
Mészáros, József 55, 71, 73
Mikoyan, Anastas 196
Millonarios 238
Mindszenty, Cardinal József 57–58
Mitropa Cup 180
Moreira, Zezé 156–157, 159
Morlock, Max 166–167
Mortensen, Stan 133, 135–136
MTK – Magyar Testgyakorlók Kőre Választmánya 300
MTK Hungária 16–20, 23–26, 28, 37–38, 50, 52, 60, 76, 78, 80, 83, 85, 90, 94, 100–104, 116, 124, 155, 172, 198, 219, 225, 228, 233, 244, 262, 264, 269–271, 291, 293
  Budapesti Textiles 85
  Vörös Lobogó 116, 133, 147, 152, 166, 177, 182, 219, 225
Munnich, Ferenc 86

Mussolini, Benito 29–30, 146

Nagy, Imre 120–121, 124, 175, 187, 193, 195–196, 200–202, 205–206, 225–227
Nagy, József 28
Nagy, Marcell 217, 220, 225–227
Népstadion 121, 144, 147, 170, 176, 196, 207, 227, 246, 254–255, 270
Norway national team 187, 227
Nógrádi, Sándor 84, 178
Nyers, István (Stefano Nyers) 65, 272–273

Olympiakos 262, 264
Olympic Games 293
1924 Paris
1948 London 49-50, 54,60
1952 Helsinki 99-100, 101, 103, 105, 114
1956 Melbourne 214, 216
1960 Rome 123, 245
Orth, György 20, 26
Owen, Syd 148
Östreicher, Emil 207, 209, 211–212, 216, 219, 221–223, 231

Padova FC 208
Palotás, Péter 124, 152, 256–260, 268
Panathinaikos 269, 274
Pelé 43, 270, 292
Peñarol 247
Péter, Gábor 76, 90–91, 116, 124, 152, 266, 268, 275
Pinheiro 157, 159
Piros, László 172, 292
Plattkó, Ferenc 233–234
Poland national team 72, 90, 99, 101, 151, 198, 256–257
Politikai Rendészeti Osztály – PRO 41
Posipal, Jupp 154, 166
Pozsonyi, Imre 234
Pozzo, Vittorio 29, 53
Purczeld, Ferenc 43, 229
Puskás, Ferenc 9–11, 40, 43–46, 53–56, 60–61, 66, 72, 74, 78, 81–84, 87, 90, 92–93, 96, 101, 104–112, 116, 119, 123–125, 127–128, 130–136, 138, 141, 144–149, 152, 154–155, 159, 161–163, 165–166, 168, 171, 173–177, 181–182, 184, 191–192, 199, 203, 207, 209, 212, 217, 220–225, 227–233, 237–242, 245–247, 249–259, 261–262, 269–270, 275, 277

Rahn, Helmut 153, 166–167
Rajk, Julia 195
Rajk, László 41, 63–64, 76, 90, 194–195, 225–226
Ramsey, Alf 10, 133, 136, 182, 291
Rappan, Karl 215
Raynor, George 123, 128, 130, 134
Rákosi, Mátyás 35, 39, 41–42, 48, 57–60, 64–65, 75, 84–86, 90, 102–103, 106–107, 112–113, 116–118, 120, 122, 124, 131, 150, 172, 174–175, 187–188, 193–198, 200, 202, 222, 246, 275, 277
Real Madrid 68, 186, 211–212, 222, 229–231, 233, 237, 240–241, 246, 251, 253, 269
Real Murcia 269
Red Star Belgrade 186
Reep, Charles 183–184
Ries, István 47, 57, 61, 75–76
Robb, George 133, 135–136
Robertson, Jacky 16–18, 20
Romania national team 99, 103, 120, 176, 257
Rous, Stanley 118–119, 129, 138–139, 292
Rowe, Arthur 100, 128, 181

Samitier, Pepe 68, 236, 238
Santos, Djalma 157–158
Santos, Nilson 157–158
Sándor, Károly 72, 74, 76, 84, 87, 91, 94–95, 103, 108, 118, 131, 133, 137–138, 142, 147, 152, 155, 166, 173, 177–179, 188–189, 191–192, 196, 198–200, 202, 205, 219, 222,

225–227, 229, 235–237, 249–250, 252, 256–259, 264, 268–269, 275
Sárközi, Mátyás 292
Sárosi, György 223, 294
São Paulo FC 231, 242
Schäfer, Hans 166–167
Scharenpeck, Ferenc 38–39
Schiaffino, Juan 160, 208
Schlosser, Imre 15–16, 20, 292
Schubert, Gyula 65–67
Schwartz, Elek 248
Scotland national team 28, 44, 151, 182, 192
Sebes, Gusztáv 10, 35, 37–41, 48–52, 54, 59–62, 70–74, 76–78, 80–81, 83, 87, 89–96, 99–107, 111–112, 115, 118–121, 123–126, 128–132, 136–139, 142–143, 145–149, 152–155, 157–159, 161–165, 169, 172–177, 179, 182, 188, 191, 193, 196–198, 216–218, 231, 245–246, 249, 254, 261–263, 274, 292
Servette FC 152, 215, 274
Sevilla FC 211
Sewell, Jackie 133, 135, 148
Sing, Karl 62, 165
ŠK (Slovan) Bratislava 66–67
Solothurn FC 152
Sos, Károly 228
Southampton FC 15
South Korea national team 151–152, 259
South Melbourne Hellas 270
Soviet Union national team 99
Sólyom, László 84
Spain national team 250–253
Spartacus FC 85, 179
Spartak Moscow 122, 184
Stalin, Josef 34–36, 58, 63, 80, 105, 114, 116–117, 122, 124, 187, 193–194, 200, 202, 204–205, 277, 291
Staniforth, Ron 148–149
Stein, Erwin 241
Sweden national team 29, 72, 74, 105, 121, 123–124, 128, 130, 134, 188, 192, 198, 203, 231, 257–259, 270
Swinbourne, Roy 185
Switzerland national team 115, 151, 177, 192, 252, 258, 273–274
Szakasits, Árpád 48, 75
Szálasi, Ferenc 31, 41
Szentendri Honvéd 267
Szigetszentmiklósi AC 266
Szokja, Ferenc 259
Szusza, Ferenc 92–93, 101, 155, 179, 198–199, 219, 222, 255–257, 272, 290
Szűcs, Nándor 44
Szűcs, Sándor 91–92, 188, 290

Tatabányai Bányász 263
Tichy, Lajos 218, 229, 231, 252, 290, 292
Tildy, Zoltán 41–42, 47–48, 57, 205
Titkos, Pál 76, 78, 80, 198
Tito, Josip Broz 63, 105–106, 194
Toldi, Géza 29, 291
Torino FC 53, 65–67
Tottenham Hotspur FC 100, 128, 133, 181
Tóth, József 147–149, 152, 157–159, 249
Tóth, Mihály 152, 155, 158, 164, 166, 173, 256, 258–260, 272
Trianon Treaty 1920 25–26, 30
Turai, István 64
Turek, Toni 166, 168
Turkey national team 105, 151, 153, 162, 192–193, 196, 257

Uruguay national team 151–152, 156, 159–160, 162, 164, 167, 260
Újpest SE 50, 52–54, 65, 83, 85, 91, 155, 164, 188, 219, 225, 272
Budapesti Dózsa 152

Vancouver Royals 269
Vas, Zoltán 171–172, 205
Vasas Győr 271–272
Vasas 20, 36, 38–39, 43, 48–49, 53, 64–66, 68–69, 73, 83, 85, 89, 119, 147, 152, 178, 207, 225, 230, 246, 271–272

Vienna Cricket & Football Club 14
Vincze, Jenő 215, 217
Vitoria 269

Wales national team 231
Walter, Fritz 121, 128–129, 134, 148, 153, 166–167
Wankdorf Stadium 152, 164–166, 243
Weisz, Agostón 38
Wembley Stadium 127
West Bromwich Albion FC 181, 282
West Germany national team 11, 151, 153, 161–162, 166–167, 171, 230, 240, 259, 266
West Ham United FC 133
Wiener AC 274
Winterbottom, Walter 121, 128–130, 134, 136, 148, 183, 291
Wolstenholme, Kenneth 134–135
Wolverhampton Wanderers FC 133, 148, 181–187, 215
Woodward, Vivian 15
World Cup 11, 28–30, 40, 64, 67, 76, 100, 118, 120, 129, 142, 150–157, 159–161, 164–166, 168–169, 171–174, 176–177, 183, 187, 192, 197, 199, 201, 203, 205, 207, 209, 211, 213, 215–216, 219, 223, 227, 229–231, 238, 240, 244, 247–248, 250–255, 266–270, 272, 274
  1934 Italy 28
  1938 France 28, 40, 76, 100, 215, 223
  1950 Brazil 67, 120, 129, 156,
  1954 Switzerland 11, 15, 151-153, 156, 166, 200, 216, 219, 231, 240, 244, 247, 251-252
  1958 Sweden 171, 197, 199, 227, 229, 231, 251
  1962 Chile 250-251
  1966 England 183
Wright, Billy 10, 130–131, 133–136, 143, 148–149, 185

Young Boys FC 24, 152, 165
Young Fellows FC 223, 228, 236

Zakariás, József 104–105, 133, 136, 147, 152, 158, 163–167, 176–177, 179, 255–260, 266–267, 293
Zsengellér, Gyula 40, 91